T0340346

THE BRAZILIAN ECONOMY

The Brazilian economy has long been defined by its enormous potential. Over the past 30 years, some of this has at last been realised. Latin America's largest economy has rapidly risen in global importance while poverty at home has declined. Yet, despite periods of progress, Brazil remains prone to economic crisis. It is also beset with stubborn inefficiencies and income disparities. This book considers the structural challenges which will need to be overcome if Brazil is to break with the past and finally embark on a path of sustained, inclusive growth.

This book aims to give the reader a clear knowledge of the nature of these structural challenges, why they exist and the effectiveness of attempts to overcome them. Through this, readers will gain a deep understanding of the contemporary Brazilian economy. The challenges discussed fall into three areas: those centring on competitiveness and the supply side, those arising from critical macroeconomic issues and those connected with environmental sustainability and social inclusion. This volume systematically examines each of these domains, highlighting such vital topics as export competitiveness, human capital formation, environmental policy and the role of financial market reform. Where appropriate, this book sets Brazil's experience in an international comparative context. It points out that many of the challenges faced by Brazil are shared by other emerging economies. In this sense, the policy lessons which stem from this volume have broader international relevance.

This book will be vital reading for all those seeking in-depth understanding of one of the world's most important, yet troubled, economies. This readership is likely to include undergraduate and postgraduate students on development economics and Latin American area studies programmes, policymakers wanting an up-to-date and coherent analysis of Latin America's largest economy, and financial professionals.

Edmund Amann is Professor of Brazilian Studies at Leiden University and Adjunct Professor, School of Advanced International Studies, Johns Hopkins University.

THE BRAZILIAN ECONOMY

Confronting Structural Challenges

Edmund Amann

Routledge
Taylor & Francis Group

LONDON AND NEW YORK

First published 2021
by Routledge
2 Park Square, Milton Park, Abingdon, Oxon OX14 4RN

and by Routledge
52 Vanderbilt Avenue, New York, NY 10017

Routledge is an imprint of the Taylor & Francis Group, an informa business

© 2021 Edmund Amann

British Library Cataloguing-in-Publication Data
A catalogue record for this book is available from the British Library

Library of Congress Cataloging-in-Publication Data
A catalog record has been requested for this book

ISBN: 978-0-367-24527-6 (hbk)
ISBN: 978-0-367-24501-6 (pbk)
ISBN: 978-0-429-28291-1 (ebk)

Typeset in Bembo
by codeMantra

CONTENTS

FIGURES

TABLES

1

INTRODUCTION – FRUSTRATED POTENTIAL

Brazil's economic performance in the long term

Introduction

The Brazilian economy presents a series of superlatives, paradoxes and contradictions. Since World War II, it has risen to be one of the world's most important centres of production, especially in agriculture, basic industries and hydrocarbons. Brazil ranks among world leaders in such esoteric technological fields as deep-water oil exploration, genomic sequencing of plants and civil aerospace. Its multinational corporations have extended their reach far beyond home shores into North America, Europe and even Sub-Saharan Africa. Brazil-based investors now lie behind such Western corporate icons as Budweiser, Burger King and Heinz. In fields of cultural production, thanks to the country's vibrant film and television sector, Brazil has exported popular drama series – telenovelas – which are enjoyed from Mexico City to Moscow. Up until very recently Brazil became renowned for its felicitous combination of rapid economic growth, poverty alleviation and narrowing income inequality.

Yet for all of these positive attributes and achievements, there is a very real sense in which the Brazilian economy's potential is far from being fulfilled. As will be later illustrated, economic performance in Brazil compared to many emerging market counterparts (notably in East Asia) has been disappointing. This is borne out whether one employs metrics on poverty alleviation, productivity growth, infrastructure, educational attainment or export growth. The sense of a failure to live up to potential could not have been more clearly encapsulated by recent events. Between 2012 and 2016, the country endured the sharpest recession since the dark days following the Wall Street Crash of 1929. In 2020, the global COVID-19 pandemic was threatening to push Brazil into deep recession once more.

The severity of recent downturns is directly attributable to the nexus of paradoxes which have long characterised the structure of Latin America's largest economy. Well documented and celebrated centres of excellence – as described above – do of course exist. Still, as if in gravitational opposition, there also sits a long tail of uncompetitive sectors marked by paltry productivity growth, low innovation and weak skills. Where strengths *do* exist – principally around natural resource-based (NRB) products – their ability to deliver resilient growth is necessarily constrained by volatile global commodity prices. This last observation resonates down the decades; indeed, as we shall see, it provided a key impetus behind the structuralist revolution in Brazil's economic policymaking in the early post-war years. The dualism characterising Brazil's productive sector finds its analogue in yawning spatial disparities, whether these relate to income and poverty, employment or export intensity. The development gap between the poor North and North East and the affluent South and South East remains stark. Equally, despite undoubted progress, on an interpersonal basis, deep poverty and income inequality are still facts of life.

Perhaps a lesser-known paradox in Brazil's contemporary political economy centres on the macroeconomic dimension. The country has rightly been celebrated for its vanquishing of hyperinflation in the 1990s. Despite the economic turbulence buffeting the continent in the latter half of the 2010s, Brazilian inflation has remained in single digits whereas in Argentina and Venezuela, it has risen vertiginously. This accomplishment, under the auspices of the Real Plan, has rested on carefully elaborated frameworks of exchange rate and, later, inflation targeting. As will be seen later, Brazil's Central Bank has proven to be a technically excellent steward of monetary policy. Yet contrastingly, in terms of fiscal policy, the track record has been distinctly unfavourable. Fiscal reform proceeded energetically in the early days of the Real Plan, with two waves of measures introduced in the decade after its launch in 1993. Subsequently, under the Lula and Rousseff administrations (2003–16), the pace of reform slackened; fiscal imbalance and the accumulation of public debt contributed to the onset of an economic crisis in the middle of the 2010s. Brazil's fiscal challenges are multi-layered and complex, as becomes abundantly clear in Chapter 5. Two of their most central components relate to the rapidly increasing cost of public sector pension provision and the byzantine and inefficient tax system (especially where indirect taxes are concerned).

Taken together, these factors have contributed to the emergence of a structural primary deficit and an associated situation in which the central government's scope for discretionary spending has increasingly been squeezed out. Following the impeachment of President Dilma Rousseff in mid-2016, the interim administration of Michel Temer (2016–18) enacted a radical measure which imposed a real-term spending freeze on the Federal government for 20 years. This has further constrained the scope of much-needed discretionary expenditure in growth-promoting areas such as education and infrastructure. Consequently, the Bolsonaro administration (2019–) has placed higher priority on pursuing a comprehensive pensions reform. This has as its objective the compression of pension costs for public sector employees, to be realised principally through the introduction of less generous entitlements. Likewise, Brazil's current administration has committed itself to reform of the indirect taxation system. The principal aim here centres on harmonising and unifying Brazil's elaborate range of sales taxes; if realised, this would not only support revenue generation but would also significantly reduce compliance costs for the private sector.

Consideration of the latter issue leads us to ponder another paradoxical feature of Brazil's contemporary political economy; the sharp divide which often exists between the economic efficiency of the public sector entities and their counterparts in the private sector. Allusion has already been made to the dualism that characterises the supply side of the Brazilian economy. Here, world-class sectors and firms coexist alongside those positioned well behind the global frontier, whether in terms of technological sophistication, productivity or competitiveness more generally. This dualism also characterises the contrasts that exist between leading elements of the Brazilian private sector and large swathes of the public sector.

While processes of economic opening and liberal reform have often succeeded in stimulating private sector competitiveness (see Chapter 2), there is widespread acknowledgement that the public sector, despite efforts at reform, remains beset by inefficiencies and processes which inhibit timely delivery of critical services. As it became starkly apparent as a result of the Lava Jato (Car Wash) scandal, public sector entities are also vulnerable to penetration by corrupt, politically connected interests who directly benefit from such "inefficiencies" as overbilling for contracts or appointment of suboptimal suppliers.

These issues form part of a broader constellation of concerns surrounding the interface between the state and the private sector. On the one hand, for many years, it has been apparent that legitimate interactions between the state and business – for example, environmental licensing or tax filings – entail far more complex bureaucratic procedures than would be typical in OECD economies. The high compliance costs so generated have come to be termed the *Custo Brasil* or Brazil Cost and are cited by industry associations such as the National Industrial Confederation (CNI) as systemic factors in retarding the country's international competitiveness.

On the other hand, thanks to the harsh light shone on business—government relations by the Lava Jato inquiry (led by Brazil's former Minister of Justice, Sergio Moro), it has become apparent how some of Brazil's largest multinational enterprises (for example, Odebrecht, Petrobras and JBS) were locked into corrupt relationships with state entities, members of Congress and the executive branch. A divide now appears to exist between "insider" and "outsider" enterprises, those who managed to survive or thrive without the patronage (corrupt or otherwise) of the state, and those whose development was intimately conditioned by it. As this volume later argues in Chapter 4, one of the most significant challenges facing Brazil's economy consists of resetting business-government relations such that they become less clientelistic, so eroding the binary divide between insider and outsider firms.

A final paradox surrounding the contemporary Brazilian economy concerns its degree of openness. As discussed in section 2 of this chapter, the period since the end of the debt adjustment crisis of the 1980s has generally been one of liberal reform. Like its BRIC counterparts over the period, Brazil has adopted far-reaching measures which have liberalised trade, opened up new sectors to foreign investment and incentivised exports. Although the Lula and Rousseff years (2002–16) saw some policy reversals in this area (notably around the capital goods sector), it is fair to characterise Brazil's approach over the past three decades as one aligned with progressive globalisation. Despite this, surprisingly, Brazil remains one of the world's most closed major economies. In 2017, Brazil's trade accounted for just 24.1% of GDP, by contrast China's stood at 37.8%. At the same time, the number of exporter firms in Latin America's largest economy was approximately equal to that of Norway, a country whose population is 40 times smaller than that of Brazil (Picanço et al., 2018).

The relatively closed nature of Brazil's economy reflects, among other things, the fact that tariff and non-tariff barriers remain high relative to international norms. In 2017, according to World Bank data, average trade-weighted tariffs in Brazil stood at 8.59%, compared with 3.8% in China and just 1.79% in the EU. The comparatively accentuated nature of Brazilian trade barriers compounds issues of poor supply-side competitiveness that have already been referred to. These, in turn, have restricted export growth outside the NRB sector. The fact that Brazil has remained such a closed economy, despite the apparent embrace of globalisation, means that it has proved to be highly vulnerable to downturns in domestic demand. This was illustrated very clearly during the 2013–16 crisis; had alternative sources of export demand been available to offset the collapse in domestic consumption and investment, there is no doubt that the recession would have been shallower and short-lived.

Having briefly discussed the achievements, frustrations and paradoxes surrounding the contemporary Brazilian economy, it is time to set out the conceptual and theoretical approaches which will inform our analysis in subsequent chapters.

Analysing the contemporary Brazilian economy: an overview of conceptual and theoretical approaches

From the discussion so far, it should be evident that Brazil has consistently faced deep-seated challenges which have frustrated attempts to place its economy on a trajectory of sustained, inclusive growth. As consecutive administrations have tried to wrestle with these issues, Brazil has often resembled a laboratory for the evaluation of new (or sometimes recycled) economic ideas (Amann, 2017). Thus, the 1980s witnessed attempts to restrain inflation through the use of heterodox measures derived from the Post-Keynesian theory (Bresser Perreira, 2018).

A decade later such approaches had been abandoned in favour of more orthodox counter inflationary measures, notably monetary restraint and exchange rate targeting. These fresh policy initiatives were strongly influenced by monetarism and rational expectations theory.

Turning away from the pursuit of macroeconomic stabilisation to that other great challenge, the attainment of global competitiveness, Brazil has witnessed similar experimentation. During the 1960s and 1970s the then military administration attempted to build new sources of comparative advantage through state-driven industrialisation strategies (Bielschowsky, 1988). These were in turn influenced by the rise of structuralist and dependency schools of economic thought, both of which had been flourishing in Latin America since the end of World War II (Ocampo & Ros, 2012). By the 1990s, with the return to civilian rule, and the Collor administration now in power, the intellectual tide had reversed completely. Market-friendly, Chicago school approaches had gained ascendancy, with Brazil rolling out comprehensive trade reforms and the world's largest privatisation programme (Baer, 2013).

The tide was to turn once more in the first decade and a half of the millennium with the PT (or Workers' Party) administrations of Presidents Lula and Rousseff embracing interventionism. Industrial strategies came back into vogue with sector-specific initiatives launched for oil & gas and shipbuilding, for example. With the impeachment of President Rousseff in 2016, the intellectual and policy climate had shifted radically once more. Under President Temer (2016–18) and his successor, President Bolsonaro (2019–), free market solutions to Brazil's long-standing competitiveness problems have come once more to the fore. In a strong echo of the Collor administration's dash for liberal economic reform in 1990–92, the Bolsonaro government has enacted an invigorated privatisation programme alongside an ambitious trade liberalisation strategy. President Bolsonaro's Brazil, with its liberal approach to trade and industrial strategy, now provides a curious counterpoint to the economic nationalism of the hemisphere's other high-profile conservative, President Trump.

The battle of ideas surrounding the economic development of Brazil helps make for a fascinating field of study. Still, by the same token, this very controversy highlights the question as to which analytical and theoretical approaches are most suited to a systematic study such as this.

This book sets out from the starting point that the economic challenges facing Brazil are practical ones, capable of alleviation, and, in fact, shared by other countries inside and outside the region. Consequently, the approach adopted by this book is guided by two principles. The first principle is that this volume's analysis and policy recommendations should be based on hard empirical assessment as to what has and has not worked. The adoption of a doctrinaire, ideological *a priori* approach is therefore eschewed in favour of a more positivist standpoint. The second key principle relates to the need to see, where possible, the Brazilian economy and its challenges in broader international comparative context. There has been a tendency in previous one-volume studies[1] to view the

Brazilian economy in relative isolation without taking into account that many of its features and structural limitations are shared by other economies, some at very different levels of development. By taking a more globally contextualised view, the intention is not only to shed powerful analytical light on Brazil's own problems but also to provide scope for internationally relevant policy lessons to be drawn.

In adopting these broad principles this volume makes two fundamental assumptions about the global economic context in which Brazil now, and in the future, will operate. The first is that, despite the protectionist inclinations of the current US administration, the global environment for trade and foreign direct investment (FDI) will continue to be characterised by relative openness. Brazil will need to function more competitively within this international economic landscape. This is hardly a contentious ideological viewpoint; it has been shared alike by every administration since the return to civilian rule in 1985. The second assumption is perhaps more controversial. It centres on the idea that Brazil, alongside other major emerging market economies, may be caught in a middle-income trap.

The notion of a middle-income trap is an important, though contested one in development economics. As Felipe (2012) points out, while the topic has been the subject of innumerable studies, there is no consensus in the literature allowing for a commonly agreed, tight empirical or theoretical definition of such a trap. In general terms, though, it can be said that the notion of a middle-income trap refers to the difficulty that many formerly fast-growing developing and emerging economies experience once their income and development levels pass a certain (empirically contested) threshold. Once this point is reached, it can become difficult to sustain previous growth levels and to finally close the gap with fully developed advanced, industrialised economies. What factors might be expected to induce such a slowdown? Eichengreen et al. (2012) argued that slowdowns are associated with high previous levels of growth, an ageing population, accentuated levels of capital investment and an undervalued exchange rate. The latter, it is argued, reduces the incentive to invest in technology and skills, preventing movement up the value chain. This in turn would inhibit productivity growth and competitiveness. This "story" appears to chime well with Chinese experience; in terms of Brazil's trajectory, the goodness of fit is less obvious. While Brazil certainly is encountering challenges associated with an ageing population (see Chapter 5) and has experienced episodes of exchange rate undervaluation, no one would argue that Chinese-style over-investment has been an issue.

However, in a subsequent paper by the authors (Eichengreen et al., 2014), it is argued that slowdowns are less likely in countries which have achieved high performance in secondary and tertiary education and in which high technology exports account for a large share of exports. This conclusion, as we will see, has particular salience for the Brazilian case where, despite undoubted economic and social progress since the 1980s, there have been considerable shortfalls in education and training. At the same time, the country's export profile has to an increasing extent become dominated by NRB as opposed to high-tech products or high value-added services. Animated by these considerations, and the need to see Brazil in an internationally comparative context, this volume takes the concept of a middle-income trap seriously. Part of this book's remit, therefore, is to assess the extent to which it may exist and whether Brazil is equipped to break out of it.

Summarising the discussion so far, this book takes as its starting point the position that Brazil's issues have counterpoints elsewhere. The need, therefore, arises to view Brazil's economic development experience, where possible, in a comparative international setting. While this volume avoids a doctrinaire ideological stance, it nevertheless takes it as given that Brazil will need to operate competitively within a relatively open international economic landscape. Within this context, it is highly probable that Brazil needs to confront a middle-income trap, a challenge shared by a range of similar, important emerging market economies. With these considerations in mind, two questions arise. First, which aspects of Brazil's economic development experience should form the focal points for the analysis? Second, and relatedly, which theoretical perspectives might be most relevant and worthy of adoption?

Turning to the first question, in order to succeed in a globalising world, Brazil needs to become an efficient, fast-growing, pro-poor market-driven economy. In order to do this, however, attention will need to be paid to the functioning of markets, the efficient and equitable operation of which remains retarded by a series of constraints. These constraints, which form the central preoccupation of the analysis, would include lack of international competitiveness, shortcomings in the development, absorption and diffusion of technology, deficiencies in human capital formation, capital market rigidities and a failure to address the environmental consequences of growth and structural change. Throughout the volume, it will become apparent that these brakes on development have stemmed from the peculiar way in which Brazil has developed as a political and economic entity. Their emergence has been influenced by factors such as deficiencies in the legal system, shortcomings in the capital market, the impact of mass illiteracy on market participation, the effect of infrastructural gaps on internal economic integration and the implications – not always favourable – of Brazil's still young democratic process for economic policymaking.

Against this background, which theoretical stance would be most relevant to frame our empirical investigation of the Brazilian economic development experience? Employing any single approach in isolation, while offering valuable insights, would orientate the analysis in such a way that not all relevant constraints and issues could be tractably investigated. Thus, this volume pragmatically draws on a range of perspectives. The theoretical optics chosen vary depending on the topic under investigation. The idea here is to select approaches based on what is most salient in their relation to a particular aspect of Brazil's economic reality.

Thus, our discussion of Brazil's counter-inflationary and fiscal adjustment strategy draws inspiration from the monetarist, rational expectations and structuralist approaches. Some examples from later in the volume serve to bear this point out. Investigating the topic of state-business relations, for example, attention is paid to the role of institutional economics and public choice theory in explaining why corruption, rent-seeking and directly unproductive activities have become so widespread. The competitiveness issue is similarly tackled through varied theoretical lenses. The analysis here takes on board neoclassical preoccupations, insofar as the need to boost static efficiency is of vital necessity. However, acknowledging that breaking out of a middle-income trap will also involve moving up the value chain and building indigenous technological capability, the discussion is also influenced by evolutionary economics and structuralist approaches.

To the extent to which this volume has a theoretical paradigm to which it gravitates more than others, this could be characterised as neo-structuralist. The reason for this lies in what this book argues to be Brazil's central dilemma: the need to overcome a series of deep structural constraints in order to compete and grow more effectively in a reasonably open global economic landscape. This fundamental interpretation of the core issue at stake accords with the tenets of a neo-structuralist approach. Against this background, it is worth considering the nature of such an approach and its relevance within the recent economic development history of Latin America.

Structuralism, neo-structuralism and development

The structuralist perspective on the economics of development has been one of the most influential in the post-war period (Bielschowsky, 1988; Kay, 1989). Its emergence as a new theoretical paradigm is distinctive. Structuralism, rather like Keynesianism, but unlike neoclassical economics, developed as an inductive response to wrenching changes in the global economy. Following the Wall Street Crash in the 1930s, collapses in commodity prices and the effective ending of access to international capital markets had seemingly rendered untenable the traditional position of less developed economies in the international division of labour. Whereas previously such economies had been able to sustain a position as exporters of primary products and importers of capital, such a potential route for development now appeared fatally compromised. The outbreak of World War II and its attendant disruption to international trade and capital markets simply confirmed many poorer economies in their view that their traditional development model was outmoded.

From this set of events there emerged slowly a new intellectual movement whose adherents would come to be known as structuralists. The object of this movement was twofold: first, to understand *how* certain economies had become underdeveloped and, second, to sketch out a new economic policy agenda appropriate to the changed global circumstances. Unlike established paradigms in economics, the intellectual heartland of structuralism consisted not of the universities of Western Europe or North America but the finance ministries and research institutes of Latin America. Of these bodies, the most influential by far in the development of structuralism would be the United Nations Economic Commission for Latin America (ECLA).

The founding of ECLA in 1949 brought together a number of outstanding researchers whose contributions in the policy arena would prove critical in accelerating Latin America down the path to industrialisation and accelerated income growth (Kay, 1989). Among the most influential of these researchers were Hans Singer (who died in 2006), Raul Prebisch and Osvaldo Sunkel. The fundamental insight of such structuralist pioneers is not that markets cannot deliver development (a characterisation of structuralism sometimes levelled by its critics) but rather that a series of institutional, political, legal and technological constraints have historically prevented markets from producing developmentally optimal outcomes in poorer economies (Bielschowsky, 1988). The solution to the entrenched problem of underdevelopment lies not in indiscriminate market liberalisation or in rampant state intervention but in a series of carefully crafted policy measures aimed at alleviating these constraints. The central message of structuralism could thus be summarised as "making markets work in the interests of development."

For the pioneers of structuralism, the central challenge was to secure sustained and rapid growth, avoiding any repetition of the policy errors of previous years. There emerged a consensus that the key problem of past policy regimes was that they ignored the perils of indiscriminate integration into the global economy. Structuralists were quick to observe that, to all intents and purposes, most developing economies fulfilled the same role in the international division of labour that they had occupied since the inception of the colonial era (Prebisch, 1949). Specifically, developing economies could be characterised as exporters of primary products and importers of manufactures, capital, technology and know-how. According to conventional trade theory, such a role could find its justification since specialisation according to comparative advantage was likely to deliver a superior outcome (in terms of welfare or efficiency) over the long term. For the structuralists, such a deductively derived conclusion was treated with scepticism, especially when set beside the evident failure of most primary product dependent economies to close the income gap with their industrialised counterparts.

In a classic piece of inductive empirical analysis, Raul Prebisch and Hans Singer demonstrated how continued reliance on primary product exports and industrialised imports would condemn an economy to long-term relative decline and underdevelopment. This was because the terms of trade for primary products tended to decline over time relative to those for manufactures. Thus, simply to maintain a given volume of imports, it would be necessary for an economy to generate an ever-increasing volume of exports. This situation was clearly not consistent with any strategy designed to boost long-term growth and development.

From this observation stemmed a radical set of policy conclusions. For developing economies to break with the past and close the gap with richer countries it would be necessary to engineer a reordering of patterns of specialisation. For the ECLA structuralists this meant in practice the adoption of a deliberate strategy of industrialisation (Kay, 1989). To the extent that such a strategy would involve a degree of trade protection, this implied a selective – and temporary – delinking of industrialising developing countries from the global economy. This policy recommendation, which stands as the most profound legacy of structuralism, underpinned the global spread of Import Substitution Industrialisation (ISI) from the 1940s to the 1970s. ISI essentially involved the substitution of goods that were previously imported by domestic alternatives.

At first, the structuralists seemed confirmed in their conclusions that industrialisation behind protective barriers offered real promise in confronting the challenge of underdevelopment. In Latin America, where ISI was pursued with especial vigour, the initial results in terms of growth and structural transformation far exceeded anything which had been previously experienced. However, after a few years it became apparent that the ISI model possessed some deep flaws. By the 1960s, Argentina, Brazil and Mexico had begun to experience failing growth, rising inflation and a deteriorating trade balance (Thorp, 1998). In the case of Brazil, as will be seen, matters became so serious that an alternative, more export-orientated strategy (known as "Post-ISI") was, with some success, temporarily adopted. Other countries, too, would encounter serious problems with ISI. The souring of the ISI miracle posed a profound intellectual challenge to the structuralists. It also seriously damaged their prestige and influence.

The passing of the years and the bitter experience of Latin American ISI prompted a critical self-evaluation within the structuralist school, a process that eventually gave rise to neo-structuralism (Kay, 1989). The waning of structuralism and the eventual rise of neo-structuralism were not only the result of inherent flaws within the cherished ISI model but also stemmed from the rising intellectual challenges posed by free market-orientated economists, whether labelled Monetarists, Chicago Boys or Neoclassicals.

Since the early 1980s, Brazil, like much of the rest of the region, has been broadly engaged in a process of dismantling the structures of ISI and has been progressively integrating itself into the global economy. In policy terms this has obviously implied an extensive programme of trade liberalisation. However, as subsequent chapters will emphasise, the transition from ISI has involved a lot more than stripping away the vestiges of protectionism. Very much in sympathy with the tenets of the liberal revolution in development economics initiated in the 1970s, Brazil along with other Latin American countries has engaged in internal market deregulation, privatisation and attempts to limit the size and scope of the state itself. Although the late 2000s and early 2010s witnessed a modest resurgence of industrial interventionism,[2] the general direction of travel has been one of gradual market liberalisation and global integration. Under the current Bolsonaro administration, this tendency has become accentuated.

Against this backdrop, not surprisingly, the new generation of structuralists – the neo-structuralists – are understandably far more sceptical (or even downright hostile) as to the wisdom of state-driven, inward-orientated industrialisation programmes. Instead, their attention is more closely drawn to one of the other major preoccupations of the structuralist tradition: the identification and alleviation of bottlenecks to efficient, equitable development (Sunkel, 1993). The attention of the state should be directed towards addressing such constraints rather than engaging in grandiose, all-embracing development programmes of the sort represented by ISI. Rather than retreating from the threat of globalisation, the proper role of the state can be seen as capacitating the productive sector (and the population) as a whole to meeting its challenges. This is likely to involve a series of pragmatic, competitiveness-enhancing market interventions. In specific terms, what are these likely to be?

First and foremost, it is worth emphasising that neo-structuralists, like their predecessors, share a preoccupation with altering the nature of developed comparative advantages (ibid.). Movement towards a concentration on higher value-added or more technologically sophisticated products is seen as a way of remaining competitive in global markets, avoiding some of the pitfalls of international protectionism and delivering enhanced growth in productivity and standards of living. Unlike some of the original structuralists, however, their successors are very sceptical as to the use of blanket ISI-style protectionist measures in order to achieve this objective.

At the same time, experience has also taught the new generation of structuralists the limitations of *dirigiste* sectoral promotion policies (an approach often characterised as "picking winners"). Instead, the emphasis is placed on interventions of a generic nature which provide private enterprise with an environment conducive to investment, risk-taking and movement up the value chain (Lall, 2000; Amann & Cantwell, 2012). This is as least as likely to involve the removal of impediments to competitiveness as the provision of concrete incentives. So, to repeat, the role of the state is to shape the policy environment in such a way that comparative advantages shift over time. However, the prime executors of this process are not planning ministries or state-owned enterprises (SOE) but rather the domestic and foreign private sectors.

Given this more circumscribed, facilitating role for the state, what is likely to constitute an appropriate set of interventions? The answer here will, of course, depend on the circumstances of individual countries. The obstacles to be overcome and the nature of appropriate incentives will clearly vary from place to place and from one historical juncture to another. This book will argue that in the case of Brazil, growth and development are being held back by a number of constraints and a lack of official incentives which the state will have to address if there is any prospect of realising a step change in economic performance. These obstacles and lack of incentives are centred in a number of areas. Each will, of course, be discussed in detail in subsequent chapters. They include an overextended public sector; a burdensome and inefficient tax regime; thin and inappropriately regulated capital markets; a disarticulated national system of innovation; low average educational attainment and skewed educational spending;

fragmented export incentives; under-investment in critical infrastructure and the growth constraining influences of mass poverty, illiteracy and poor health. Before examining these issues in-depth, however, it is worth setting them in context by offering a concise review of Brazil's development as an economy. This comprises a brief historical overview followed by a quantitative portrayal of Brazil's economic performance in the contemporary period.

Brazil's economic performance in the long-run context

Beginnings – from colonial times to World War II

The rise of the Brazilian economy to global prominence has been a protracted process punctuated by crisis, seismic changes in political regime, variations in the degree of external orientation and profound shifts in the role of the state. As in the case of its Latin American counterparts, the emergence of the contemporary Brazilian economy has been conditioned by the colonial experience. Between its initial occupation by Europeans in 1500 and independence in 1822 Brazil formed the largest of Portugal's overseas possessions.

During these long three centuries, three distinctive features characterised the colonial economic experience. The first centred on the placement of Brazil within the mercantilist system, whereby the colony's external economic interactions – principally trade – were almost exclusively channelled through Portuguese trading houses (Baer, 2013). This facilitated revenue raised by the Portuguese crown, political control and protection against foreign incursion. The second key feature relates to the role of Brazil – mediated through Portuguese commerce – in the global division of labour. As the colonial economy developed, its pattern of exports became characterised by specialisation in natural resource-based commodity exports, the two most important products being precious stones and cotton.[3] The third feature, which continues to exercise malign economic, social and political effects to this day, centred on the use of slave labour most especially in the key commodities export sectors. As Versiani (2018) indicates, the colonial period saw Brazil become one of the key participants in the Atlantic slave trade. Well over two million people were forcibly transported from Africa to provide labour for colonial Brazil's fast-expanding agricultural and mining sectors; not until the late 19th century – 1889 in fact – was slavery finally abolished.

The transition from colony to becoming an independent Empire in the 1820s initially brought surprisingly little economic change. Brazil remained an economy characterised by a strong dependence on commodity exports. However, thanks to independence and the growing role of the British, Brazil began to embrace the 19th-century doctrine of free trade. By the 1890s, Brazil's first decade as a republic, new commodities – notably rubber and coffee – had come to supplant the traditional staples of minerals and cotton as the most dynamic export products. The growth of the coffee sector, in and around the city of São Paulo kick-started a period of rapid urbanisation, European labour migration and industrialisation in Brazil's South East. By the opening decade of the 20th century, as Abreu (1990) points out, Brazil, within the context of a liberal international economic order, was manifesting clear signs of development with growing income per capita, a rising share of industry in GDP and the development of urban middle and working classes. To meet increasing capital investment demands that could not be met through domestic savings, Brazil, like Argentina, experienced a dramatic surge in inward FDI. Brazil's not unimpressive development trajectory was only briefly interrupted by the outbreak of World War I. Once the conflict ended, global trade patterns returned to normal and, by the mid-to-late 1920s, Brazil was benefitting from a strong upsurge in global demand.

The Wall Street Crash and its aftermath were to have profound implications for Brazil which continue to resonate to this day. Following the crash in 1929, Brazil soon found access to international capital markets severely restricted while a combination of global depression and protectionist measures – principally in the United Kingdom and the United States – put a harsh brake on Brazil's traditionally strong export sectors (Baer, 2013). The response to these events by the Vargas dictatorship, which came into power in 1931, was to radically alter the course of Brazil's development strategy. Eschewing the liberal approach to economic management which had characterised the period since independence in the early 19th century, President Getúlio Vargas expanded the role of the state[4] and embraced ISI. The latter strategy involved increasingly concerted efforts to replace industrial product imports by domestically produced alternatives. At first this was achieved by the dint of currency devaluation and ad hoc protectionism. Later, after World War II, the pursuit of ISI took on a more strategic character as a comprehensive industrial policy rapidly took shape.

Another long-term consequence of the Vargas administration relates to the labour and state-business relations. The corporatist ideology practised by the regime deliberately fostered the emergence of representative interest groups from among relevant economic actors: industrial workers, big business and agriculture. Thus, the 1930s saw rapid expansion in formal trade union representation as well as a rise in the salience of business associations (Schneider, 2004). As part of this process, the links between the state and business were strengthened as both worked in tandem to pursue industrialisation and development goals. The authorities also began to intervene more extensively in Brazil's agricultural sector, instigating the coffee valorisation programme. The latter involved, as Europe's Common Agricultural Policy later would, the purchase and sale of buffer stocks so as to stabilise market prices. The Vargas era also saw profound labour market reforms. The launch of the labour code – which still provides the legal basis for contemporary employment relations – aimed to improve workers' rights and access to social benefits. Politically, this helped to bind the increasingly numerous working classes[5] to the Vargas administration, bolstering its perceived legitimacy.

Structural transformation and the state: 1945–80

The four decades after the end of World War II proved to be a period of rapid growth and structural transformation for Brazil's economy. In a broad sense, the country during this time retained in place the essential elements of economic strategy bequeathed it by Vargas in the 1930s: import substitution industrialisation, and a pivotal role for the state in the economy. As Brazil departed the 1940s and embarked on a phase of civilian rule, policymakers fell increasingly under the influence of the structuralist economists (Bielschowsky, 1988). This resulted in a more phased, strategic approach to the pursuit of industrialisation with sectoral priorities identified. At the same time, macroeconomic management came to be dominated by a technocratic elite; it was increasingly subject to scrutiny by the newly created international financial institutions, the International Bank for Reconstruction and Development (The World Bank) and the International Monetary Fund (IMF).

In many ways, the 1950s proved a golden decade for Brazil's economy. Under Presidents Vargas[6] and Kubitschek, Brazil enjoyed average annual GDP growth in excess of 7%. The industrialisation process which had accelerated in the 1930s picked up further speed as Brazil began to develop a comprehensive consumer durables sector. The Kubitschek administration (1956–60) stepped up investment in infrastructure and famously created a new capital city, Brasília, out of the semi-arid central Planalto plateau. Yet, despite the pace of progress, all was not entirely well. The ISI process failed to generate export growth sufficient to meet the rising demand for key imported inputs. At the same time, structural bottlenecks began to make themselves felt as increased aggregate demand pressed against deficient infrastructure and an inadequate skills base. As a result, by the early 1960s, growth was faltering and inflation rising (Abreu, 1990).

As an indirect result of these economic setbacks, the military came to power in March 1964 for what would prove to be a protracted, 20-year period. Unlike the case of Chile nine years later, the military, on taking power, did not dismantle the structures of ISI. Neither, by the same token, did they attack the thicket of corporatist ties binding the state to organised labour and big business (Schneider, 2004). Instead, between 1967 and 1973, the military government experimented with a reformed version of ISI, sometimes referred to as Post-ISI. This attempted, via limited trade reform and capital market liberalisation, to unleash Brazil's export potential.

For a while, this strategy proved highly effective, with growth rates touching 8% and 9% in the early 1970s. This era came to be known as the Brazilian Economic Miracle; it seemed at last that Brazil was living up to its long-held promise. Unfortunately, however, this pace of expansion could not be maintained following the OPEC I oil price hike in 1973. In the wake of this, arguably the greatest external shock to hit the Brazilian economy since 1929, the country's current account deficit rapidly expanded as external markets entered recession and the oil import bill surged. Rather than engage in a programme of painful stabilisation and structural adjustment though reduced domestic absorption, the military government doubled down on state-driven industrialisation. Under the terms of the Second National Development Plan (PND II), launched in 1974, Brazil set out to develop its own capital goods sector (Amann, 2000) while investing heavily in transportation and energy infrastructure. The adoption of this strategy involved the assumption of increasing levels of external debt, not only to finance a string of grandiose investment projects[7] but also to address a structural trade deficit. The latter was fuelled by high domestic absorption in the face of depressed global demand for Brazil's exports.

The debt with growth strategy embodied in the PND II was forced to an abrupt halt at the start of the 1980s thanks to a further oil price hike instigated by producer countries (OPEC II in 1979). OPEC II not only inflated Brazil's oil import bill; it also sparked a global recession which adversely affected demand for Brazilian exports. This time round, escape was no longer possible through external debt accumulation; tightened monetary policy in the Western economies had sharply pushed up interest rates on international financial markets. As a result, and given Brazil's already substantial stock of foreign debt, little alternative remained but for the country to embark on an IMF-sanctioned debt adjustment strategy (Thorp, 1998). This emphasised fiscal retraction and reduced domestic absorption. Even this did not prove sufficient to prevent the eventual default on foreign debt which occurred in 1987.

The lost decade, civilian rule and the path to globalisation: 1980–93

The 1980s in Brazil and throughout Latin America has become known as the lost decade. This label seems only appropriate when one considers the sharp contraction in national output and rise in poverty and inequality which characterised the era. Yet the decade saw the planting of the seeds of reform which were to bear fruit in the 1990s and beyond, as Brazil cautiously embraced globalisation and, eventually, pro-poor growth. With the need to limit debt growth uppermost in the minds of domestic policymakers and their counterparts in the IMF and World Bank, the 1980s were marked by a stringent fiscal adjustment. However, the most immediate challenge, from the public's perspective at least, was the need to choke off hyperinflation.

The latter, by the late 1980s, had firmly taken hold in Brazil, propelled by structural bottlenecks, ballooning public debt, missteps in the formulation of monetary policy and, relatedly, chronic currency weakness. Attempts to hold inflation in check during this period centred on a range of approaches, some more macroeconomically orthodox in tone. Others, by contrast, such as the Bresser Plan and the Summer Plan, rested on heterodox foundations.[8] Lacking credibility among economic agents and replete with conceptual flaws, one by one these plans failed (Ayres et al., 2019). None would succeed, in fact, prior to the launch of the Real Plan well into the 1990s.

Despite macroeconomic frustrations, reform and change were in the air. In 1985, military rule ended after 21 years. The new indirectly elected civilian president, José Sarney, under pressure from the Washington-based international financial institutions, launched a cautious programme of trade liberalisation and privatisation. His directly elected successor, Fernando Collor de Melo, while failing to tame the rampant inflation[9] nevertheless succeeded in introducing ambitious microeconomic reforms comprising a wide-ranging privatisation programme (Programa Nacional de Desestatizção) and a rolling four-year timetable of trade reforms known as the *Abertura Comercial* (Amann, 2000). The latter involved the progressive elimination of non-tariff barriers and an average reduction of tariff barriers by 50%. Thus by 1992, the year President Collor was removed from office on corruption charges, Brazil had firmly turned its back on decades of structuralist-influenced state-driven industrialisation strategy. In favour now was progressive integration with the global economy and primacy for the private sector.

Stabilisation and growth: 1993–2012

By the beginning of 1993, the Brazilian economy had firmly established itself on a trajectory of microeconomic reform and progressive international integration. However, inflation remained at chronically high levels. Output growth was also subdued. Against this challenging backdrop, newly appointed President, Itamar Franco, and his Finance Minister, Fernando Henrique Cardoso, set out to develop a comprehensive solution to Brazil's inflationary problem (Giambiagi & Moreira, 1999). The solution, in the form of the Real Plan, launched in 1993, proved to be effective and long-lasting. At its core the Real Plan recognised that previous attempts to rein in inflation had failed due to an inability to gain the credibility of economic agents and influence their expectations.

The new counter-inflationary plan tackled these issues head-on by the phased introduction of shadow currency, the Real Unit of Value (URV, to use its Portuguese acronym). This was pegged to the US dollar within tight bounds. While the old, conventional currency, the Cruzeiro Real, continued to circulate, prices were also posted in URV terms, allowing agents to adjust, over time to the notion of a currency unit whose value was not eroding, either in terms of domestic purchasing power or in terms of the dollar. This ingenious "soft launch" of a new currency was accompanied by monetary and fiscal tightening according to a pre-announced plan. Consequently, when the URV's real-world incarnation, the Real, began circulation in July 1994, the public was suitably prepared. As a result, the Real gained rapid acceptance (Amann & Baer, 2000). Pegged to the US dollar as it was, credibility among agents was sustained. Between 1994 and 1997 consumer price inflation on an annualised basis fell from almost 2000% to just 7%. At the same time, confidence in the new macroeconomic framework proved sufficient to trigger a rapid recovery in consumer and investment demand. Between 1993 and 1998 growth averaged 3% per year, well above anything which had been achieved during the 1980s.

By the late 1990s, it appeared as if the Brazilian economy had definitively turned the corner. Structuralist-influenced state-driven industrialisation strategy and heterodox remedies for price instability had been abandoned. The new approach was rooted in a combination of global economic integration and a currency bound to an exchange rate anchor. It appeared to be delivering the desired combination of accelerating growth and declining inflation. The Real proved robust enough to survive the rigours of the 1997–98 emerging markets crisis.[10] Following the accession to power of President Luiz Inácio Lula da Silva (Lula) in 2003, the Real remained the cornerstone of Brazil's macroeconomic policy framework. Still, the arrival of Lula and his left-leaning PT (Workers' Party) in power raised the question of whether there would be yet another fundamental shift in approach regarding Brazil's development strategy. Would there be a return to state-driven industrialisation or even autarchic development strategy? The answer here turned out to be broadly "no" albeit with some qualifications.

The Lula years – stretching from 2003 to 2010 – proved to be a period of accelerated economic expansion in which, for once, the poor were not left behind. Price pressures remained under control thanks to the maintenance of tight monetary policy, nested within an inflation-targeting framework (Ayres et al., 2019). Simultaneously, output was buoyed by booming global demand for Brazil's key commodity exports. The new administration broadly conserved the macroeconomic framework bequeathed by its predecessor while experimenting with a more activist industrial policy in selected sectors, including oil and gas.

Despite the rising tide of interventionism, there was no significant rollback of the trade reforms accomplished in the 1990s while, perhaps surprisingly, the privatisation programme continued. On the social plane, Brazil successfully pioneered a conditional cash transfer programme, the Bolsa Família. This, in tandem with stable prices and growing employment, drove declines in the incidence of poverty and interpersonal income inequality. By the end of the 2000s, it appeared that Brazil was finally on the verge of realising its long-held potential; GDP growth was closing in on 10% per annum while FDI poured in. *The Economist* famously captured this economic exuberance when, in 2009, it depicted Rio's famous Christ the Redeemer statue launching into space on a plume of steam and smoke.

Crisis and reform: 2012–present

Lula's successor, Dilma Rousseff, elected in 2010, inherited what appeared to be a favourable set of circumstances. However, within four years Brazil's economy had entered a profound crisis. Within six, part-way through her second term, President Rousseff had been impeached, having been found guilty of misrepresenting the true state of Brazil's parlous public finances. At the root of the Brazilian economy's descent into steep recession and crisis lay three factors. In the first place, the global commodity price boom came to an end in 2013. Second, and in the face of this, there was a failure to tap alternate sources of growth in an economy beset by structural constraints and, across many sectors, lack of competitiveness (Amann & Cantwell, 2012). Third, a failure to embrace systemic fiscal reform had left the public accounts in a worsening state. Proactive political leadership and the swift articulation of a fresh growth strategy could have softened the external shock imposed by the commodity slump. However, the Rousseff administration did not prove effective in these terms. Indeed, in the run up to the President's impeachment in August 2016 its ability to effect economic reform was increasingly compromised by Brazil's largest-ever corruption scandal, the *Lava Jato* or Car Wash crisis. *Lava Jato*, which will be the subject of an extensive review in Chapter 8, saw the veil lifted on long-standing and corrupt linkages between state organs, politicians and large enterprises (Netto, 2016).

The end of the Rousseff administration saw the President's replacement by Michel Temer, a member of the centrist PMDB party. This political change saw a reversion to a more market-fundamentalist reform agenda. This in many ways resembled the type pursued by President Collor de Melo in the early 1990s. On assuming office in August 2016, President Temer moved to accelerate the privatisation programme, prioritising the sale of assets in the transportation infrastructure sector. During its short, two-year, tenure the new administration adopted the most far-reaching fiscal reform measure since the 1990s, imposing a 20-year real-term freeze on federal expenditures (Oreira & de Paula, 2019). Progress on other reforms, notably pension and social security reforms were frustrated, however, amidst the ongoing political fallout from the Lava Jato scandal.

Whatever its shortcomings, the Temer administration succeeded in restoring sufficient confidence among economic agents such that, by 2017, Brazil had begun to emerge from recession, its steepest since the 1930s. Going to the polls in October 2018, Brazil's electorate decisively endorsed an economically and socially conservative candidate, Jair Bolsonaro. The election results amounted, in effect, to a rejection of the PT's more interventionist and progressive agenda. Since taking office in January 2019, the Bolsonaro administration has continued down the path of intensified liberal reform instituted by its predecessor. Privatisations have been stepped up, plans for a new wave of trade reforms announced and, perhaps most prominently, a detailed programme for pension and social security reforms announced (and partially accomplished).

Up until 2020 and in tandem with these developments the economy continued its (weak) recovery. However, the advent of the COVID-19 global pandemic in 2020 has imparted a great shock to the Brazilian economy, driving output down and unemployment up. Against this background, the authorities have been obliged to temporarily revise their approach to macroeconomic policy, introducing a programme of quantitative easing. It remains to be seen whether the effects of the pandemic will, over the long term, slow the pace of reforms or indeed set policy in a different direction. Further discussion around these issues will take place in the concluding chapter.

The Brazilian economy in long-term, comparative perspective: a brief quantitative portrait

Growth

Taken as a whole, the post-World War II period can be viewed as one in which Brazil, by historical standards, grew very rapidly and underwent substantial structural alteration. However, as Figure 1.1 indicates, average growth rates tended to be much higher prior to 1980 than subsequently. During the initial ISI phase that lasted from the late 1940s to the early 1960s, GDP growth not only remained positive but rarely dipped below 5% p.a. As the previous section argued, the replacement of ISI with the Post-ISI strategy after 1964 produced even more positive results as Brazil embarked on its so-called "economic miracle." Even with the advent of the oil crisis in 1973 and the reversion to more traditional ISI, continuing capital inflows enabled the economy to expand at rates exceeding 5% p.a.

The emergence of the debt crisis in the early 1980s marks something of a watershed in Brazil's growth performance. After a sharp recession in 1981–84 growth rebounded but, thanks to near hyper-inflation, could not be sustained. In response to growing price instability, the late 1980s and early 1990s saw the implementation of a series of stabilisation initiatives (Ayres et al., 2019). One of these, under the Collor administration in 1992 saw bank accounts frozen and a corresponding massive contraction in output and demand. Although, as already argued, the Real Plan (launched in 1993) proved much more successful in its counter-inflationary objectives, average rates of GDP growth have subsequently proved far less impressive than those achieved in the earlier ISI and Post-ISI periods.

Whereas the latter periods typically saw average annual growth exceed 5%, since 1993 only in four years (1994, 2004, 2007 and 2010) has GDP growth matched this performance. The fact that growth has failed to take off despite

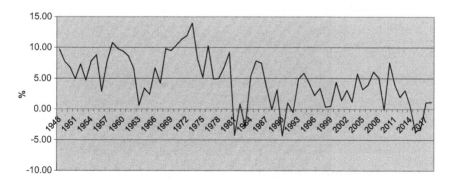

FIGURE 1.1 Brazil: annual growth in Real GDP 1948–2018.
Source: Author elaboration on the basis of IBGE/IPEA data.

the implementation of an ostensibly successful stabilisation plan is a troubling phenomenon and one which, of course, forms a point of departure for this book. The long-run underperformance in relation to GDP growth should not deflect us from noting the highly negative consequences for output engendered by Brazil's 2013–16 recession. This was the steepest in the country's history and saw GDP contract by 3.55% in 2015 and 3.47% in 2016. Recovery, subsequently, has proven weak: GDP growth in 2017 and 2018 stood at barely over 1% p.a.

The less than spectacular growth performance enjoyed by Brazil in the last decade or so stands at odds with that of the other BRIC or emerging economies. Figure 1.2 reveals the evolution of GDP per capita over the postwar period. It will be noted that since the start of the 1980s both India and, especially, China have rapidly closed the gap with Brazil. Whereas in 1980 Chinese and Indian GDP per capita stood at US$524 and US$875, respectively, that of Brazil was substantially greater at US$7567. Almost 40 years later in 2017, Chinese and Indian GDP per capita had risen in constant dollar terms to US$ 15308 and US$ 6427, respectively. This represented a more than 30-fold increase in the case of China and an 8-fold increase in the case of India. In the case of Brazil, GDP per capita had reached US$ 14103 by 2018 implying only a roughly two-fold increase since 1980. The achievement of India and China in raising per capita GDP is all the more impressive when one considers the fact that their populations were increasing much more rapidly than that of Brazil during the period in question. In the case of Russia (for which data are only available from 1989 onwards), per capita GDP went into steep decline in the immediate aftermath of the collapse of the Soviet Union. However, since the mid-1990s, GDP per capita has strongly recovered, partly on the back of increasing commodity prices. As a result, average Russian income per head now comfortably exceeds that in Brazil.

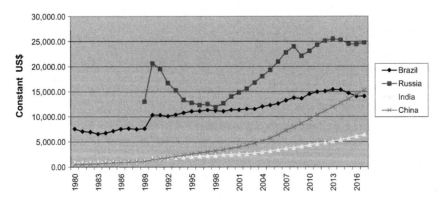

FIGURE 1.2 Evolution of GDP per capita in the BRIC economies.
Source: Author elaboration on the basis of IPEA/World Bank data.

Structural change

The relatively high rates of growth in the post-war period up until the early 1980s were associated with substantial structural change in the Brazilian economy (Baer, 2013). As Figure 1.3 indicates, the proportion of GDP accounted for by the industrial sector rose substantially during this time. Between 1960 and 1980, industrial value as a percentage of GDP rose from 25.4% to 30.25%. Significantly, the period since 1980 – which, as we have seen, has been associated with lower average rates of growth – saw something of a contraction in the share of industrial GDP. By 2017, industrial value-added as a percentage of total GDP had declined to 10.15%. However, the component of output represented by mining (effectively a lower value-added industrial sector) actually rose. Whereas mining accounted for just 1.1% of GDP in 1980, by 1990 it had reached 1.7% and by 2018 accounted for 4.3%. In the case of agriculture, between 1980 and 2017, the percentage contribution to GDP fell (from 9.95% to 4.57%). However, the share of GDP accounted for by agricultural value added has remained more or less stable since the middle of the last decade.

The analogue of these trends is, of course, a rising share of output accounted for by the services sector. The contraction in the relative shares of agriculture and industry is a phenomenon by no means confined to Brazil (see Bernard et al., 2017). Similar structural trends are, of course, readily observable in Europe, North America and Japan. In one sense what might loosely be termed "de-industrialisation" could be construed as a sign of economic "maturity." Unfortunately, in the case of Brazil – unlike the United States or the United Kingdom – for example, the relative shrinking of the industrial base appears not to have had its counterpart in the emergence of dynamic non-industrial activities capable of raising long-term growth. In the latter economies, the rise of financial and professional services and information technology have facilitated an acceleration in average growth rates following the end of the great recession of 2008–10.

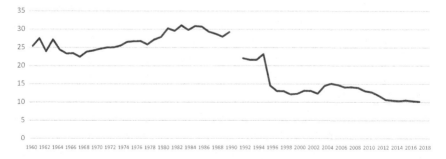

FIGURE 1.3 Brazilian industrial value-added as a percentage of GDP, 1960–2017.
Source: Author elaboration on the basis of World Bank data.

Savings and investment

In attempting to understand any country's growth performance, a common starting point centres on the savings and investment constraints (Agenor & Montiel, 2015). Since, with given production technology, the maximum feasible growth rate will be set by the availability of capital, an examination of the national evolution of saving and investment behaviour can be illuminating. The period of relatively favourable growth performance up until the early 1980s was associated with a rising investment share of GDP. Between 1959 and 1980, the share of investment in overall GDP rose from 17.78% to 23.35%. Up until the early 1970s, the growth in investment was almost exclusively financed out of domestic savings.

However, as argued in the previous section the remainder of the 1970s proved a period of debt-led growth in which foreign savings assumed a much more important role in the financing of investment. This enabled overall gross domestic fixed capital formation to run ahead of saving for several years (Figure 1.4). With the advent of the debt crisis in the early 1980s, the inflow of foreign savings tapered off sharply, a development that became associated with a reduction of the incidence of investment in overall GDP. Since the late 1980s, and despite the successful stabilisation brought into being by the Real Plan after 1993, investment as a proportion of national output has failed to pick up, hovering at around 20% of GDP. Throughout the 1990s and up until 2018, savings as a proportion of GDP generally trailed investment, the difference being made up by a recovery in foreign capital inflows (many of which were associated with privatisation-related FDI).

The Brazilian track record on investment can be put into further perspective if one considers the case of China. China's outstanding growth since 1980 is paralleled by its investment performance: between 1980 and 2017 investment as a

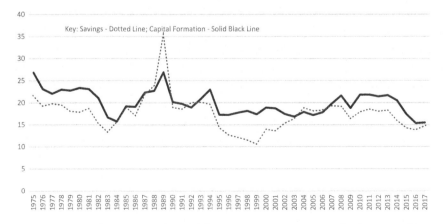

FIGURE 1.4 Brazil: savings and capital formation as a percentage of GDP, 1975–2017.
Source: Author elaboration on the basis of IBGE data.

percentage of overall GDP rose from an already impressive 27% to 44%. As in the case of Brazil, foreign capital inflows (especially in the form of FDI) have come to play an important role in financing Chinese investment.

It should be evident from the discussion thus far that Brazil's economic performance in the period since the debt crisis has proved disappointing in relation to that which preceded it. However, in regard to at least one vital respect – inflation – such an assessment would be unfair and inaccurate.

Inflation

As Figure 1.5 indicates, whatever the success in terms of growth associated with the ISI and Post-ISI experiments, there was a heavy price to pay in terms of high and accelerating inflation. During the 1970s, increasing international indebtedness went hand in hand with accentuated price instability. Despite the fiscal retrenchment and recession associated with the debt adjustment crisis of the early 1980s, price instability became an increasingly ingrained feature of the Brazilian macroeconomy. In an effort to tame inflation, the late 1980s and early 1990s saw a series of so-called heterodox stabilisation programmes. These programmes – the most notable of which were the Bresser Plan, the Summer Plan, the Rice and Beans Plan and (most infamously) the Collor plans I and II – singularly failed in their anti-inflationary objectives.

Given the track record of previous stabilisation attempts, observers were understandably sceptical when Finance Minister Fernando Henrique Cardoso announced the anti-inflationary Real Plan in 1993. As already suggested, the policy mix and timing of the Real Plan meant that it succeeded where other stabilisation plans had failed. Consequently, inflation fell sharply after 1993 and has remained in abeyance despite the effective ending of the dollar peg in 1999 (Ayres et al., 2019). The continued success of the Real Plan in its current inflation-targeting incarnation means that Brazil today enjoys historically low single digit levels of inflation which are more reminiscent of those in OECD economies.

FIGURE 1.5   Brazil: general prices index (IGP-DI) 1945–2018.
Source: Author elaboration on the basis of IPEA data.

Trade and the external balance plus the role of FDI

The adoption of the exchange rate anchor, although successful in lending impetus to the anti-inflationary successes of the late 1990s, proved costly to maintain, not least because of the competitive burdens it placed on the export sector. The deterioration of the trade balance, alongside fiscal disequilibria proved critical factors in the economic crisis of 1998–99 which ultimately resulted in the floatation of the Real and the switch to the inflation-targeting regime. As Figures 1.6 and 1.7 illustrate, the abandonment of the exchange rate anchor ultimately has had far from unfavourable consequences.

For much of the post-war period Brazil remained prone to periodic balance of trade crises, a tendency strongly accentuated by the competitive problems implicit in ISI (Abreu, 1990). By the mid-to-late 1970s the trade deficits had grown to record proportions, a situation that was only able to persist thanks to unprecedented capital inflows. With the debt adjustment crisis of the early 1980s, the authorities were obliged to reduce drastically domestic absorption with the result that the trade balance sharply swung into surplus (Figure 1.6). However, improvements in the trade balance, resulting as they did from reduced domestic demand rather than improving underlying competitiveness, could not be sustained once demand picked up or the currency strengthened. By the late 1990s, accelerating growth, allied to a strong Real, had given rise to substantial trade deficits.

The decision to float the Real in 1999 led to a sharp depreciation against the US dollar (see Figure 1.7). This, together with the strengthening of commodity prices in the 2000s, proved fortuitous for the evolution of the Brazilian trade balance, although a temporary reversal was experienced in relation to the commodity price slump after 2011. As Figure 1.6 indicates, in more recent years Brazil had begun to register larger trade surpluses.

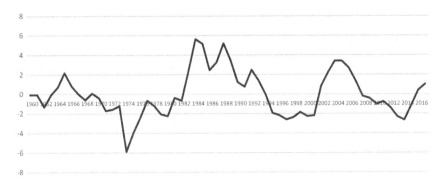

FIGURE 1.6 Evolution of Brazil's trade balance, 1960–2017 (% GDP).

Source: Author elaboration on the basis of World Bank OECD, National Accounts data.

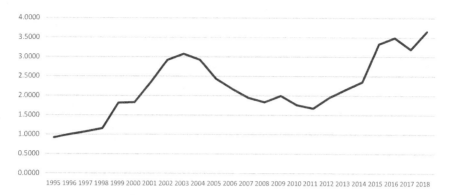

FIGURE 1.7 Brazilian Real per US dollar, 1995–2018 (annual average).

The relatively favourable recent external performance of the Brazilian economy represents an important achievement. However, as will later be noted, the long-term sustainability of this achievement is questionable given its dependence on buoyant commodity demand. To ensure that Brazil's recent trade successes can survive future downturn in such prices, it will be argued that more needs to be done to strengthen the competitiveness of non-traditional export sectors. This is at least as likely to involve systemic competitive reforms as more "traditional" targeted industrial policy.

Poverty and distribution

Whatever Brazil's long-term economic achievements regarding growth, inflation or the external balance, they need to be seen in the context of an ingrained tendency towards highly uneven distributional outcomes. Still, as Figure 1.8 demonstrates the past 15 years or so have witnessed a marked reduction in the Gini coefficient for interpersonal income distribution. Although Brazil has made significant progress in reducing income inequality, the country still ranks among the most unequal on earth.

In tandem with the reduction in the value of the Gini coefficient, Brazil has also made progress in driving down the incidence of poverty as Figure 1.9 indicates. As a share of the population, those classified as poor on the basis of falling within the World Bank's US$3.20 a day (in 2011 dollars) poverty headcount ratio declined from 37.2% to 9.6% between 1992 and 2017. This compares favourably with performance realised in other emerging and developing economies though the fall in China was more dramatic. Between 1993 and 2015, measure by the same criterion, the share of the population qualifying as poor shrank from 83.4% to just 7%. As will be discussed in Chapter 7, the factors resulting in favourable outcomes regarding poverty and distribution are numerous and do not centre entirely around Brazil's vaunted Conditional Cash Transfer Programme, the Bolsa Família. Low inflation and employment generation have proved to be

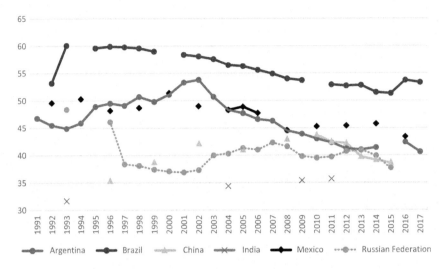

FIGURE 1.8 Variations in the Gini coefficient, selected countries 1991–2017.
Source: Author elaboration on the basis of World Bank data.

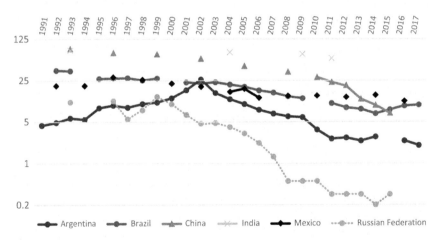

FIGURE 1.9 Poverty headcount ratio at $3.20 a day (2011 PPP) (% of population).
Source: Author elaboration on the basis of World Bank data.

vital drivers (Ferreira et al., 2017). Given this, it is not surprising that progress in tackling poverty and inequality received a sharp setback as a result of Brazil's recent recession.

Conclusions

This chapter has aimed to set out the scope for this book, its conceptual framing as well as to offer a brief comparative overview of the performance of Brazil's economy. It was established that Brazil, despite its emergence as a major global economy, continues to face serious challenges. These are exemplified in its proneness to crisis and, over the past five years at least, a notable fall off in growth performance. In explaining the background to these issues, the central argument has been that Brazil faces ingrained structural impediments to accelerated, inclusive and sustainable growth. These have emerged over several decades and have prevented Brazil from realising its undoubted potential. Thus far, they have proved very hard for policymakers to tackle.

Given all of this, the purpose of this book is to evaluate in detail the nature of the structural challenges that will need to be overcome if Brazil is to break with the past, escape what may well be a middle-income trap and do better by its (often) hard-pressed citizens. Over the course of the next few chapters, the challenges to be examined broadly fall into three areas: those centring on competitiveness and the supply side, those arising from critical macroeconomic issues and those connected with environmental sustainability and social inclusion. In systematically examining each of these domains, the key topics highlighted centre on competitiveness (Chapter 2), human capital formation (Chapter 3), state-business relations (Chapter 4), fiscal adjustment (Chapter 5), investment and the role of monetary policy (Chapter 6), poverty, distribution and social inclusion (Chapter 7) and environmental considerations (Chapter 8). It will be argued that such issues were never thoroughly addressed by policymakers even when windows of opportunity were created during periods of progress and expansion. This especially applies to Brazil's chronic failure to tackle deficiencies surrounding training, education and productivity growth.

Notes

1 See, for example, Baer (2013), an excellent study which, however, offers only limited comparative perspective.
2 With, for example, special policy initiatives launched to favour import substitution in the petroleum exploration and production sector.
3 Brazil's role as a major coffee exporter would only become cemented in the post-independence 19th century.
4 Most famously through establishing state-owned enterprises such as the National Steel Company (CSN) in 1941.
5 At least those with formal employment contracts.
6 This time democratically elected.
7 The most famous being the Itaipú hydroelectric scheme on the frontier with Paraguay, at the time the world's largest.
8 Here the emphasis was placed on non-monetary measures such as price freezes and alterations in the elaborate system of price and wage indexation which had grown up by this time.
9 A particularly notable failed attempt to address hyperinflation comprised the Collor I plan, launched in 1990. This involved, among other measures, a temporary freeze of bank accounts in an attempt to engineer a monetary shock.
10 Although the aftermath of this crisis saw the authorities dispense with an exchange rate targeting framework in favour of an inflation-targeting mechanism.

2

PUBLIC POLICY, COMPETITIVENESS AND THE EVOLUTION OF BRAZIL'S PLACE IN THE INTERNATIONAL DIVISION OF LABOUR

Introduction

The previous chapter characterised the Brazilian economy as one defined by superlatives, contradictions and paradoxes. Emerging from this kaleidoscopic picture surges an essential truth: whatever the undoubted achievements that have propelled it to the position of the seventh largest economy on earth, Brazil has still failed to live up to its obvious potential. Growth and progress on living standards have demonstrably failed to match that experienced in large parts of the emerging market world, especially East Asia. Chronic poverty and a highly skewed income distribution remain grim facts of life despite two decades of ambitious pro-poor reforms. Lastly, as starkly illustrated in the recent recession, Brazil's economy remains painfully prone to crisis and vulnerable to the impacts of external shocks. A fundamental driver of suboptimal performance across all of these dimensions has been lack of competitiveness in key sectors and areas of the supply side. This has hampered attempts to advantageously and proactively shift Brazil's position in the global division of labour. The purpose of this chapter is to examine the interconnected issues of competitiveness and Brazil's place in the global economy.

The economic issue of competitiveness has become a central policy preoccupation across the world, Brazil being no exception. Its rise to prominence is at least partly the result of flourishing academic interest in the topic over the past 30 years. The publication in 1990 of Michael Porter's landmark volume, *The Competitive Advantage of Nations* represented one of the seminal events in the evolution of post-1945 economics and business studies. Porter argued that nations could be considered to be in competition with one another on the global economic stage and their effectiveness in this contest rested on the extent to which they possessed particular attributes. The latter, nested within Porter's famous Diamond

Framework, comprised factor conditions, demand conditions, the presence of related and supporting industries and firm strategy, structure and rivalry.

Porter's volume developed a series of famous country case studies. The impact of these was such that the research broke out of the academic debate and into the public sphere, inspiring a new generation of policymakers. While Porter's work triggered some opposition within the international economics discipline (see Krugman, 1991), others were more enthusiastic. The following three decades have seen a mushrooming of academic and policy-orientated work on the competitiveness theme, the research focusing not just on the national level, but on sectors, firms, regions among other levels of aggregation. A particularly vibrant branch of this research, especially as far as emerging markets such as Brazil are concerned, has focused on the development of innovative capability at sector and enterprise level (e.g. Lall, 1992; Amann & Cantwell, 2012).

As might be expected given the plethora of research and its diverse levels of aggregation, there is no settled definition as to what constitutes competitiveness or how it should be measured. Instead, there is broad acknowledgement that certain factors, such as higher labour productivity, moving up the value chain of a given sector, or enhancing investment in human capital, are vital in unlocking new market opportunities, enhancing the terms of trade or attaining a more advantageous position in the international division of labour (Cimoli & Stiglitz, 2009). The precise importance attributable to these or other individual factors would vary dependent on the level of aggregation in question (firm, sector, region, etc.). In the Brazilian context, Figueiredo et al. (2018, pp. 41–3) draw a distinction between improvements in competitiveness arising from factor accumulation and productivity rises, on the one hand, and structural change on the other hand. The nearest we have to an "industry standard" definition, at least in terms of measurement, is embodied in the annual World Economic Forum's Global Competitiveness Report. The latter presents a widely quoted composite index of competitiveness based on 12 pillars, the latter comprising institutions, appropriate infrastructure, stable macroeconomic framework, good health and primary education, higher education and training, efficient goods markets, efficient labour markets, developed financial markets, ability to harness existing technology, market size (both domestic and international), production of new and different goods and innovation (product and process) (World Economic Forum (WEF), 2018a). On this basis, the 2018 report ranked Brazil 72nd out of 140 economies surveyed. Whatever the theoretical or methodological critique that one may level at the WEF's conception and measurement of competitiveness, it is by far the most widely cited global index and one which exercises significant influence among policymakers and in the wider public debate.

Brazil's poor standing in the index, if nothing else, should alert us to the kinds of structural, competitive factors that are impeding its progress and rendering its economy liable to repeated crises. This chapter will examine issue by issue, the kinds of competitiveness challenges which Brazil faces and will need to overcome if its economic performance is to improve on a sustainable and recurrent basis. Prior to this, so as to provide relevant background and context, it is worth detailing the evolution of the policy environment over the post-war period. In doing so the objective is to depict the sharp shifts in policy regime that have occurred as consecutive administrations have grappled with the need to enhance competitiveness, foster new forms of integration with the global economy and enhance economic resilience.

The policy environment: rupture or continuity?

Viewed over the long term, there is a case to be made that all of Brazil's economic policymaking teams, from the days of President Getúlio Vargas in the 1930s to the present, have faced a common fundamental challenge. This derives from the need to achieve sustained growth in output and living standards while being faced with the reality of an economy which could be characterised in informal terms as lopsided – or to use more formalised structuralist nomenclature – dualistic (Kay, 1989). As this chapter will demonstrate, the Brazilian economy has been accordingly characterised by the coexistence of pockets of genuine world-class competitiveness alongside sectors which have struggled to gain traction whether in terms of static efficiency, the building of innovative capability or the ability to gain presence in the global marketplace. In broad terms, those sectors of the economy which might be characterised as "globally competitive" have tended to cluster around poles of natural comparative advantage, principally agricultural and extractive activities. Those sectors which have time and again struggled in competitive terms have typically – though not without exception – centred on "non-traditional" activities, especially manufacturing, business services and high technology.[1]

While the nature of this challenge has remained broadly constant, the response of policymakers has varied considerably over the years. These shifts in response have derived variously from ideological impetus, evolution of the underlying structural characteristics of the domestic economy and changes in the level and patterns of global demand.

The import substitution era

The adoption of policies of import substitution and state-driven industrialisation in the 1930s under Vargas represented the first concerted attempt by Brazilian policymakers to build new sources of competitive advantage and so re-orientate the country's position in the global division of labour. This was to be achieved through means of interrelated policies of import compression and the encouragement of new patterns of specialisation, in particular, the establishment of productive activities in the manufacturing and key industrial input sectors (Baer, 2013). What began as a somewhat reactive and disparate effort, had, by the late 1950s under President Juscelino Kubitschek, transformed into a carefully planned and executed endeavour. Favoured sectors – in particular, consumer durables such as automobiles – were granted elevated effective rates of protection (ERPs) in which tariffs and quotas on final output greatly exceeded those of their counterparts on intermediate inputs. During this period ERPs for these emergent sectors could comfortably exceed 50%. For some products, automobiles and personal watercraft among them, imports were effectively prohibited. Perhaps the most surprising feature of the industrial and trade policy regimes spanning this epoch – sometimes characterised as formal ISI (Colman & Nixson, 1994) – was the paradox embodied in the simultaneous compression of imports with an open-door approach to inward FDI in newly emerging sectors. From white goods to automobiles, from steel to chemicals Brazil rapidly established new industrial capacity heavily underpinned by foreign capital.

Thus, during this era, such global industrial giants as Ford, Siemens and Esso (later Exxon Mobil) established or expanded operations to meet growing domestic demand and to replace that output which could no longer be viably imported. Of course, the formal ISI provided opportunities for domestic capital which were actively taken up whether by the private sector or an increasingly salient SOE sector. The scope of the latter expanded significantly in the 1950s following the foundation of Petrobrás (which remains Brazil's largest public enterprise) and a slew of nationalisations in the network industries (Roett, 2011; Baer, 2013). Meanwhile, Brazil's new state development bank, the BNDES (National Economic Development Bank), founded in 1953, facilitated public and private sector industrial development projects through taxpayer-backed loans on advantageous terms (Torres, 2016).

As indicated in Chapter 1, the ISI period, despite its successes in establishing new sectors, consistently failed to reconcile structural transformation with efficiency or meaningful economic resilience. By the mid-1960s, rising inflation and stubborn trade deficits prompted the new military administration to adopt a more liberal approach to trade policy. The new approach, which came to be known as Post-Import Substitution Industrialization (Colman & Nixson, 1994) attempted to unleash the export potential of the new industrial economy which had grown up over the previous 30 years. Alongside limited trade liberalisation, principally targeted at imported inputs, a series of stepped currency devaluations was implemented, the objective being to boost export competitiveness in foreign currency terms. At the same time, capital market liberalisation was promoted in an attempt to unlock barriers to investment and thereby to boost productivity (Abreu, 1990).

This modified ISI strategy for a while proved very successful. While Brazil had by no means fully opened its economy to trade or – in respect to certain strategic sectors, foreign investment – the 1960s were nevertheless a period of cautious liberal reform. For a while the macroeconomy responded very favourably with growth and exports rising in tandem during a period which later became known as the Brazilian Economic Miracle (Baer, 2013). The 1960s also saw the first concerted attempts to improve systemic competitiveness through dedicated industrial innovation policies. During this period the architecture of institutions and policy initiatives which would go on to forge the framework of Brazil's national system of innovation began to take shape.

As we saw in the previous chapter, a trebling of oil prices in 1973 and an associated global downturn spelt the end of Brazil's economic miracle and, with it the drift towards trade and market liberalisation. The response of the military authorities in 1974 to the worsening economic crisis was a doubling down on the original ISI strategy under the guise of a new framework, the PND II. Rather than trying to induce enhanced competitiveness and sectoral change through intensified exposure to the global marketplace, the new plan erected fresh trade barriers and elevated the state's role as a fomenter of industrial capacity (Amann, 2000). Under this new policy regime, the principle objective was to address Brazil's external constraints by developing new import replacing activities (especially capital goods) while underpinning competitiveness across all sectors through enormous state-driven infrastructural investment (ibid.). Thus, it was in this period, the mid-to-late 1970s that we saw the emergence of such iconic mega projects as the Itaipú hydroelectric scheme, the Trans Amazonian Highway and the Rio-Niteroí bridge (Baer, 2013).

While the demand side push from accelerated fixed capital investment propped up economic activity, the new strategy, like others before it, proved incapable of being sustained indefinitely. The principal reason for this lay in the fact that Post-ISI did not prove effective in addressing the external imbalance. Instead, it compelled Brazil to cover the resulting deficits with funds borrowed from international capital markets. Once international monetary conditions tightened, as we saw in the previous chapter, policymakers were obliged to rapidly change course, ushering a lengthy period of liberal reform.

Liberal reform: the Washington consensus and beyond

The 1980s proved a watershed in the political economy of Brazil and nowhere did this find its expression more than in the authorities' fresh approach to industrial, trade and technology policy. Following the intervention of the World Bank, as part of a structural adjustment package, the new civilian administration of President José Sarney adopted a cautious programme of trade reforms starting in 1987. This resulted in downward adjustments in tariffs across the almost 13,000 products embraced by the country's tariff schedule (Castelan, 2010, p. 583). The Sarney administration also launched a privatisation programme which aimed to induce greater competitiveness and market contestability by enabling the sale of publicly owned assets to the private sector.

Despite the bold rhetoric, the actual results proved to be quite modest in terms of privatisations achieved. By the end of the Sarney administration in March 1990, just 18 state-owned enterprises had been sold to the private sector compared with a total of 140 which had been earlier identified by the Special Privatization Committee as suitable for sale (Pinheiro, 2011). Privatisation and trade reform aside, efforts to support the competitive evolution of the productive sector were very limited during the 1980s. This had partly to do with the scale of the fiscal adjustments being undertaken which prevented technology policy initiatives, for example, from being funded as generously as previously. The only glaring exception to this was the so-called market reserve policy for information technology products which provided funding for innovation in this sector amid attempts to create a home-grown mini-computer (Ferraz et al., 1992).

The cautiousness of this initial phase of liberal reform may partly be explained by the fact that the authorities' attention was heavily absorbed by the implementation of failed macroeconomic stabilisation attempts. However, the Sarney administration itself hardly represented an ideological break with the past, being populated with politicians and technocrats marinated in the country's developmentalist institutional structures.

The boldest attempted break with Brazil's developmentalist traditions (at least prior to the election of the current President) came with the accession to power of Fernando Collor de Melo in 1990. President Collor was the first directly elected head of state in almost 30 years. Coming from the previously obscure North Eastern state of Alagoas, Collor was also something of an outsider, having fewer ties with established institutions and political parties than his predecessor. Collor, like his contemporary Carlos Menem of Argentina, can be viewed as the quintessential "neoliberal" President, ideologically committed to a programme of rolling back the state and opening up the economy to foreign competition, trade, and investment. The most important trade reforms since the Vargas era in the 1930s were implemented under Collor in a programme known as the *Abertura Comercial* or "Trade Opening." The *Abertura* constituted a rolling four-year timetable of trade liberalisation comprising two main axes: a 50% average reduction in tariff levels[2] across the board, and a comprehensive rolling back of non-tariff barriers (Kume, 1996). The latter, in fact, had formed the main bulwark against imported competition for decades and their scaling back, allied to the tariff reduction, contributed to a much more liberalised trade regime (Amann, 2000).

President Collor during his brief two and a half years in office[3] also pressed forward with the privatisation programme initiated under his predecessor. Under a new title, the Programa Nacional de Desestatização – National Privatization Program – the Collor administration along with its immediate successor[4] proved much more successful than had President Sarney in selling off state assets. Between 1990 and 1994, 33 companies were privatised, generating US$ 8.6bn in revenue. This was 12 times as much as achieved in the entire previous decade (Pinheiro, 2018, p. 710). Assets sold included such Brazilian corporate icons as Embraer, one of the world's leading aircraft producers.

The commitment to open markets and microeconomic reform was broadly maintained by the administrations of President Fernando Henrique Cardoso (1995–2002), although with a social democratic rather than neoliberal inflexion. The policy emphasis around competitiveness and redefining Brazil's place in the global economic order shifted from trade policy towards internal supply-side reforms. The most striking element of President Cardoso's rebalanced approach lay in an unprecedented acceleration of the privatisation programme. By the late 1990s, this became the world's largest one, involving the transfer of assets across the network and process industries, transportation and finance (Giambiagi, 1999). Among the most noteworthy privatisations were those of the publicly owned telecommunications sector in 1998, the mining giant CVRD in 1997 and several regional or municipal electricity generators or distributors, such as Rio de Janeiro's Light in 1996 (Baer & McDonald, 1998). Between 1995 and 1998, the revenue resulting from such sales reached US$ 60.1bn, significantly helping to facilitate the ongoing fiscal adjustment.

In tandem with the privatisation programme, the Cardoso administration did more than any other since the 1960s to actively attract inward FDI. Barriers to foreign ownership were scaled down and removed in the public utilities, and, most dramatically in the upstream oil and gas sector. The latter development followed a constitutional reform in 1997 (Giambiagi & Moreira, 1999). As a result, foreign multinationals such as Shell, Exxon Mobil and BG group became major players in the Brazilian energy sector, especially in offshore exploration and production.

In contrast to these notable developments, the pace of trade reform slowed. Whereas weighted average applied tariffs for all imports fell from 31.9% in 1989 to 13.3% in 1994, by the end of President Cardoso's second term in 2002 they had fallen further by only just over three percentage points. The only obvious exception to slowing trade liberalisation was the consolidation of the regional customs union, Mercosul. The latter had been created by the signing of the Treaty of Asunción in March 1991 and, by the late 1990s had significantly reduced regional barriers to trade, in particular, facilitating commerce between Brazil and its largest economic neighbour, Argentina.

Throughout the Cardoso years and, indeed beyond, lay a central question which remained, and still remains, only partially addressed in policy terms. Given the opening up of the Brazilian economy, how might enterprises be capacitated to build competitiveness, cope with an increasingly contested domestic market and leverage opportunities in the wider global economy? Compared with its predecessor the Cardoso administration had fewer doctrinaire scruples as far as industrial or technology policy interventions were concerned. Still, its response was rather muted. While the technological policy architecture built up during the 1960s and 1970s remained in place (with some recovery in funding after 1994), there was little enthusiasm for experimentation with new industrial policy initiatives, no matter how market-friendly. The only real exceptions to this proved to be the Programa Brasileiro de Qualidade e Produtividade (PBQP – Brazilian Quality and Productivity Program) – effectively a lightly funded network-based awareness-raising initiative (Amann, 2000). There was also a special managed trade regime in automotive products established between Brazil and its Mercosul partner, Argentina. Neither of these policies, or other lesser targeted initiatives of the period, turned out to be competitive game changers.

Developmentalism makes a comeback

In 2002, politics in Brazil took a decisive turn with the election of President Luiz Inácio Lula da Silva, erstwhile trade unionist and head of the Workers' Party (the PT). Over the following dozen years or so President Lula and his PT successor and protégé, Dilma Rousseff, adopted a far more sceptical approach to liberal reform than had their predecessors in the 1980s and 90s. While Brazil remained broadly aligned with the tenets of macroeconomic orthodoxy,[5] policymakers proved willing to experiment with more interventionist forms of industrial, technological and even trade policy. Schneider (2015, p. 127) terms this "21st Century Developmentalism." The new philosophical economic disposition of the PT administration drew on the intellectual leadership of heterodox economists, especially Guido Mantega (who served as finance minister between 2006 and 2015) and Luciano Coutinho who, between 2007 and 2016, presided over Brazil's mighty BNDES development bank.

The new direction of microeconomic policy, in particular, the approach to building competitiveness drew strong inspiration from neo-structuralist insights. At a metalevel, the new strategy attempted to use the power of the state to facilitate competitive change across the supply-side using targeted, broadly "market friendly" initiatives (Arbix, 2019). Rather than reimplementing blanket ISI, as first-generation structuralists may have been inclined to do, there was a focus on fomenting the accumulation of productive and technological capability in new and established sectors. This was to be accomplished via the creation of knowledge networks, the provision of fiscal and financial incentives for private sector innovation and the strengthening of public sector research institutes and sectoral industrial policies. The latter was strongly targeted at the oil and gas sector, establishing local content requirements around refineries and equipment and vessels to be deployed in the offshore sector (Netto, 2016). This policy marked the return of ISI (at least as far as one sector was concerned). However, it was to have profound political consequences. With the state and the private sector ever more tightly bound by a nexus of financial, regulatory, and personalistic relationships, the oil and gas sector became the focal point for a corruption scandal that was eventually to strip the PT of power.

The corruption surrounding one facet of the industrial policy during the 2003–16 period should not obscure the institutional innovation and intriguing experimentation which characterised the authorities' efforts to grapple with some of the issues retarding Brazil's competitiveness. The focal point here lay in attempts to induce greater innovativeness in the productive sector. This objective had long been a focal point of public policy. Schwartzman et al. (1995) in their comprehensive study reveal the complex and fragmented nature of Brazil's science and technology policy architecture. This comprised – and continues to comprise – a multi-agency approach, with initiatives undertaken by the states, in addition to the federal level of government. Alongside SOE-based research divisions associated with the network and energy industries, there exist publicly funded standalone research institutes such as Embrapa in the agricultural sector and Fiocruz in life sciences. The work done in such settings is often at the global frontier and has helped propel enterprises such as Embraer and Petrobrás into world leaders in their fields (Amann & Figueiredo, 2012). Besides this, there exists a network of funding agencies, most notably FINEP (Financing Agency for Studies and Projects) (which supports industrial Research and Development (R&D)) and CAPES (Coordinating Agency for the Improvement of Higher Education Personnel) and CNPq (National Council for Scientific and Technological Development) which target research in academic institutions. State-level bodies such as FAPESP (São Paulo Research Foundation) and FAPERJ (Rio de Janeiro Research Foundation) also exist and support innovation and research carried out by private and public sector entities within state boundaries.

Prior to the mid-2000s the operation of these agencies within Brazil's National System of Innovation was typified by a somewhat *dirigiste* approach in which policymakers identified and then funded areas deemed to be of strategic priority (Ferraz et al., 1992; Dahlman & Frischtak, 1993). Taking inspiration from the neo-structuralist perspective and related approaches in the burgeoning innovation studies literature, a more market-driven approach emerged after 2003. According to Arbix (2019) two foundational pieces of legislation, the Innovation Law of 2004 and the "Lei do Bem" of 2005 updated Brazil's approach to innovation policy, allowing closer engagement between universities and firms, the launch of incentive programmes to support risky ventures in the private sector and subsidies to allow the placement of researchers within firms (ibid., p. 78). The budgets behind innovation ventures were also increased with the result that government spending on R&D rose from 0.54% to 0.64% of GDP between 2000 and 2015 (Frischtak, 2019 p. 94).

The growing priority attaching to innovation undoubtedly represented a step forward in terms of addressing Brazil's supply-side impediments. However, the end of the 2000s and the beginning of the 2010s saw the country's economy rocked by the global financial crisis. With this, the locus of industrial trade and technology policy shifted in a more traditional, top-down, import-substituting direction. The Productive Development Policy of 2008 and the Greater Brazil Plan of 2011 both encouraged priority sectors through subsidies, tax incentives and tariff measures among other measures. According to Arbix (2019), they could be seen as essentially counter-cyclical initiatives in which the priority accorded to the building of competitiveness through enhanced innovation was secondary. In this sense it is probably fair to say that throughout the Rousseff administration (2011–16) serious engagement with issues around innovation and competitiveness entered a period of decline.

A return to liberal reforms? The Temer and Bolsonaro eras

The economic and political crisis that ended the administration of President Rousseff in 2016 provided the impetus, both financially and ideologically, for the repudiation of the cautious return to developmentalism that had marked the PT's years in power. The new President, Michel Temer, in an attempt to win back market confidence, instituted a series of orthodox macro- and microeconomic reforms. Introduced over the 2016–18 period they principally comprised a 10-year real-terms federal government spending freeze, an accelerated privatisation programme (focusing on transportation infrastructure), a recommitment to trade reform,[6] and the removal of the obligation of Petrobrás to have a substantial stake in new exploration and production contracts.

The economically liberal response of the Temer administration to Brazil's crisis was in many ways measured and trepidatious compared with the approach adopted by President Collor a quarter of a century earlier. With the election of President Jair Bolsonaro in October 2018, however, a more radical approach was countenanced. The new administration's economic policymaking team is heavily influenced by the Chicago School which not only advocates the primacy of free markets and free trade but also remains sceptical as to the extent to which the state should or could effectively regulate their operation. Chicago school economists were influential in encouraging financial deregulation in the United States during the 1990s and early 2000s (for example, the replacement of the Glass-Steagall Banking Act separating commercial and investment banking) and a more liberal approach to merger and acquisition transactions (Ebenstein, 2015). Brazil's Minister of Finance, Paulo Guedes, is a Chicago-trained economist and functions within this tradition, advocating market-based solutions for the structural challenges impeding Brazil's growth and development. Politically, the Minister and his team draw support from an anti-developmentalist faction, the *Movimento Brazil Livre*, which emerged as a campaign group during the PT years and wishes to see the state rolled back throughout the economy. Accordingly, the pursuit of greater competitiveness and a more advantageous position in the global division of labour are seen as requiring market-based solutions. These involve the retraction of the state and the exposure of the economy to greater global competition.

Approaching the mid-point of President Bolsonaro's first term this liberal reform agenda has advanced and almost compares in scale and speed with that implemented by President Collor in his first few months in office. Aside from the focus on macroeconomic orthodoxy,[7] the priority of the new administration has centred on reigniting the privatisation programme. This involves a plan to privatise more than 100 SOEs including Eletrobrás, Brazil's largest electricity utility. The full privatisation of Petrobrás has also been mooted. If successful, this programme would effectively pick up the momentum of divestment of pubic assets which was lost when the Cardoso administration left office in 2002.

The most striking aspect of the new administration's proposals, however, concerns the issue of trade reform. Days into his first term, President Bolsonaro, addressing the WEF at Davos in January 2019, highlighted trade liberalisation as one of his administration's priorities (*Financial Times*, 22 January 2019). Under Presidents Lula and Rousseff (2003–16) progress on trade reform had proven glacial. Brazil remained a comparatively closed economy and its trade-weighted average tariff rates for all imports had declined by just 1.52 percentage points over this period.[8] A concrete demonstration of the new administration's intent to resume progress came at the end of June 2019 with the signing of a free trade agreement between the European Union (EU) and Mercosul. The agreement, which requires ratification by national legislatures, is by far the most sweeping since the foundation of Mercosul in 1991; indeed, it represents the most ambitious development in Brazil's trade reform agenda in almost 30 years. For years, progress on the negotiations (started in June 1999) languished, impeded in part by the Argentinean and Brazilian administrations' then sceptical approach to trade reform. The arrival of more market-friendly administrations of Mauricio Macri in Buenos Aires and Jair Bolsonaro in Brasília appears to have changed the dynamics of the process, spawning an acceleration in talks.

The agreement mandates the elimination of tariffs on 93% of Mercosul's exports to the EU and grants preferential treatment for the remaining 7% (*Financial Times*, 30 June 2019). For EU exporters, the agreement will eventually lead to the elimination of tariffs on 91% of their exports to Mercosul economies (ibid.). Perhaps as significantly, the agreement opens up public procurement contracts, extends the scope for free trade in services, while offering protection and special status for regional food specialities. From a Brazilian perspective the agreement, providing it comes into force, will offer unparalleled access to the EU market, especially for its highly competitive agricultural products. By the same token, however, Brazil's less competitive industrial economy will be exposed to an unprecedented external challenge, not least in the previously heavily protected automotive sector.

Another competitive challenge that the Bolsonaro administration has committed to tackle concerns the taxation of business, especially the issue of indirect tax. At present multiple indirect taxes are levied on goods and services ranging from the federal industrial products tax (IPI) to the municipal tax on services (ISS) and the state-level ICMS tax. State and municipal taxes are levied at different rates dependent on locality and, in addition, there are a series of complex federal payroll taxes which employers need to navigate. Oliveira and Biasoto (2015) highlight the competitive impediment these taxes impose, not least regarding the promotion of exports.

A particularly serious issue surrounds the cumulative nature of the taxes, which is a peculiarly Brazilian feature. The scope for indirect tax exemptions on products or services destined for the export market is very limited compared to most major economies and is a feature that needs urgently addressing (ibid.). Against this background the Bolsonaro administration and members of Congress are exploring proposals to simplify tax structures with a view to remedying these issues (E & Y Americas Tax Centre, 2019). The centrepiece of current proposals (approved by the tax reform committee of the Lower House of Congress in December 2018) would replace a multiplicity of state, local and federal taxes with a single, unified federal value-added tax, the IBS or Imposto sobre Bens e

Serviços (Tax on Goods and Services). Final approval of this measure will require the agreement of both houses of Congress.

Summing up the experiences of the past eight decades of Brazil's policy experiences, the overwhelming sense that emerges is one of discontinuity and time inconsistency. Episodes of state-driven, *dirigiste* developmentalism gave way to periods of market fundamentalism, to be supplanted in due course by the re-embrace of statism (Amann, 2017). Only at certain points of time, such as the late 1960s and the early-to-late 2000s, was this pattern disrupted. Here, thanks to benign external conditions and fortuitous changes in the political climate, more pragmatic, measured attempts were made to wrestle with Brazil's competitive challenges (ibid.). These exceptional epochs aside, external shocks and swings in the ideological pendulum combined to create an unstable policy environment. This has been characterised by lack of pre-dictability, uncertain funding and a multiplicity of short-lived, ill-planned initiatives. The question which now emerges is whether the Bolsonaro ad-ministration can engineer a break with this legacy. Could a more stable and better-considered policy environment emerge; one which provides a firmer basis for enterprise planning, and hastens the resolution of Brazil's enduring competitive challenges? To begin answering this question it is necessary to understand better, from an international comparative perspective, the nature of the competitive challenges facing Brazil.

Analysing Brazil's competitive challenges

In order to analyse the competitive issues facing Brazil, this section adopts the following structure. In the first place, using WEF data, it examines in broad the-matic terms where Brazil's competitive strengths and weaknesses lie in relation to peer group economies. Having accomplished this, the section next investi-gates Brazil's competitive performance through the optic of international trade. Examining patterns of specialisation and employing measures such as Revealed Comparative Advantage (RCA), we analyse the extent to which Brazil has suc-ceeded in building competitive strength in global markets, such as, for example, by establishing new niches or comparative advantages.

Following this analysis, we then consider an important driver of trade perfor-mance: the evolution of productivity. Both aggregated and disaggregated meas-ures of productivity are employed in international comparative context so as to gauge Brazil's global standing, and to identify where the real challenges exist. In a final analytical sub-section, the focus shifts towards the issue of innovation. Since innovation is a vital ingredient in any attempt to move up the global value chain and establish non-price-based forms of competitive advantage, this issue is of key significance. Accordingly, and once more in international comparative terms, we focus both on aggregate measures of innovative capability and on the reality at sectoral level. Given the strongly heterogeneous nature of technological intensity and capacity even within given sectors, an examination of firm-level evidence is also indispensable. Therefore, some firm-based case study material also forms part of the analysis. The chapter draws to a close by considering the challenges posed to competitiveness around infrastructure. It also discusses what the phenomenon of Brazil-based multinational corporations can tell us about the nature of the nation's underlying competitiveness.

Brazil's competitive challenges: an overview

As indicated in the earlier discussion, the WEF's Global Competitiveness Indicators (GCI) provides a very commonly referenced gauge of a country's global competitive standing. While the GCIs are not without their methodological limitations, they nonetheless provide a valuable indication of where key challenges and strengths lie for any given country. In the case of Brazil which, in 2018 lay at 72nd place (out of 140 countries) in the overall rankings, even a brief perusal of the data flag up some very important and troubling issues. The first point to emerge stems from the evolution over time of Brazil's summary ranking compared with relevant peer group economies. Between 2007 and 2018 Brazil's position in the rankings stayed at a constant 72.[9] India, by contrast, saw its rank fall to 58th place (from 42nd), Russia's rose to 43rd (from 58th) while that of China also increased to 28th place (from 34th) (WEF, 2018a). The failure of Brazil to sustainably ascend through the rankings reflects its unimpressive performance in the component indicators that combine to generate the overall rankings. These component indicators are termed "pillars." Examining the extent to which ranking accorded to each pillar differs from the overall ranking makes interesting reading. In the critical areas represented by the Institutions (93rd position), Infrastructure (81st positions), Macroeconomic Stability (122nd position), Skills (94th position), Product Market (117th position), Labor Market (114th position) and Business Dynamism (108th position), Brazil's performance in 2018 trails substantially its overall ranking. Only in the categories ICT Adoption (66th position), Health (73rd position), Financial System (57th position), Market Size (10th position) and Innovation (40th position) do the individual pillar rankings exceed or approximate Brazil's overall global standings (ibid.).

What immediately emerges from this analysis is the sense that Brazil's competitive challenges are not confined to niche areas but are instead characterised by a multiplicity of sources, all of which have structurally deep roots. At the same time, it can also be said that the nature of the structural difficulties facing Brazil is, to a certain extent, interrelated and systemic. Analysts from the WEF have attempted to understand this complex reality further by conducting a special study focusing exclusively on Brazil. The report entitled *Brazil Competitiveness and Inclusive Growth Lab Report* (WEF, 2018b), identifies particular issues around the effectiveness of innovation and the national innovation system, poor performance on productivity, the relative closedness of the economy and, as an overarching challenge, the implications of excessive regulation and counterproductive government intervention in the economy.

The diagnosis of the WEF reports hardly breaks new ground or makes starkly original claims. This is not a criticism of the report but rather an indication that the same issues, time and again, have been identified across numerous studies, but then left ignored or insufficiently addressed by policymakers. Thus, for example, the Confederação Nacional de Indústria – National Confederation of Industry (CNI) in its most recent competitiveness report (CNI, 2019) also identifies a series of issues around government intervention (especially the burden of taxation and related compliance costs) and infrastructure, while expressing concern around the topic of innovation and technological dynamism. The CNI study in some ways is more illuminating than its WEF counterparts. This is because its international comparative focus concentrates on emerging market, newly industrialised and resource-rich economies which, in principle, makes for more meaningful contrasts and comparisons with Brazilian experience.

Reports of much earlier vintage have highlighted very similar competitive challenges. Aside from the CNI's biannual competitiveness reports (which stretch back over two decades), landmark studies such as the McKinsey Institute Report on Productivity (1998) and the Fundação Dom Cabral, Federal University of Rio de Janeiro, Unicamp Report on Competitiveness in Brazilian Industry (1993) pointed to important themes such as deficiencies in national and sectoral innovation systems, low productivity growth, lack of export dynamism, and the burden placed on the productive sector by the complexity of the taxation system and high compliance costs associated with government regulations. The latter issue is frequently summarised in the literature and, by industrial lobby groups such as the CNI and Federação Industrial do Estado de São Paulo (FIESP) as the *Custo Brasil* or "Brazil Cost." It can be argued that the Brazil Cost, or more precisely attempts to circumvent it, has been a principal driver of the corrupt practices which have come to characterise state-business relations. This issue will be discussed at length in Chapter 4.

Analysis of Brazil's competitiveness challenges founded solely on studies of the type mentioned above would leave one open to the criticism that any conclusions reached would be based on reliance on ad hoc methods, with an associated lack of rootedness in more rigorous microeconomic and trade theory. Partly for this reason, but also to gain deeper perspectives on some of the key issues at stake, we now evaluate Brazil's evolving competitive position through the optic of shifting patterns of international trade.

International trade and export competitiveness

As discussed at length in the previous section, the evolution of Brazil's economy since the 1930s can be characterised by repeated attempts to build new sources of competitive strength. Through this, it was hoped that fresh areas of comparative advantage could be established, thus advantageously shifting Brazil's place in the international division of labour. The developmentalist policy agenda, which held sway up to the 1980s and then once more during the PT years (2003–16) placed special emphasis on enhancing competitiveness in "non-traditional" activities, especially those which could be broadly considered "high technology" (Amann & Figueiredo, 2012; Arbix, 2019). These would include key sectors such as pharmaceuticals, information technology products and services and aerospace. Through reshaping the form of Brazil's global trade as a result of these endeavours, the objective was to render the country less vulnerable to the vicissitudes of international commodity price fluctuations. Relatedly, an increasing emphasis on the export of higher technology products held out the potential to improve Brazil's terms of trade at an aggregate level, improving in turn growth potential.

Did these shifts in the pattern of trade materialise? A very widely used metric which may be used to address this question comprises Bela Belassa's Revealed Comparative Advantage (RCA) index. The index, developed in the mid-1960s by Bela Belassa and Mark Noland (Belassa, 1965), divides the share of a country's exports of a particular class in its total exports, by the share of that class of exports in total world exports. If the value so derived exceeds one then a country may be said to have a revealed comparative advantage in that product. If the value is less than one then the country has a comparative disadvantage in terms of the product in question.

The World Bank World Integrated Trade Solution (WITS) database enables us to chart the evolution of Brazil's RCA over the long-term, with annual observations stretching from 1989 (at the very start of the liberalisation experiment) to 2017 (the year following the end of the Rousseff administration). Table 2.1 indicates the extent to which the hoped-for shifts largely failed to materialise effectively despite or because of fairly favourable rates of overall export growth.

What quickly becomes apparent from even cursory scrutiny of Table 2.1 is that Brazil's RCAs veer strongly towards sectors associated with underlying sources of natural comparative advantage. Thus minerals (with RCA values of 8.1 in 1989 and 8.81 in 2017), vegetable products (3.35, 1989; 4.97, 2017) and raw materials (1.9, 1989; 3.59, 2017) stand out as product categories where RCA is the strongest. Interestingly, revealed comparative advantage in these areas actually *increased* over the three-decade period in question, partly illustrating the extent to which primary product-related sectors were able to build on existing strengths through investment and innovation. This is a theme to be taken up in the following two sections. The flipside of this highly impressive performance is a far more subdued picture in the case of non-traditional export activities. Thus, machinery and electrical equipment saw its already low RCA value drop from 0.25 to 0.22 between 1989 and 2017. For transportation equipment and capital goods – two areas benefitting from special industrial policy measures during the PT era – the RCA values did in fact increase between 1989 and 2017. However, as Table 2.1 makes plain, with the values in question less than unity by the end of the period, from an RCA perspective at least, Brazil remained far from competitive in these areas.

Turning to data on export shares Table 2.2 reveals the extent to which the share of exports in traditional, primary product-related areas expanded at the expense of non-traditional manufactured products over the 1990s and 2000s. Most

TABLE 2.1 Revealed comparative advantage by export product category in Brazil, 1989–2017

Product group	1989	1990	1991	1992	1993	1994	1995	1996	1997	1998	1999	2000	2001	2002
All products	1	1	1	1	1	1	1	1	1	1	1	1	1	1
Capital goods	0.23	0.35	0.47	0.48	0.53	0.51	0.5	0.51	0.53	0.57	0.54	0.59	0.59	0.55
Consumer goods	0.5	0.56	0.68	0.71	0.77	0.71	0.66	0.67	0.68	0.7	0.73	0.75	0.7	0.65
Intermediate goods	1.8	1.75	1.78	1.64	1.61	1.63	1.72	1.81	1.67	1.53	1.66	1.64	1.52	1.59
Raw materials	1.9	1.84	1.64	1.72	1.7	1.86	1.89	1.81	2.06	2.34	2.2	1.89	2.2	2.34
Animal	0.78	0.8	1.1	1.15	1.29	1.01	1.03	1.19	1.08	1.29	1.6	1.88	2.29	2.76
Chemicals	0.5	0.62	0.68	0.62	0.7	0.64	0.67	0.73	0.74	0.7	0.7	0.72	0.58	0.54
Food products	4.81	4.46	3.82	4.49	4.13	4.48	4.48	5.35	4.76	4.63	5.01	4.68	4.66	4.58
Footwear	2.11	1.95	4.76	4.83	4.68	3.38	3.15	3.13	2.9	2.76	2.87	3.24	2.93	2.68
Fuels	0.04	0.03	0.17	0.15	0.24	0.23	0.11	0.1	0.08	0.12	0.14	0.19	0.29	0.34
Hides and skins	1.08	1.62	1.07	1.2	1.19	1.16	1.41	1.69	1.71	1.74	1.71	1.85	1.9	2.03
Mach and elec	0.25	0.32	0.42	0.39	0.42	0.39	0.4	0.4	0.41	0.4	0.39	0.41	0.41	0.41
Metals	2.97	2.89	2.92	2.37	2.36	2.09	2.08	1.98	1.77	1.61	1.76	1.72	1.43	1.56
Minerals	8.1	10.3	8.8	8.54	8.8	8.3	8.95	9.29	8.79	9.93	9.89	10.4	9.38	9.65
Miscellaneous	0.08	0.17	0.3	0.44	0.39	0.38	0.29	0.26	0.26	0.28	0.35	0.21	0.21	0.21
Plastic or rubber	0.42	0.5	0.68	0.62	0.82	0.75	0.7	0.7	0.67	0.67	0.69	0.77	0.66	0.61
Stone and glass	0.38	0.56	0.78	1	0.59	0.58	0.7	0.79	0.78	0.69	0.76	0.85	0.74	0.76
Textiles and clothing	0.65	0.67	0.66	0.57	0.47	0.43	0.4	0.38	0.34	0.31	0.31	0.35	0.35	0.33
Transportation	0.18	0.35	0.4	0.52	0.62	0.65	0.6	0.64	0.83	1	0.87	1.12	1.12	0.92
Vegetable	3.35	2.61	2.31	2.46	2.35	3.22	2.95	2.66	3.96	3.45	3.56	3.67	4.26	4.05
Wood	0.84	0.95	1.09	1.15	1.42	1.62	1.95	1.72	1.75	1.75	2.04	2.27	2.02	2.08

(Continued)

Product group	2003	2004	2005	2006	2007	2008	2009	2010	2011	2012	2013	2014	2015	2016	2017
All products	1	1	1	1	1	1	1	1	1	1	1	1	1	1	1
Capital goods	0.55	0.56	0.61	0.59	0.55	0.52	0.44	0.43	0.42	0.41	0.39	0.35	0.35	0.38	0.36
Consumer goods	0.63	0.59	0.6	0.57	0.54	0.47	0.48	0.44	0.41	0.42	0.43	0.39	0.39	0.41	0.41
Intermediate goods	1.6	1.57	1.51	1.5	1.42	1.34	1.37	1.29	1.24	1.23	1.2	1.27	1.31	1.31	1.26
Raw materials	2.38	2.33	2.13	2.21	2.45	2.48	2.91	2.94	2.76	2.76	2.92	3.13	3.77	3.8	3.59
Animal	2.79	3.05	3.29	3.36	3.7	3.51	3.51	3.48	2.99	3.26	3.52	3.38	3.58	3.51	2.89
Chemicals	0.53	0.51	0.52	0.55	0.55	0.56	0.55	0.57	0.53	0.59	0.59	0.57	0.57	0.53	0.53
Food products	4.21	4.07	3.99	4.27	3.99	3.92	4.12	4.22	4.18	4.11	4.08	3.78	3.54	3.49	2.98
Footwear	2.43	2.35	2.13	1.94	1.74	1.47	1.26	1.08	0.8	0.72	0.71	0.68	0.65	0.69	0.65
Fuels	0.43	0.36	0.38	0.45	0.45	0.48	0.57	0.61	0.57	0.55	0.42	0.57	0.68	0.74	0.83
Hides and skins	2.04	2.05	1.98	2.25	2.22	1.78	1.37	1.51	1.45	1.52	1.81	2.13	2	1.89	1.54
Mach and elec	0.42	0.4	0.45	0.46	0.39	0.38	0.32	0.28	0.28	0.28	0.26	0.24	0.23	0.22	0.22
Metals	1.56	1.58	1.49	1.37	1.23	1.19	1.08	0.91	0.97	0.96	0.85	0.93	1.03	1	1.03
Minerals	9.25	9.11	9.2	9.37	9.59	10.4	10.3	10.8	10.6	10.5	10.2	10	9.34	9.14	8.81
Miscellaneous	0.18	0.22	0.22	0.19	0.27	0.27	0.33	0.33	0.33	0.38	0.35	0.37	0.37	0.42	0.4
Plastic or rubber	0.67	0.61	0.66	0.69	0.71	0.59	0.65	0.57	0.56	0.56	0.53	0.51	0.54	0.57	0.55
Stone and glass	0.73	0.74	0.67	0.71	0.62	0.46	0.42	0.36	0.29	0.36	0.47	0.57	0.54	0.58	0.56
Textiles and clothing	0.38	0.39	0.37	0.34	0.34	0.32	0.27	0.28	0.3	0.4	0.29	0.26	0.27	0.29	0.2
Transportation	0.91	1.01	1.1	1	0.98	0.91	0.83	0.88	0.81	0.76	0.81	0.65	0.71	0.87	0.86
Vegetable	4.26	4.39	3.89	3.72	4.02	3.98	4.31	3.85	4.1	4.66	5.41	5.35	5.46	4.98	4.97
Wood	2.15	2.18	2.13	2.24	2.09	1.95	1.9	2.13	1.76	1.83	1.95	2.09	2.5	2.52	2.57

Source: Author's elaboration from WITS database.

TABLE 2.2 Brazil: share of total exports by product (%)

Product group	1989	1990	1991	1992	1993	1994	1995	1996	1997	1998	1999	2000	2001	2002	2003
All products	100	100	100	100	100	100	100	100	100	100	100	100	100	100	100
Capital goods	15.968	15.453	16.033	17.291	18.18	18.338	16.912	17.362	18.884	20.606	20.619	23.823	22.579	20.606	19.181
Consumer goods	19.821	20.812	20.03	22.891	23.612	21.329	21.429	22.026	21.966	23.301	22.48	22.865	23.482	22.332	21.634
Intermediate goods	40.161	39.008	39.317	38.173	37.539	37.596	41.664	39.555	35.025	32.457	33.091	31.693	29.266	30.759	32.171
Raw materials	20.738	21.372	22.2	19.299	18.536	20.011	17.977	18.93	22.048	21.772	21.297	19.661	22.627	24.265	25.318
Animal	1.84	2.071	2.6354	3.0736	3.2906	2.8805	2.5821	3.0617	2.8291	2.846	3.6503	3.5203	5.0701	5.3941	5.8731
Chemicals	4.6133	4.8883	4.8765	4.8999	4.8522	4.7153	5.4591	5.7164	5.627	5.7137	5.7524	5.6689	4.8049	5.0063	5.006
Food products	15.263	16.833	14.503	15.476	15.045	15.201	16.846	18.545	16.206	15.335	14.655	11.273	13.124	12.982	12.08
Footwear	3.8307	3.783	3.9472	4.113	5.0469	3.7468	3.2342	3.465	3.0162	2.7192	2.801	2.9399	2.8976	2.5167	2.2253
Fuels	2.4785	2.1728	1.3799	1.6083	1.6689	1.8182	0.8834	0.8817	0.6011	0.691	0.8421	1.648	3.59	4.883	5.1858
Hides and skins	0.833	1.0291	1.0909	1.22	1.1858	1.169	1.3449	1.55	1.5266	1.444	1.3891	1.5038	1.6408	1.7756	1.6157
Mach and elec	11.076	11.171	11.423	11.123	12	11.791	11.779	12.071	11.917	11.836	12.045	13.164	12.799	12.157	12.056
Metals	18.41	17.171	19.157	17.464	16.381	14.573	14.757	13.681	11.978	11.176	11.052	11.199	9.0951	10.134	10.519
Minerals	7.5319	8.9269	9.5154	7.3875	6.7355	6.0394	6.2055	6.4524	6.098	7.1579	6.5939	6.4259	5.8267	5.7592	5.5365
Miscellaneous	1.9962	2.4276	2.5142	2.5763	2.5975	2.8042	2.9527	2.9169	3.1411	3.0102	3.8306	4.0897	4.0604	3.8719	3.4486
Plastic or rubber	2.5534	2.5608	2.8182	2.98	3.203	3.1898	3.2346	3.0555	3.029	2.8958	2.9599	3.1439	2.6874	2.6317	2.9123
Stone and glass	1.3155	1.3728	1.4113	1.4532	1.8619	2.1243	2.491	2.8759	2.6048	2.4134	2.5785	2.4719	2.2387	2.4563	2.2452
Textiles and clothing	4.0142	3.9733	4.2975	4.0789	3.5725	3.2222	3.0996	2.706	2.3912	2.1766	2.1033	2.2202	2.2467	1.9687	2.2756
Transportation	8.8577	7.3205	7.0102	9.5605	8.8698	8.7378	7.1738	7.793	10.606	12.632	11.438	14.623	13.841	12.13	11.144
Vegetable	10.39	9.0153	8.0262	7.275	7.3931	11.346	9.6376	8.8015	12.313	11.81	10.878	8.7558	9.7111	9.9575	11.105
Wood	4.9971	5.2828	5.3932	5.7115	6.2969	6.6412	8.3197	6.427	6.1162	6.144	7.4313	7.353	6.3676	6.3774	6.7716

(*Continued*)

Product group	2004	2005	2006	2007	2008	2009	2010	2011	2012	2013	2014	2015	2016	2017
All products	100	100	100	100	100	100	100	100	100	100	100	100	100	100
Capital goods	21.299	21.834	20.651	19.49	18.508	14.945	14.275	13.474	14.31	15.923	13.303	14.641	16.4	14.069
Consumer goods	20.125	19.825	19.75	18.859	16.636	16.678	14.619	12.816	13.193	13.399	12.697	12.824	13.416	13.203
Intermediate goods	30.977	29.689	30.311	29.01	28.164	29.498	27.293	26.648	26.691	25.212	26.868	28.985	29.55	27.746
Raw materials	26.064	26.799	27.376	29.965	34.252	37.048	41.934	45.078	43.482	43.468	45	41.975	39.485	43.743
Animal	6.5092	6.7216	5.9227	6.7237	7.0598	7.3368	6.699	5.9423	6.3332	6.8713	7.787	7.5775	7.5014	7.0632
Chemicals	4.6583	4.5779	4.7707	4.9629	4.7748	5.2792	5.0625	4.7571	4.74	4.5809	5.0781	5.1872	4.9365	4.8487
Food products	11.315	10.912	11.894	11.031	10.983	14.938	13.4	12.415	12.872	12.51	11.556	11.689	13.191	11.569
Footwear	1.9733	1.6783	1.4307	1.2736	1.0267	0.9679	0.8187	0.5875	0.5325	0.5242	0.5527	0.5856	0.6313	0.5895
Fuels	4.5739	5.9905	7.6849	8.277	9.4418	8.9268	9.8277	10.464	10.912	7.3635	9.1739	7.1932	6.2522	9.747
Hides and skins	1.4914	1.3168	1.4807	1.4612	1.0302	0.8411	0.924	0.8436	0.8988	1.0772	1.3549	1.2412	1.1597	0.9215
Mach and elec	11.545	12.852	12.576	10.702	9.8209	8.71	8.0315	7.5087	7.7521	7.2268	7.5272	7.8536	8.0363	7.9366
Metals	11.106	11.131	11.112	10.477	10.285	8.013	7.1378	7.3977	7.1069	6.1171	7.1651	7.9874	7.2374	7.4927
Minerals	5.9097	7.2218	7.549	7.9379	9.849	9.8381	15.629	17.573	14.021	14.826	12.966	9.1063	8.8971	10.6
Miscellaneous	3.2901	3.4309	3.3767	4.0999	3.6713	3.1758	2.9834	2.928	3.3767	2.9747	3.2036	2.7344	2.3798	1.2199
Plastic or rubber	2.6966	2.893	3.0354	3.0836	2.5063	2.9099	2.6457	2.582	2.5201	2.3171	2.4579	2.6829	2.7658	2.5064
Stone and glass	2.1787	2.0721	2.2197	2.0719	1.7385	2.0538	1.9584	1.8298	2.0436	2.1186	2.1121	2.4455	2.8197	2.3828
Textiles and clothing	2.1669	1.8742	1.5302	1.4614	1.2251	1.2392	1.122	1.1768	1.4002	0.9817	1.1306	1.2446	1.1974	1.092
Transportation	13.547	12.918	11.657	11.869	11.309	8.4987	8.5545	7.6455	8.0125	10.979	7.1698	8.4986	10.745	9.1141
Vegetable	10.823	8.9247	8.5083	9.6696	10.904	12.876	10.877	12.775	13.903	15.706	16.518	18.727	16.898	17.801
Wood	6.215	5.4848	5.2526	4.8987	4.3741	4.3965	4.3287	3.5742	3.5751	3.8259	4.2469	5.2462	5.3518	5.1163

Source: Author elaboration from WITS database.

strikingly, the share accounted for by raw materials more than doubled (from 20.7% to 43.7%) between 1989 and 2017 while exports of machinery and electrical equipment fell as a percentage of total exports from 11.1% to 7.9%. All of the data, both in terms of export share and RCA point fairly unambiguously towards a process of "re-primarisation" of the Brazilian economy following the end of the import substitution period in the 1980s. Data presented by Chiarani and da Silva (2019) lend support to this conclusion but there are important nuances which the authors highlight. First of all, while the overall share of industrial products in total exports declined, the authors identify a sub-category – "high-tech products" where there was a modest rise in participation (5.11% in 1996 rising to 7.26% in 2010) (ibid., p. 162). However, it is established that exports in this sub-sector, by 2010 were heavily (slightly over 50%) skewed towards aerospace products, the latter being generated by Embraer, one of Brazil's most famous companies (ibid.). Significantly, Embraer, unlike many of its counterparts in other branches of industry, continued to benefit from industrial policy measures, even during the trade and market liberalisation era of the 1990s. The sector is thus, to an extent, exceptional.

Examination of import data reveal an interesting counterpoint to the export story just discussed. The most striking finding centres on the shrinkage in the proportion of imports accounted for by raw materials: between 1989 and 2017 this declined from 33.7% to 9.1% of the total, a truly dramatic change (WITS database[10]). The single most important factor underpinning this development relates to the emergence of Brazil's upstream oil and gas sector over the past three decades. Having been a significant net oil importer in the 1970s,[11] by 2018 the country was approaching self-sufficiency in crude oil production.[12] This development augurs well for Brazil's ability to weather future external shocks resulting from oil price spikes on global markets. The import shares accounted for by other NRB product categories also declined. This occurred, for example, in the case of vegetable products, minerals, and wood. Just as a relative-terms import compression has been associated with NRB products, there has been a rise in the relative importance of imports of higher value-added manufactured products, especially those which fall into the high technology category. Between 1989 and 2017 the share of capital goods in total imports rose from 27% to 32.2%. Imports of machinery and equipment rose from 22.3% of total imports to 25.2% over the same period. Setting the import and RCA data side by side with one another, it is hard to escape the conclusion that the past three decades have seen a competitive shift away from industrial and manufactured products and towards those based on primary activities.

By extension, it would be easy to arrive at the further conclusion that the re-primarisation of Brazil's export profile is simply the result of poor industrial competitiveness, the de-industrialising effects of globalisation, and the natural consequences of a sustained commodity price boom. With respect to the latter, in particular, it was always practically inevitable that the surge in commodity prices experienced between the early 2000s and the mid-2010s would translate into the accentuated presence of NRB products in Brazil's overall export profile. What such a conclusion ignores, however, were the strong structural improvements in competitiveness in export-leading sectors, especially mining and agriculture (Mueller & Mueller, 2016). As subsequent sections will make clear, these sectors, far from passively riding a wave of buoyant external demand, proactively engaged in significant investment and innovation. In so doing unit costs were contained, productivity strongly boosted, and value added to the commodities being produced. The other point which needs to be borne in mind – and which will be explored further in the sub-section focusing on technology – is that it would be incorrect to label the entire manufacturing/non-traditional exports sector – as a competitive laggard. Pockets of this sector performed extremely well, demonstrating that attempts to boost Brazil's competitiveness in global markets going forward need not be confined to areas of traditional strength.

Productivity

In the quest to drive up living standards over time, the central challenge faced by any economy centres on the need to achieve sustained gains in productivity whether in single-factor (i.e. labour or capital) or total-factor terms. The achievement of such productivity growth, for many countries – even advanced ones – has proven extremely difficult. In the case of the UK economy, for example, the period since the international financial crisis of 2008–9 has witnessed something of a productivity slump with output per hour worked increasing by just 0.4% per annum compared with an average of 2.3% for the 1980 to 2007 period (*Financial Times*, 13 August 2018). The difficulties of raising rates of productivity growth reflect the complex structural drivers at work, in particular, the fact that over the long-term, improvements in productivity depend on the adoption of new techniques, the accumulation of knowledge and even the emergence of entirely new productive sectors (Gordon, 2016). All of these require significant long-term investment and, where innovation is concerned, the ability of an economy to assume and manage risk. In the case of the middle-income trap, described in Chapter 1, a failure to sustain productivity growth is one of the central factors preventing emerging economies from closing the income per capita gap with their advanced counterparts. In Brazil, the structural complexity and economic salience of the productivity issue has, as argued earlier, triggered a plethora of public policy initiatives aimed at tackling it. As this sub-section demonstrates, however, the results on the ground have not always proved favourable, whether in relation to Brazil's past performance or in comparative international terms.

Quian et al. (2018) provide some stark indications concerning productivity trends at the aggregate level. The authors estimate the contribution of total factor productivity[13] (TFP) to economic growth in Brazil over the past quarter century. Between 1996 and 2015 GDP growth averaged 2.6% per annum. According to the authors' growth accounting exercise, 39% and 38%, respectively, of this growth was simply the result of increased inputs of capital stock and labour with

24% the product of increased human capital per unit of labour. TFP for this period was actually *negative* standing at −1%. In other words, and perhaps shockingly, TFP since the mid-1990s has actually acted as a drag on growth (ibid., p. 4). The corollary of this, of course, is that in aggregate terms economic efficiency has failed to improve, despite public policy initiatives, a surge of inward investment and the opportunities presented by an increasingly open global marketplace. By contrast in the United States, a far more mature economy, OECD data reveal that TFP growth averaged 0.93% per annum over the same (1996–2015) period. To gain deeper insight into the important productivity dynamics associated with the Brazilian economy it will be necessary to examine the evolution of single-factor productivity on a sectoral basis, both over time and in the international comparative context.

Tables 2.3–2.5 reveal the extent to which Brazil's single-factor productivity performance, at least in terms of labour, has been broadly disappointing over the past three decades. For the industrial sector Table 2.3 reveals quite a remarkable stagnation in labour productivity growth between 1991 and 2018; output per employee in real terms over this period tended to hover at just under US$25,000 with the broad exception of the 2009–13 sub period where it briefly exceeded US$27,000. The latter period was associated with a rapid, though not sustained, acceleration in output growth propelled largely by a commodity price boom. By 2018, output per employee was back under US$25,000, very little changed from what it had been approximately three decades earlier in 1991. In comparative terms, Brazil's productivity stagnation in industry is not so exceptional when set alongside the performance of neighbouring Argentina. However, the performance is notably unfavourable in comparison with Chile and Latin America's second-largest economy, Mexico, both of which have aggressively pursued trade and investment liberalisation since the 1980s. Compared with India and China, Brazil's performance appears worse still: between the beginning of the 1990s and 2018, the world's two most populous countries saw their industrial output per employee in industry rise by approximately ten and two-fold, respectively.

Sharpening the focus on manufacturing industry, Morceiro (2018) highlights what amounts to be something of a productivity crisis. Between 2003 and 2013, just before the recession hit, labour productivity in manufacturing as a whole declined by −0.5% on an average per annum basis. In low and medium low technology sub-sectors the decline was even more accentuated (−0.5%) while in high and medium high technology sub-sectors it was a more modest −0.2%.

Turning to the services sector, the data also indicate stagnating output per employee over a three-decade period in the case of Brazil. Between 1991 and 2018, remarkably, the output produced by each unit of labour declined by around US$500 in real terms (Table 2.5). Again, this contrasts with the rapid growth seen in China, India and even Argentina (though not Mexico). Services productivity growth regarding labour was also much more impressive in the United States and, indeed, in the OECD overall. The only area where Brazil's performance stands out as favourable, let alone impressive, is in the agriculture, forestry

TABLE 2.3 Industry, value added per worker (constant 2010 US$)

	1991	1992	1993	1994	1995	1996	1997
Argentina	14,224.22	15,751.17	18,379.35	20,170.57	21,985.64	24,233.34	24,398.38
Brazil	24,387.23	22,859.23	23,876.32	25,028.92	25,715.60	25,549.51	25,930.15
Chile	30,606.08	31,265.76	32,734.92	34,731.27	36,996.09	38,832.73	39,663.68
China	2,231.22	2,614.44	2,968.84	3,338.10	3,622.83	3,893.83	4,247.95
India	2,914.53	2,929.32	3,024.24	3,205.27	3,460.54	3,571.29	3,603.06
Mexico	34,875.55	35,677.46	35,072.15	37,435.68	34,074.03	34,904.08	35,886.20
OECD members					56,329.15	57,572.60	62,046.02
Russian Federation	18,895.89	15,227.62	13,908.03	12,436.60	12,769.71	12,788.43	14,602.71
United States							73,031.82
South Africa	29,193.96	28,282.90	27,907.51	27,629.97	27,270.60	27,190.27	27,275.90

	1998	1999	2000	2001	2002	2003	2004
Argentina	24,409.42	24,052.04	24,372.85	24,306.56	24,050.48	23,717.57	24,202.89
Brazil	25,104.74	24,711.38	25,334.83	24,787.59	24,263.96	24,460.13	25,425.82
Chile	43,423.60	49,133.12	50,586.31	50,055.83	49,657.70	49,938.94	50,046.07
China	4,621.95	5,035.35	5,493.22	6,013.89	6,656.52	7,407.29	7,897.68
India	3,641.46	3,735.53	3,854.29	3,779.61	3,867.63	3,930.54	4,014.23
Mexico	33,649.98	32,527.58	31,639.59	31,794.04	31,980.66	32,260.62	32,478.48
OECD members	62,907.15	64,655.05	66,693.99	66,619.45	68,280.20	70,150.63	72,934.31
Russian Federation	14,672.79	15,198.63	16,357.61	16,770.79	16,976.30	18,574.08	20,490.44
United States	74,865.47	78,252.53	80,779.64	80,252.42	84,398.18	87,834.65	91,997.43
South Africa	26,340.84	25,929.58	26,315.53	25,802.59	26,365.59	27,208.60	26,645.63

	2005	2006	2007	2008	2009	2010	2011
Argentina	24,377.58	25,180.13	26,011.09	26,400.91	25,323.18	27,108.33	27,287.88
Brazil	24,789.74	24,629.97	25,208.26	24,718.73	24,133.81	26,615.68	27,828.15
Chile	50,302.93	49,847.13	48,191.65	47,068.71	46,892.87	46,163.55	44,555.10
China	8,542.84	9,358.28	10,516.82	11,426.72	12,437.86	13,796.58	14,884.62
India	4,153.77	4,503.74	4,638.16	4,676.02	4,928.65	5,111.22	5,036.90
Mexico	31,052.15	30,949.77	30,504.51	30,458.44	29,519.72	30,148.45	30,437.83
OECD members	73,835.47	75,309.60	77,552.60	77,155.54	74,960.50	79,984.17	80,409.38
Russian Federation	21,075.24	22,151.53	22,718.56	23,173.58	22,395.82	23,431.17	24,918.78
United States	92,284.78	94,460.30	96,623.20	96,362.29	99,226.73	1,04,013.72	1,03,292.27
South Africa	26,775.81	26,632.46	26,998.32	27,214.40	26,890.98	29,975.26	30,132.65

	2012	2013	2014	2015	2016	2017	2018
Argentina	26,765.28	26,347.80	25,167.87	25,804.42	24,612.92	25,497.05	24,802.22
Brazil	25,612.98	26,089.56	24,983.77	23,982.22	24,831.73	25,012.94	24,812.16
Chile	44,881.23	45,779.32	46,151.40	46,132.16	45,994.25	45,586.32	46,825.65
China	15,995.92	16,915.67	17,837.46	19,055.79	20,232.22	21,498.97	23,077.91
India	5,024.56	5,124.92	5,378.76	5,806.24	6,165.60	6,377.32	6,715.66
Mexico	30,551.31	29,700.17	29,544.49	28,746.82	27,618.60	26,735.51	26,356.26
OECD members	80,501.59	80,982.83	81,572.84	82,477.64	82,650.02	87,096.22	
Russian Federation	25,216.07	25,323.51	24,680.66	24,836.22	25,626.97	25,968.49	26,853.80
United States	103,074.67	103,254.38	103,011.10	103,956.28	102,855.47	103,342.12	
South Africa	30,446.53	30,041.09	29,628.64	28,282.81	28,654.16	28,409.03	27,846.73

Source: Author's elaboration from the World Bank World Development Indicators.

TABLE 2.4 Agriculture, forestry and fishing, value added per worker (constant 2010 US$)

	1991	1992	1993	1994	1995	1996	1997
Argentina	392,306.05	328,109.07	303,817.33	324,802.77	266,298.28	206,439.33	189,324.24
Brazil	3,329.31	3,443.11	3,394.81	3,576.98	3,724.53	4,035.38	4,016.93
Chile	3,273.05	4,192.37	4,104.88	5,001.49	4,752.81	5,001.46	5,442.82
China	716.11	752.91	806.52	859.56	926.85	989.91	1,023.80
India	803.16	840.96	853.69	876.51	857.82	929.07	891.60
Mexico	3,299.54	3,109.62	3,088.33	3,194.57	3,425.07	3,656.68	3,231.94
OECD members				11,744.36	11,434.41	12,186.50	14,063.20
Russian Federation	6,077.03	5,110.14	5,020.54	4,480.81	4,298.67	4,260.08	5,722.35
United States							33,184.07
South Africa	7,134.94	5,078.29	6,194.21	6,531.83	5,121.66	6,266.75	6,232.75

	1998	1999	2000	2001	2002	2003	2004
Argentina	204,224.94	215,733.93	232,902.00	194,153.72	164,198.10	114,677.09	103,232.48
Brazil	4,235.57	4,299.86	4,318.08	4,447.56	4,620.86	4,899.79	4,693.66
Chile	5,629.46	5,669.05	5,982.54	6,591.82	6,827.36	6,691.05	7,510.25
China	1,049.94	1,061.51	1,073.71	1,099.19	1,123.32	1,165.27	1,282.35
India	935.00	952.19	936.53	978.63	901.56	971.91	964.52
Mexico	3,940.71	3,743.40	4,311.36	4,481.86	4,404.31	4,880.48	4,922.86
OECD members	14,857.46	15,417.27	17,816.67	17,697.95	18,265.42	18,939.83	20,826.65
Russian Federation	4,965.37	4,266.12	4,817.99	6,459.84	6,888.56	7,138.44	7,678.85
United States	34,177.49	39,455.76	67,148.37	69,173.73	63,862.28	72,153.60	76,110.39
South Africa	5,798.81	6,111.87	6,318.22	6,171.22	5,973.07	6,613.51	7,078.35

	2005	2006	2007	2008	2009	2010	2011
Argentina	139,002.19	162,781.13	162,707.46	147,957.20	105,043.64	140,340.96	267,743.30
Brazil	4,757.51	5,123.87	5,474.59	5,908.89	5,788.33	6,410.23	7,033.91
Chile	8,279.63	8,935.21	9,212.15	10,013.25	10,052.60	10,123.03	11,095.55
China	1,400.37	1,532.81	1,646.82	1,782.78	1,924.05	2,076.50	2,272.34
India	1,000.51	1,038.53	1,107.79	1,114.60	1,122.82	1,241.46	1,376.78
Mexico	4,863.89	5,228.19	5,502.19	5,439.60	5,270.73	5,256.66	5,028.69
OECD members	21,637.80	21,932.38	22,116.38	23,569.08	24,475.40	23,523.30	23,412.24
Russian Federation	7,452.74	7,808.06	8,570.61	9,358.59	9,845.71	9,353.35	10,650.14
United States	87,081.25	82,531.19	74,971.60	72,543.71	83,627.46	77,789.98	70,444.86
South Africa	8,872.21	8,323.12	8,521.21	10,878.54	12,267.17	13,133.88	13,887.80

	2012	2013	2014	2015	2016	2017	2018
Argentina	238,374.77	262,055.31	304,102.51	676,057.44	1,333,314.53	2,873,483.74	2,513,749.27
Brazil	8,940.51	9,793.61	10,723.03	11,246.11	11,007.54	13,230.31	13,218.45
Chile	10,730.41	11,069.42	11,028.92	11,537.59	11,528.57	11,800.26	12,423.32
China	2,453.60	2,719.82	3,008.16	3,221.86	3,429.95	3,653.16	3,818.40
India	1,455.75	1,523.74	1,509.70	1,511.22	1,594.93	1,669.34	1,717.86
Mexico	5,155.91	5,217.17	5,312.91	5,420.05	5,631.73	5,694.28	5,779.46
OECD members	23,013.91	24,593.16	25,417.09	26,159.66	26,373.76	27,629.51	20,903.63
Russian Federation	10,942.03	12,048.45	12,928.80	13,358.80	13,661.02	15,880.16	15,802.00
United States	69,466.01	84,826.89	81,618.62	81,909.33	84,256.06	79,108.00	
South Africa	13,109.91	12,885.35	14,476.43	10,817.65	9,787.24	12,025.47	11,766.73

Source: Author's elaboration from World Bank World Development Indicators.

TABLE 2.5 Services, value added per worker (constant 2010 US$)

	1991	1992	1993	1994	1995	1996	1997
Argentina	13,114.59	13,655.74	14,337.32	14,927.28	15,318.27	15,100.33	15,595.27
Brazil	21,655.09	21,144.87	20,990.18	21,129.78	21,026.61	21,627.90	21,552.84
Chile	14,319.38	14,857.55	15,529.01	15,453.92	16,579.99	17,995.10	18,677.22
China	3,222.36	3,422.04	3,568.01	3,696.77	3,807.08	3,909.10	4,165.01
India	2,482.27	2,544.30	2,653.47	2,708.87	2,911.58	3,052.77	3,260.88
Mexico	25,186.68	24,954.33	24,495.06	24,490.24	23,071.89	22,797.43	23,469.15
OECD members							72,775.00
Russian Federation	20,113.06	18,478.27	15,162.77	15,050.21	13,151.97	12,721.97	12,173.00
United States							85,120.48
South Africa	20,139.96	19,407.77	20,916.18	20,686.91	20,722.33	20,897.62	20,741.90

	1998	1999	2000	2001	2002	2003	2004
Argentina	15,463.86	14,965.95	14,779.80	14,260.27	12,923.23	12,866.00	13,359.82
Brazil	21,250.83	20,975.46	20,981.73	20,693.10	20,790.41	20,557.39	20,929.85
Chile	18,649.77	18,730.29	19,339.86	19,981.51	20,397.25	20,629.88	21,559.64
China	4,407.01	4,743.50	5,074.00	5,518.24	6,001.55	6,361.20	6,591.18
India	3,438.04	3,728.33	3,822.90	3,946.07	4,120.37	4,290.95	4,518.31
Mexico	23,280.70	24,353.83	24,665.12	24,089.94	23,394.66	23,059.21	22,930.45
OECD members	73,675.92	74,735.29	75,725.27	76,189.68	76,495.69	76,850.68	77,491.31
Russian Federation	11,783.72	11,996.03	12,370.28	12,480.76	12,688.67	13,609.57	13,766.06
United States	87,149.46	89,157.30	90,069.71	91,203.81	92,549.20	94,300.28	95,904.58
South Africa	20,460.08	20,704.65	20,918.70	21,545.96	23,562.46	23,819.79	24,204.46

	2005	2006	2007	2008	2009	2010	2011
Argentina	14,191.00	14,932.33	16,037.99	16,780.04	16,094.10	17,110.45	17,790.63
Brazil	21,140.28	21,222.83	22,027.64	22,490.47	22,624.96	23,402.87	23,758.77
Chile	21,948.36	22,803.49	23,569.15	23,869.26	23,665.03	23,585.86	24,336.88
China	7,011.70	7,581.35	8,388.10	8,999.29	9,510.51	10,096.47	10,626.45
India	4,754.52	4,997.25	5,293.21	5,551.97	5,944.76	6,310.51	6,446.28
Mexico	22,901.90	22,950.87	22,937.75	22,864.55	21,382.88	22,247.32	22,596.85
OECD members	78,096.72	78,627.99	79,109.48	78,420.13	77,188.86	78,178.67	78,971.13
Russian Federation	14,675.30	16,046.98	17,466.35	18,463.50	17,425.92	17,843.79	18,212.30
United States	97,895.52	98,719.49	99,116.16	98,956.50	99,591.93	1,02,026.13	1,03,043.47
South Africa	23,281.32	23,503.41	24,142.56	21,780.12	22,236.83	23,043.43	23,391.56

	2012	2013	2014	2015	2016	2017	2018
Argentina	17,647.52	17,891.30	17,598.91	17,618.66	17,232.86	17,266.19	17,175.68
Brazil	22,895.42	23,031.62	22,612.86	21,894.04	21,587.12	21,230.48	21,157.50
Chile	25,330.70	25,616.32	25,762.60	25,917.09	26,188.12	25,979.74	26,537.82
China	11,145.10	11,545.12	12,001.98	12,632.92	13,301.24	14,037.49	14,941.58
India	6,711.40	7,004.09	7,421.25	7,840.44	8,230.62	8,632.40	9,016.96
Mexico	22,657.16	22,850.85	23,455.09	23,839.19	24,352.57	24,736.55	24,891.20
OECD members	79,266.33	79,484.87	79,892.35	80,392.11	80,308.36	81,548.25	
Russian Federation	18,799.40	19,318.06	19,351.02	18,949.34	18,806.50	19,060.17	19,533.98
United States	103,411.88	103,606.74	104,304.46	105,558.91	105,700.76	106,184.96	
South Africa	23,353.95	23,293.02	23,316.99	23,291.60	23,518.78	23,074.89	22,793.09

Source: Author's elaboration from World Bank World Development Indicators.

and fishery sector (Table 2.4). Here, output per employee in real terms rose by a factor of four between 1991 and 2018, a performance matched only by Chile. The sectoral variations in productivity performance and, in particular, the exceptional showing of agriculture, very much tie in with the RCA data reviewed earlier. Brazil's strengthening competitiveness in agriculture – at least as evidenced by single-factor productivity – has been accompanied by an overall rise in its revealed comparative advantage. By contrast, at an aggregate level at least, industry appears to be in retreat, with declining relative participation in overall exports and what, without exaggeration, could be described as an ongoing productivity crisis.

In overall aggregate terms, across all sectors, Quian et al. (2018) underscore and elaborate on the low labour productivity growth that has characterised the Brazilian economy in recent years. The authors estimate that between 1996 and 2014 (after which productivity declined in lockstep with a deep recession) labour productivity increased by just 0.6% per annum. The authors further estimate that of the increase in value added per capita over this period, productivity improvements arising from labour movements from low productivity to high productivity sectors accounted for 25% of the change, while improvements in productivity *within* sectors were responsible for just 18% (ibid., p. 13). In other words, inter-sectoral resource transfers have proved more of a driver of aggregate productivity improvements than have structural changes taking place inside sectors. This adds weight to the argument that more needs to be done to improve the competitiveness of individual sectors rather than simply relying on the necessarily finite scope of Lewis-style labour transfers to deliver growth in productivity and, ultimately, living standards.

The disappointing productivity performance that generally characterises the Brazilian economy demands an explanation. However, while there is agreement around the fact that Brazil faces something of a productivity crisis, there is little consensus surrounding its causes (Morceiro, 2018, p. 254). Nevertheless, Cavalcante and De Negri (2015), in their exhaustive study, highlight some of the factors that they argue are at work. These include difficulties in mobilising resources from low to highly productive sectors, deficiencies in infrastructure provision, insufficient training and education, under-investment in technology and the high compliance and efficiency costs imposed by the nature of Brazilian bureaucracy. The latter, representing the "Brazil Cost" discussed earlier, is a particular focal point of industrial associations and feature strongly in their analyses of the factors inhibiting improvements in competitiveness and productivity (see, for example, CNI, 2019). In respect to the Brazil Cost policy agenda promoted by industry there is a particular focus on the role of labour market rigidities and ancillary employment costs as factors inhibiting the growth of labour productivity. These concerns met with some response as the Temer administration, in 2017, secured the passage of legislation that made it easier to hire labour on a flexible, part-time basis. This represented the most significant change to Brazil's Vargas era labour legislation in decades.

Another set of issues highlighted by Morceiro (2018) focuses on the issue of under-investment compared with competitor nations. The author reveals data by the ABIMAQ machine tools trade association which indicates that in 2015 Brazil's installed machinery averaged 17 years in age, twice of what was typical of industrialised countries (ibid., p. 255). The capital stock per employee in Brazil, according to Morceiro is around a quarter of his or her Japanese or American counterpart. The reasons for under-investment are numerous but an important component of the explanation here is connected with the evolution of Brazil's capital markets: this will form the subject matter of Chapter 6. Other chapters will focus on further drivers of productivity change, among them, the crucial role of training and education (Chapter 3) and the evolving nature of state-business relationships (Chapter 4) For the moment, however, this chapter turns to another important determinant of productivity: technology and innovation.

Innovation and technological change

As should be evident from the first half of this chapter, the stimulation of innovation and technical change has long been an objective of policymakers. Various mechanisms have been employed to this end over the years, ranging from direct public investment in research and development programmes to more indirect fiscal incentives aimed at the private sector. The logic underlying all these initiatives rests on the axiom that the pursuit of new forms of competitive advantage in the global economy necessarily requires the accumulation of technological capabilities and the development of new products and processes. To what extent have the hopes and objectives of policymakers been met in these regards? As in the measurement of competitiveness more generally, there is no generally agreed metric or standard for gauging technological success or its lack thereof. Instead, authors in the innovation studies field rely on a range of indicators and, especially in regard to the firm level, on individual case studies. Such approaches offer rich insight and evidence and have been employed in a substantial and growing literature on the Brazilian case. In what follows, an attempt is made to distil the key findings from this literature and to provide, where necessary, a sense of how Brazil's performance fares against relevant comparator countries.

In terms of gauging the relative technological intensity of economies a very broad – and widely used – indicator is provided by spending on R&D in relation to overall output. Table 2.6 reveals the extent to which Brazil performs quite well compared to its emerging market counterparts, notably those located in Latin America. Whereas R&D spending in Brazil typically accounts for just above 1% of GDP, the figures for Argentina, Chile, and Mexico, the region's other most industrialised economies, invest less than half of that in proportional terms and lesser still in absolute terms.

Nonetheless, Brazil's performance in ramping up its R&D spending has been considerably less impressive than that of China where over a decade and a half following the turn of the millennium the proportion of R&D in relation to GDP

TABLE 2.6 Expenditure on research and development as a percentage of GDP

	Argentina	Brazil	Chile	Mexico	India	China	Russia	South Africa	OECD
2000	0.40	1.05		0.31	0.77	0.89	0.98		2.12
2001	0.39	1.1		0.32	0.75	0.94	1.09	0.72	2.16
2002	0.36	1.01		0.37	0.74	1.06	1.16		2.13
2003	0.38	1		0.38	0.73	1.12	1.19	0.76	2.14
2004	0.40	0.96		0.39	0.77	1.21	1.07	0.81	2.11
2005	0.42	1		0.40	0.84	1.31	0.99	0.86	2.14
2006	0.45	0.99		0.37	0.82	1.37	1.00	0.90	2.17
2007	0.46	1.08	0.31	0.43	0.82	1.37	1.04	0.88	2.20
2008	0.47	1.13	0.38	0.47	0.87	1.45	0.97	0.89	2.27
2009	0.59	1.12	0.33	0.52	0.84	1.66	1.16	0.84	2.32
2010	0.56	1.16	0.35	0.53	0.82	1.71	1.05	0.74	2.28
2011	0.57	1.14	0.36	0.51	0.83	1.78	1.01	0.73	2.31
2012	0.64	1.13	0.36	0.49		1.91	1.03	0.73	2.31
2013	0.62	1.2	0.39	0.50		2.00	1.03	0.72	2.33
2014	0.59	1.27	0.38	0.53		2.03	1.07	0.77	2.35
2015	0.62	1.34	0.38	0.52	0.62	2.07	1.10	0.80	2.34
2016	0.53	1.27	0.37	0.49		2.12	1.10	0.82	2.34
2017	0.54		0.36			2.15	1.11		2.37

Source: Author's elaboration from World Bank, OECD, and MCTIC data.

has more than doubled. Perhaps surprisingly, and as a matter of some internal debate, R&D effort in India stagnated over this period. Set in this overall context, it may be said that Brazil, in broad relative terms, has maintained its commitment to investment in innovation despite the challenges of the past few years. This conclusion is lent further support when one examines data on the numbers of those involved in R&D activities in Brazil: between 2005 and 2014 this doubled from approximately 160,000–320,000 employees according to Ministry of Science and Technology data.

In breaking down the R&D expenditure numbers, one key feature quickly becomes apparent: the accentuated role of the public sector compared with the world's most innovative economies. Thus, for example, of the 1.27% of GDP allocated to R&D expenditure in Brazil in 2016, 52.4% was accounted for by the public sector, with the remaining 47.6% resulting from private sector investment. By contrast, in the United States, only 25% of expenditures originated in the public sector, while in South Korea, Japan and China, the public sector contributed 23%, 15% and 20%, respectively (Marques, 2019).

The data here reflect a couple of factors which have long been features of the landscape of the science, technology and innovation landscape in Brazil. First of all, from the 1960s onwards, as the first half of this chapter made clear, the state has set the acquisition and development of key technologies as a national priority and has pursued this objective with a fair degree of consistency despite recurrent fiscal pressures. Second, and possibly serving as a partial explanation for the statist orientation of Brazil's innovative trajectory, large swathes of the private sector have long proved reluctant to commit significant resources to what is often viewed as a risky form of investment activity (Amann & Figueiredo, 2012). Despite this, Brazil has developed what amounts to the most highly funded and comprehensive national system of innovation (NSI)[14] in Latin America (Cassiolato et al., 2014). Brazil's NSI comprises an elaborate network of research institutions, universities and enterprises through which research is conducted. As subsequent discussion will make clear, this has facilitated the creation of world-leading technological capabilities in selected areas.

Turning away from the question of resources injected into innovative activities, what of the eventual outcomes? One of the most widely used metrics, though far from a comprehensive indicator of technological achievement, centres on the number of patents sought and granted. Table 2.7 provides such data, based on registrations at the US Patent Office, and indicates the extent to which Brazil has succeeded in ramping up its patenting activity in recent years. Again, its track record compares favourably with that of its key Latin American counterparts, Argentina and Mexico. Once again, however, China has far outstripped Brazil, or indeed any other country in accelerating its patenting activity over the 1999–2017 period. The data on India are interesting in that the sharp rise in patenting activity appears at odds with the stagnation in expenditure on R&D noted earlier. This leads us to consider a very important issue: the productivity of R&D expenditures. How does Brazil fare in comparative terms in this regard? Frischtak (2019, p. 101) presents some interesting evidence drawn from the World Bank and World Intellectual Property Organization data.

Regarding patents granted per US$ 100m spent on R&D, Brazil, achieved an average of 1.2 patents in 2005 compared with 1.1 in 2015. For an average of 25 relevant comparator countries the equivalent figures for 2005 and 2015 were 25.7 and 19.3, respectively, set against 174.5 (2005) and 103.1 (2015) for a group of "frontier" countries. In this context, and against a background of internationally dwindling "patent productivity" Brazil's performance does not appear especially favourable. One of the factors constraining the efficiency with which Brazil translates innovative effort into tangible outputs concerns the costs associated with conducting R&D in that country. Compared with other emerging market locations, notably China, Brazil has a high-cost index rank for accomplishing R&D. In 2012 this stood at 95.4 compared with 56.8 for Mexico, 65.4 for Russia, 54.3 for China, and 43.9 for India (where the US index value comprises the base at 100) (ibid., p. 111).

The numerical indicators presented so far cannot fully illuminate the realities of the technological landscape in Brazil, inherently characterised as it is with qualitative as much as quantifiable change. For this reason, it is worth briefly grappling with the large qualitative, case-study-based literature which has sprung up around innovation in the Brazilian economy in recent years.

TABLE 2.7 US patents applied for and granted by country of residence of the applicant, 1999–2017

		1999	2000	2001	2002	2003	2004	2005	2006	2007	2008
Argentina	Applied for	96	137	137	95	125	103	94	117	150	138
	Granted	44	54	51	54	63	46	24	38	37	32
Brazil	Applied for	186	220	219	243	259	287	295	341	375	442
	Granted	91	98	110	96	130	106	77	121	90	101
China	Applied for	257	469	626	888	1,034	1,655	2,127	3,768	3,903	4,455
	Granted	90	118	195	288	297	403	402	659	770	1,223
South Korea	Applied for	5,033	5,705	6,719	7,937	10,411	13,646	17,217	21,685	22,976	23,584
	Granted	3,562	3,314	3,538	3,786	3,944	4,428	4,351	5,908	6,295	7,548
India	Applied for	271	438	643	919	1,164	1,303	1,463	1,923	2,387	2,879
	Granted	112	131	178	249	342	363	384	481	546	634
Mexico	Applied for	147	190	196	157	185	179	180	213	212	248
	Granted	76	76	81	94	85	86	80	66	56	54
Russia	Applied for	388	382	433	377	341	334	366	412	444	547
	Granted	181	183	234	200	203	169	148	172	188	176
South Africa	Applied for	179	209	231	241	224	246	197	231	252	265
	Granted	110	111	120	113	112	100	87	109	82	91
United States	Applied for	149,825	164,795	177,511	184,245	188,941	189,536	207,867	221,784	241,347	231,588
	Granted	83,906	85,068	87,600	86,971	87,893	84,270	74,637	89,823	79,526	77,502

		2009	2010	2011	2012	2013	2014	2015	2016	2017
Argentina	Applied for	146	134	156	141	160	126	159	164	203
	Granted	45	45	49	63	75	71	66	82	84
Brazil	Applied for	464	568	586	679	769	810	855	931	892
	Granted	103	175	215	196	254	334	323	310	374
China	Applied for	6,879	8,162	10,545	13,273	15,093	18,040	21,386	26,026	29,674
	Granted	1,654	2,655	3,174	4,637	5,928	7,236	8,116	10,462	13,243
South Korea	Applied for	23,950	26,040	27,289	29,481	33,499	36,744	38,205	37,341	35,565
	Granted	8,762	11,671	12,262	13,233	14,548	16,469	17,924	19,494	20,717
India	Applied for	3,110	3,789	4,548	5,663	6,600	7,127	7,976	8,739	9,222
	Granted	679	1,098	1,234	1,691	2,424	2,987	3,355	3,657	4,163
Mexico	Applied for	220	295	306	355	357	481	593	618	638
	Granted	60	101	90	122	155	172	172	224	288
Russia	Applied for	522	606	719	888	959	1,007	991	1,219	1,125
	Granted	196	272	298	331	417	444	440	436	432
South Africa	Applied for	318	320	339	318	415	375	352	359	352
	Granted	93	116	123	142	161	152	166	–	–
United States	Applied for	224,912	241,977	247,750	268,782	287,831	285,096	288,335	295,327	293,904
	Granted	82,382	107,791	108,622	121,026	133,593	144,621	140,969	143,724	150,949

Source: Author elaboration from data provided by USPTO/MCTIC.

Much of the qualitative literature has focused on the experience of individual sectors and, to a growing extent, on enterprises themselves. As context to these studies it is worth beginning by noting that formalised R&D activity is not widely dispersed throughout the Brazilian productive sector. Although compared to its regional counterparts, Brazil expends relatively significant resources on R&D, this is sectorally quite concentrated and, what is more, this is quite focused on a select grouping of enterprises (Amann & Figueiredo, 2012). Data provided by Brazil's Ministry of Science, Technology, Innovation and Communications (MCTIC) make this point pithily: in the year 2000, of 72,006 enterprises surveyed, just 4.4% claimed to host ongoing in-house R&D programmes. By 2014, the proportion so engaged fell to just 3.6% (out of a population size of 117,976).

A very brief review of the qualitative literature swiftly reveals, in sectoral and enterprise terms, the focal points of innovation. Major studies from Ferraz et al. (1992), Amann, and Figueiredo (2012), Figueiredo et al. (2018) to Reynolds et al. (2019) reveal a technological landscape characterised by high degrees of R&D investment and technological achievement in key areas, notably life sciences and agricultural technology, aerospace, oil exploration and production, NRB product processing and, to a more restricted extent, enterprise software development. These focal points are often – though not exclusively – characterised by proximity to activities rooted in natural comparative advantage. In particular, agriculture, whether in terms of animal husbandry or arable cultivation, has seen significant innovation driven by an active and well-funded state agency, Embrapa. This has facilitated profound changes in the agricultural sector and helps to explain why agricultural productivity growth has outstripped that of other sectors or indeed that of other major economies (Mueller & Mueller, 2016).

Association between targeted state support and technological intensity, both in terms of investment made and capabilities built is also seen in the aerospace and oil and gas sectors. Here two enterprises, Petrobrás and Embraer (one state-controlled, the other privatised), have acquired world-leading capabilities in their respective fields, allowing them to expand their global scale as multinationals (Mussachio & Lazzarini, 2014). This theme will be further examined in the next section. Outside these lead sectors, pockets of excellence, both in enterprise and sectoral terms do exist. Thus, for example, technologically advanced, frontier-defining enterprises exist in the automotive sector (e.g. Marcopolo bus and coach) and electrical equipment (e.g. WEG electric motors). However, as the aggregate data and case study material make clear, such cases tend to be the exception rather than the rule. For all intents and purposes, the bulk of Brazil's productive sector, not least that engaged in manufacturing, undertakes no formal R&D. In particular, Brazil lacks a secondary tier of technologically leading small- and medium-manufacturing enterprises such as may be encountered in the United States, or, famously in Germany's *mittelstand*. Instead, as if to mimic historical patterns of wealth distribution, technological capability in Brazil is highly concentrated in scope and is often at least the partial result of nurturing by the state.

Brazil's multinationals

Thus far, much of the discussion has centred on dimensions of competitiveness related to trade, productivity and innovation. However, much focus on cross-border investment flows has been missing. In this connection, it is important to note that another illustration of a nation's competitiveness stems from the performance of firms, and, especially the extent to which these prove capable, not only of confronting foreign competition at home but of taking the battle abroad. The rise of outward foreign direct investment (OFDI) from emerging markets-based enterprises over the past three decades has represented one of the most dynamic features of the global economy. Brazil has most certainly formed part of this process with significant overseas expansion across a range of sectors and investment locations.

The rise of the emerging market multinational corporations (EMNC) phenomenon represents an important juncture in the evolution of the global economy. Whereas, in the first four decades after World War II, OFDI was almost exclusively the preserve of multinational corporations (MNCs) based in Western Europe, North America and Japan, since the 1980s the role of OFDI from developing and emerging market countries has become far more significant. The fact that EMNCs have expanded to such an extent has altered patterns of global investment flows. However, it has also begun to reshape the geopolitical landscape. Countries such as Brazil and China – which play host to numerous home-grown MNCs – are now able to exercise soft power through outward investment, a capability once solely in the hands of the advanced industrial economies.

However, the causes of the EMNC boom are at least as worthy of note as any potential impacts on global investment flows or, indeed, the international balance of power. In this regard, what the rise of EMNCS illustrates is that emerging economies such as Brazil now possess – in particular quarters at least – the requisite access to capital, managerial skill and technology with which to gain entry to markets around the world. In this sense, the evolution of OFDI can tell us quite a lot about the underlying competitiveness of a particular country. In particular, close study of a nation's MNCs can help indicate where comparative advantages lie, where technology and pools of skill exist and where new capabilities are being developed.

With these considerations in mind, this section will consider the Brazilian EMNC phenomenon in the following manner. In the first place, to set the discussion in an appropriate theoretical context and to demonstrate the link to the competitiveness theme, contemporary theories of international production are briefly considered and their relevance to emerging market settings evaluated. Following this, the discussion focuses on the empirical reality of the Brazilian MNCs and attempts to gauge what the key determinants of the phenomenon have been. The discussion also considers what patterns of sectoral specialisation among these enterprises can tell us about underlying competitive conditions in Brazil itself. Finally, given the apparent retraction in Brazilian OFDI in the final part of the 2010s, consideration is given to what the future may hold for Brazilian MNCs.

Whereas theories of trade date back to the earliest days of economics, at the beginning of the 19th century, fully formed theories of international production, in particular, in relation to the MNC are a rather more recent phenomenon. The dawn of such theories can be traced to the work of Stephen Hymer in the 1960s. Hymer (1976), partly drawing inspiration from theories of the firm expounded by Bain and Chamberlain, argued that in order to expand, gain market share and displace the competition, enterprises require an ownership advantage. The latter would effectively represent the source of monopoly rents and can be thought of as the set of attributes that enable the firm effectively to avoid always having to engage in price-based competition. What factors might constitute such an ownership advantage? The answer here would normally centre on such features as technical knowledge, intellectual property and brand identity; in other words, knowledge-based assets which provide a given firm with a unique set of advantages. Assuming a firm has such advantages, it would then potentially be able to leverage them on a global scale to reap the associated monopoly profits. In this sense, the metamorphosis of a firm into an MNC can be thought of as a rational response to the potential rewards to be gained by the international deployment of – often expensively created – ownership advantages.

Hymer's insights stimulated a lot of academic debate and provided the basis for a more elaborate theory of international production that would emerge later. The theory in question, developed by John Dunning (Dunning & Lundan, 2008) and termed the OLI (or Ownership, Location and Internalisation) approach, has become effectively the standard approach to examining the MNC phenomenon. The OLI theory incorporates Hymer's notion of ownership (O) advantages: without these it would not be possible for a firm to become an MNC. Assuming a firm is in possession of such advantages, the question arises as to whether the rents potentially arising from them could be better generated through the internalisation (the "I" of the OLI schema) of production (i.e. through FDI) or through licensing a third party (for example, through a franchise arrangement). The answer here will depend on a range of factors but is likely to be swung heavily by such issues as capital availability, the extent of local market knowledge, the rule of law and the potential for principal-agent issues to arise. In general terms, the more complex the technologies involved, the greater the potential for information asymmetries and associated principal-agent issues, the more likely it is that FDI through a wholly owned subsidiary will take place.

Assuming the firm has decided to internalise through FDI, the most influential part of Dunning's analysis focuses on where, geographically, investments are likely to take place and, relatedly, what the specific objective of the investment is. This is where the location (the "L" in the OLI schema) decision arises. Dunning and Lundan (2008) argue that FDI flows fall into four main categories, efficiency-seeking, market-seeking, resource-seeking and strategic asset-seeking. Efficiency-seeking investments are motivated by the ability to produce efficiently in a foreign location, perhaps because of good infrastructure, skills or cost-effective labour. On the other hand, resource-seeking investment (which is especially important in the Brazilian and broader Latin American context) occurs because the MNC identifies in its target location the opportunity to extract natural resources. By contrast, market-seeking investment is driven by the opportunities that exist to gain access to a customer base in a given location while strategic asset-seeking behaviour is impelled by the requirement to acquire particular assets – often ownership advantages – in a foreign location (ibid.). The beauty of the OLI framework is that it allows us to characterise and categorise MNC behaviours and potentially draw conclusions surrounding the underlying competitiveness and strategic logic of the enterprises concerned.

Having considered the theoretical background, what of the Brazilian experience itself? The first point to note is that, compared to its Latin American peers Brazil has, on average, in recent years constituted the largest single foreign investor (Table 2.8). In 2018, for example, Brazil contributed roughly 40% of all the OFDI undertaken by all countries in the region. It will be noted, however, that the FDI flow data depicted in the table are highly volatile year-on-year. This is, in fact, fairly typical for countries across all regions since FDI flows can be dominated in any given year by large, lumpy transactions, especially large takeovers. Another reason for the volatility typically observed relates to the phenomenon of intracompany loans. These would involve overseas subsidiaries raising loans in foreign capital markets and then repatriating the proceeds to the parent company. Such measures can often be deployed where home country financial market conditions are stressed. In the case of Brazil, the steep dive in OFDI flows between 2017 and 2018 is largely attributable to this phenomenon (World Investment Report, 2019, p. 53). Another complicating factor in interpreting and indeed obtaining accurate data concerns the role of offshore centres. These are frequently used for tax or other purposes to obscure the true origin of the ultimate investors.

Still, even with these caveats in mind, it is obvious that Brazilian corporations have become significant overseas investors. Some even have become household names (e.g. Embraer), while some, such as 3G Capital exercise controlling interests in major corporations responsible for such well-known consumer brands as Burger King, Budweiser and Stella Artois. The big question concerns how Brazil has become such a vibrant centre for MNCs, having been previously renowned for being more of a destination for foreign FDI. The answers to this question are complex and need to be related to the individual motives of the MNCs concerned, the sectors within which they operate and how ownership advantages have been developed. A good starting point to understand the general logic behind the expansion of Brazilian MNCs is to consider the Columbia Center for Sustainable Investment (CCSI) and Getúlio Vargas Foundation (FGV) ranking of the largest enterprises by foreign assets. The latest version of this was published in 2018 (CCSI-FGV, 2018).

TABLE 2.8 Latin America and the Caribbean (selected countries): foreign direct investment outflows, 2010–18 (millions of dollars)

	2010	2011	2012	2013	2014	2015	2016	2017	2018
Brazil	26,763	16,067	2,083	15,644	20,607	3,134	14,693	19,352	14,060
Chile	9,461	20,252	20,556	9,888	12,800	15,931	6,994	5,172	1,949
Colombia	5,483	8,420	−606.2	7,652	3,899	4,218	4,517	3,690	5,122
Mexico	8,038	12,398	18,700	13,605	7,130	11,891	6,013	3,181	10,457
Uruguay	60	7	3,869	−2,034.0	1,319	1,605	619	4,794	3,339
Venezuela (Bolivarian Republic of Venezuela)	2,492	−370.0	4,294	752	1,024	n.d.	n.d.	n.d.	n.d.
Other	1,293	2,006	3,458	1,606	4,376	1,673	2,828	1,503	1,141
Latin America and the Caribbean	54,554	60,268	53,409	48,003	53,075	39,327	37,452	38,846	37,870

Source: Adapted by the author from ECLAC data.

Of the 20 largest Brazilian MNCs by foreign assets the report points out that 90% of the assets in question are located in the food, mining, oil & gas, pulp & paper and other extractive activities (ibid., p. 1). In other words, the largest Brazilian corporations tend to operate within, or close to, the primary product sector. The top three companies listed (Petrobrás (oil & gas), Vale (mining) and JBS (foods), accounted for almost two-thirds of the total overseas assets of the 20 largest Brazilian MNCs combined. The overrepresentation of the enterprises engaged in primary product processing and extraction among Brazil's largest MNCs is strongly reflective around the importance of natural comparative advantage (access to natural resources) in providing a springboard to internationalisation.

Thus, perhaps paradoxically for a country so rich in natural resources, its largest overseas investors are generally engaged in resource-seeking behaviour, according to the OLI schema. Another interesting feature of the data is that they indicate that, among Brazil's top ten MNCs by overseas assets, no fewer than four were, or currently are (in the case of Petrobrás) state-controlled companies. The others, Vale (mining), CSN (steel) and Embraer (aerospace), started life as SOEs. Why might state-ownership – past or present – appear to be such an important characteristic of Brazil's largest MNCs? One explanation here is that state support, in a savings constrained economy, formed a vital means of acquiring the scale, through capital investment, to make internationalisation through outward investment a practical reality for many Brazilian companies traditionally (see Chapter 6), lack of access to capital is an important factor in explaining their failure to grow. However, there is another important explanation linking the role of the state with the expansion of Brazil's largest MNCs. This has to do with the fundamental point that state support – either past or current – helped to facilitate the creation of ownership advantages, especially through innovation.

As will be recalled from the earlier discussion of the OLI framework, intellectual property and innovation form two vital elements in the presence of ownership advantages; they are in effect the source code for the creation of rents. Without possession of proprietary technologies and related intellectual property, enterprises seeking to internationalise through OFDI would be forced to rely on licensing or strategic asset-seeking modes of investment. In relation to the latter modality, this is indeed what many Chinese and Indian enterprises have successfully accomplished (Ramamurti & Singh, 2009). The purchase of the United Kingdom's Jaguar Land Rover by India's Tata Group more than a decade ago is a case in point.

In the case of Brazil, however, it is much harder to find examples of strategic asset-seeking investment. In examining the major overseas investors, their investment objectives tend to centre on gaining access to markets and natural resources. Thus, the case must be that the ownership advantages are being created locally. That this is the case may seem surprising for an economy traditionally considered as languishing in the global periphery. However, the fact is that there is a rich literature documenting the creation of ownership advantages in Brazil, especially through the acquisition of domestic technological capabilities. Thus, for example, Amann and Figueiredo (2012), Fleury et al. (2013) document the processes whereby Brazilian MNCs have painstakingly developed their own technologies in a variety of fields ranging from life sciences, to oil exploration and production, to aerospace. Studies such as these point out that, in many cases, an active programme of state support proved vital in fomenting the technological capability necessary to enter new fields and, in some cases, to close on and reach the global frontier.

In the case of Petrobrás, for example, as was true of many large SOEs including the national telecommunications enterprise, Telebrás, the electrical utility, Petrobrás and the aerospace firm, Embraer, publicly funded research laboratories were set up within these enterprises – or, in the case of Embraer in proximity to them. This was done in order to develop complex technologies and transfer them to wherever they would be required. This enabled Petrobrás, for example, to go on to win world records for offshore deep drilling and in the case of Embraer, facilitated it in penetrating the complex and demanding world of civil jet transports (ibid.). Even when privatisation occurred (which it did, for example, with Embraer, Telebrás, Vale and others) a research tradition was continued and support for laboratories sustained (ibid.). With the capabilities created in the pre-privatisation era, that continued beyond it, the basis for the formation of ownership advantages was firmly established. The prominence of former SOEs and, indeed other forms of enterprises that benefited from innovation policy among Brazil's MNC is testament to the importance of these measures.

Notwithstanding these insightful cases, it should be recognised that by no means do all Brazilian MNCs fit the pattern of current or former SOEs grounded in the extractive sector. Beyond the top 20 list, and even as part of it, one can find enterprises with a diverse range of activities, not least in manufacturing. Although Brazilian OFDI in manufacturing pales beside that of, say, China, there are cases of successful global Brazilian MNCs operating in buses and commercial vehicles (Marco Polo) and electric motors (WEG), for example. These cases show the potential that exists for Brazilian MNCs to prosper even when there appears to be no underlying natural comparative advantage providing forward momentum.

Looking to the future, the prospects for Brazilian MNCs are currently clouded thanks to low commodity prices globally. Were these to rise then, with additional resources, enterprises such as Vale and Petrobrás could resume international expansion. More generally though, in the spirit of diversifying the productive base of the economy, it will be important for new MNCs to sprout from non-traditional sectors. This is true, especially in such areas as business services and high technology, where Brazilian OFDI is currently light. All of this will form another policy issue for the current and future administrations to grapple with.

Infrastructure

Over the decades since the inception of President Vargas' *Estado Novo* (New State) in the 1930s, the development of infrastructure capable of facilitating structural economic change has been a recurrent policy objective for one administration after another. That this is the case stems from a number of factors. On the one hand, as part of the structuralist/developmentalist economic ideology that permeated civilian and military governments alike up until the 1980s, investment in infrastructure was seen as a means of binding the nation together, fortifying strategically vulnerable regions on Brazils northern and western frontiers, and, most of all, supplying critical inputs for the related processes of industrialisation and urbanisation. The rise of corporatist mechanisms for industry representation (Schneider, 2004) institutionalised and further embedded the pro-infrastructure tendency at the heart of Brazil's administrative and industrial élite.

As part of this, major construction and capital goods producers were able to maintain constant pressure on the state to develop new projects so as to try and keep order books full. In fact, whether one considers oil & gas, highways, ports or electricity generation and transmission, the evidence shows that the commissioning of infrastructure projects acted to bring state and business together, rather as was the case with technology policy.[15] In this sense, the infrastructure development campaign acquired a logic of its own. This was born of the shared interests of contractors and politicians, both of whom were anxious to favour their constituents with the jobs, business opportunities and patronage that went with large contracts. The political expediency of large infrastructure projects as a means of building up a support base and of financially lubricating the political process is not to be underestimated. In fact, this very issue forms the subject matter for Robert Caro's classic account of the acquisition and deployment of political power, *The Power Broker.* This compelling volume charts the career trajectory of Robert Moses, the individual responsible for much of the New York metropolitan area's parks and major highways (Caro, 1974).

While the lobbying networks advocating for infrastructural investment never went away, the 1980s and 1990s, as Chapter 1 made clear, saw the waning of the structuralist and developmentalist influences on economic policymaking. Nonetheless, the pursuit of improved infrastructure remained a priority, even if the solutions were to be found through attempts to encourage greater private sector provision. The theoretical impetus behind fresh infrastructure projects was now to be imparted less from developmentalist attempts to engender structural transformation and more from a desire to improve Brazil's competitive standing and boost its growth prospects.

Justifying this new-found preoccupation with the infrastructure issue were a number of studies, notably Fereira & Araujo (2007). This uncovered significant growth impacts resulting from a rise in infrastructure stocks. At the same time, as Brazil moved into the 2000s, the rise of GCI raised the policy profile of infrastructure once more. In fact, infrastructure forms one of the 12 pillars of the WEF's GCI (WEF, 2018). For governments across the world, it had become clear that the quality and availability of infrastructure in their economies would be one of the key factors by which their business climate would be judged and decisions – especially around FDI projects – made. With the more developmentally inclined PT in power from 2003 to 2016, infrastructure advocates could then draw on justification from both traditional statist and so-called "neoliberal" standpoints, a rare confluence!

Against this background of relatively consistent political and ideological support for the infrastructure development process, it might be thought that Brazil would have performed well in regard to investment in, and completion of, such projects. In fact, the evidence suggests that the country has struggled, especially in recent years and that, in international terms it is at a significant disadvantage compared with peer countries. To take one important indicator as an example, consider how Brazil ranks internationally in the WEF's infrastructure pillar, 1 of 12 which collectively combine for the GCI. In 2018 Brazil ranked 81st out of 140 countries. China and India, by comparison, stood at 29th and 63rd position, respectively, while regional peers, Argentina, Chile and Mexico achieved 68th, 41st and 49th position, respectively. To take another example, examining patterns of spending over time, it becomes clear that despite growing pressures to be competitive, the relative proportion of GDP accounted for by spending on infrastructure has declined quite significantly. In the early 1980s, just before Brazil was obliged to take on far-reaching structural adjustment packages, investment in infrastructure stood at 5.2% of GDP. By 2013, this proportion had fallen by over half to 2.25% (Garcia-Escribano et al., 2015, p. 11).

Further insight can be gleaned if the situation of individual infrastructural sectors is considered. One of the most (in)famous cases concerns ports, where, because of deficient investment and poor operational practices, delays are common. For example, according to Micco and Perez (2002, p. 159), tariffs in Brazilian ports are five to six times higher than international averages. Not only this: only one of Brazil's ports – Santos – features among the top 100 in the word (Garcia-Escribano et al., 2015, p. 10). These issues are associated with delays in supply chains as trucks queue for hours to load and unload. This further limits the competitive attraction of Brazil as an export platform, hence, so much of the inward FDI that occurs focuses on resource-seeking or market-seeking activities.

As a result of this, port reform and related infrastructural improvements have risen up the list of political priorities. Despite this, Doctor (2016) indicates that progress on accomplishing actual change has been slow because of the weight of institutional vested interests. One solution may be to construct new ports in fresh locations with different working practices and more up-to-date methods. In the United Kingdom, during the 1960s this is exactly what occurred with the establishment of Felixstowe, a port geared to the new phenomenon of containerisation. It conveniently lacked the labour unrest which had blighted the competitiveness of more traditional terminals such as Liverpool or the Port of London. In the case of Brazil, such an initiative has been realised with the construction of the port of Suapé in Brazil's North-eastern state of Pernambuco. However, modern though Suapé is, it is located more than 1000 miles north of Brazil's main industrial and population centres.

Another interesting example is provided by the experience of the railway sector.[16] Prior to the 1950s and 1960s Brazil used to have a reasonably comprehensive system of local and long-distance passenger railways, at least in the more populated South and South East. Subsequently, however, the strategic priority ascribed to road vehicle transport as part of the ISI programme, and the accelerated development of civil air transport saw the curtailment of most passenger services (except for urban rail). Up until the 1990s, most Brazilian rail infrastructure was in the hands of a Federal Government concern, RFFSA. Following privatisation, the lines were sold off to different interests, including foreign groups. While some modernisation has taken place, rail remains almost overwhelmingly concentrated on freight and the system itself is fragmented, being comprised of stretches of tracks with different (often non-standard) gauges. Remarkably, for two great centres of population less than 400 km apart, no passenger rail service now links Rio de Janeiro and São Paulo. The plans for connecting the two cities with high-speed passenger rail are yet to come to fruition, despite the original intention of completing this project by the 2016 Rio Olympics. As a result, Brazilians travelling between both cities must make use of congested highways or air services, both less than environmentally sustainable.

Another infrastructural challenge facing Brazil concerns its highway networks. It might be expected that these would be highly developed and of a good standard, given the priority ascribed to motor vehicle transport by consecutive development plans in the 1950s, 1960s and 1970s. In the case of the South East, especially in the state of São Paulo, this is partly true. In this region, major centres of population are linked by modern multilane highways. Since the 1990s, the quality of these has improved thanks to private investment, as previously publicly owned motorways have been sold off to private sector concessionaires. However, no such multilane highways link the South East with the North East, a factor which can be argued to be one of a number holding the latter region back. More broadly, only 18% of Brazil's 1.75 million km of highways are paved (World Bank, 2012).

Another major infrastructural challenge is presented by Brazil's electricity generation and transmission sector Bolognesi (2018). Like the highways sector, this has confronted considerable reform as a result of market liberalisation, specifically privatisation. Whereas Brazil's electricity generation and transmission utilities used to be in the hands of state, municipal and federally owned companies, now it comprises a mixture of public and private enterprises, the latter including some foreign participants. The emergence of a more liberalised market for electricity generation and transmission, which involved the creation of a new regulator, ANEEL (National Agency for Electrical Energy), has led to a diversification of power sources. As Chapter 8 will indicate, Brazil's historical reliance on hydroelectricity has lessened over the past three decades as new providers have established thermal generating capacity, notably using newly established natural gas resources. However, given the fact that well over half of Brazil's electricity is generating using hydro sources, the nation's power supply remains vulnerable to periods of drought. In the past, these have resulted in power outages and rationing, notably during 2001–2 and again in 2013.

The experiences of the sectors here, recounted only very briefly, find their analogue elsewhere in areas such as water & sanitation, airports, waste disposal and so on (Oliveira, 2018). These challenges and the reduction in spending on infrastructure relative to GDP since the 1980s may seem surprising given the high political profile of infrastructure and its lack of ideological contentiousness. So, what factors explain the difficulties in increasing infrastructural provision?

In the first place, it is impossible to understand the factors which have retarded infrastructural investment since the return to civilian rule in the mid-1980s without first taking into account the financial consequences of structural adjustment. Throughout the 1980s and 1990s, the requirement to meet fiscal targets imposed severe spending constraints on consecutive administrations. Cuts were targeted on non-discretionary areas of spending, especially public investment (Amann, 2000). As a consequence of what amounted to the fiscal exhaustion of the state, from the 1990s onwards new models of infrastructural provision emerged. These featured an enhanced role for the private sector. It was hoped that by tapping the resources of private enterprises and capital markets, the spending gap on infrastructure left by the retreating public sector could be filled. Achieving this would require the development of infrastructure provision models which had to walk a delicate tightrope. On the one hand, such models had to provide returns attractive enough to draw on private sector participants. On the other hand, the tariffs provided to users by the new participants would have to be reasonable. Added to this was the desirability that the new entrants created net new capacity rather than simply sweated existing assets.

In attempting to reconcile what could be conflicting objectives the state took on a new role as a regulator (Pinheiro, 2011). Depending on the sector it would privatise assets, launch concessions, establish public-private partnerships and/or simply open up markets to new entrants. The experiences of these processes varied quite greatly from sector to sector. Often, but not always, the much-needed capacity failed to come online quickly enough or at all.

Whereas telecommunications liberalisation and privatisation, initiated in 1998, has generally led to favourable outcomes – far more consumer choice, better pricing and improved technology – this was not necessarily true in other sectors, where problems were realised (Oliveira, 2018). For example, as already recounted, the electricity sector has experienced difficulties in matching capacity with demand. The sector also developed a highly complex ownership structure. Thanks to political opposition, some utilities – for example, Eletrobrás and Cemig – have so far remained under public sector control (though privatisation plans exist). Others – for example, Tractebel Energia and AES Tiête – have come under foreign, private control. Partial privatisation of the port system has not resolved all its difficulties (Doctor, 2016).

Responding to all of this, the Lula and Rousseff administrations attempted to boost infrastructure spending through more direct public co-financing of projects which would, nevertheless, still involve hefty private sector participation. This was often through modalities such as public-private partnerships. The first Accelerated Growth Programme (PAC 1) in 2007, and then its successor (PAC II) in 2010 targeted almost R$ 1.5 trillion for infrastructure spending. More recently, the current administration, emphasising privatisation to a greater degree, has announced initiatives to improve the port, rail and highway networks. Nevertheless, problems remain. Spending as a proportion of national income stands well below what it was four decades ago.

What factors explain this? Clearly the roots of the problem are complex, as studies such as Oliveira (2018), World Bank (2012) and Mourougane and Pisu (2011) make evident. However, some commonly observed features do emerge. The first concerns the availability of financial resources. As Chapter 6 will make clear, Brazil remains a savings-constrained economy and one in which a concentrated financial sector can make raising credit difficult through domestic private sector sources. Second, adding to the difficulties, macroeconomic uncertainty and regulatory risk,[17] may put off both infrastructure operators and those who might finance them. Responding to this critical issue, in January 2019 the WEF and the Inter-American Development Bank published an important report in which they argued that there was a need for the BNDES development bank to issue project guarantees and so mitigate risk. The idea here is that the Bank, rather than always lending directly, acts in ways which "crowd in" private sector investors (IDB-WEF, 2019). Such a shift in BNDES focus appears a very sensible move: thanks to the 20-year spending cap now in place,[18] achieving extra public investment will be extremely challenging.

Another common issue, and one which applies especially to projects in environmentally sensitive areas, concerns the time taken to obtain licenses. This has especially affected hydroelectric schemes, notably the Belo Monte scheme in the Amazon. This ran into considerable delays at the licensing stage. The argument here is not in favour of abandoning licensing arrangements but rather one supporting streamlining processes, and preventing the emergence of regulatory uncertainty. The latter often occurs as competing federal and local agencies seek to impose often contradictory requirements. Most of all, however, investors in infrastructure need to feel confident that the market in which they are committing resources will deliver adequate returns over the years ahead. Given Brazil's track record of volatile growth and macroeconomic fragility, it is not surprising that infrastructural investment has been muted. For this reason, there should be even more motivation to proceed with the other aspects of structural reform which are necessary to secure Brazil's economic future.

Conclusions

This chapter has demonstrated that despite three decades of reform initiatives, Brazil still remains beset by profound competitive challenges. As, from the late 1980s, the direction of policy shifted towards trade and market liberalisation, then in the direction of state-led developmentalism and finally – from 2016 – back to liberal reforms, Brazil's competitiveness failed to take off, despite the emergence of major global opportunities. The performance of productivity outside agriculture, in particular, has proved highly disappointing.

The precise determinants of this poor performance are complex and contested but revolve around some familiar themes. These include, but are not limited to, under-investment in human capital, wilting fixed capital, and infrastructural investment and, relatedly, technological inertia. Regarding the latter feature, this chapter made clear that while nodes of world-leading technological capability exist, these tend to be exceptional and are characterised by their proximity to sources of natural comparative advantage and state support. This is exemplified in the case of some of Brazil's most successful MNCs. Lack of competitiveness in non-traditional activities, allied to booming commodity prices (at least up to 2014) helps to explain one of the most striking features of the contemporary Brazilian economy: its re-primarisation. This has led Brazil towards being more reliant on a select group of commodities exports as it has attempted – not unsuccessfully, it must be said – to address its external constraint. Tackling the vulnerability implied by Brazil's recent evolution in the global division of labour will be a challenging and long-drawn-out affair. It must necessarily involve broadening the scope of competitive excellence which currently characterises only a select few sectors and enterprises.

Notes

1 See Morceiro and Guilhoto (2019) for a comprehensive account of deindustrialisation and the long-term competitive predicament of Brazil's manufacturing sector.
2 The dispersion of tariff rates was also significantly reduced.
3 He resigned in December 1992 in an attempt to halt an impeachment trial launched after wide-ranging allegations of corruption surfaced.
4 The administration of President Itamar Franco (1992–94).
5 Inflation and primary surplus fiscal targeting remained in place throughout the PT years.
6 In June 2016 the government requested that Brazil join the TiSA (trade in services agreement). The Temer administration also set in train negotiations for Brazil to join the OECD and to engage with the WTO's Agreement on Public Procurement initiative (*Americas Quarterly*, 7 September 2017).
7 This centres in policy terms on the quest for pensions and social security reform (see Chapter 5).
8 Author's calculation based on World Bank data.
9 However, this masks an elevation to 48th place in 2012 before the economic and political crisis took hold and brought Brazil back to where it had started back in 2007.
10 World Integrated Trade Solutions – a trade database retained by the World Bank.
11 The series of events leading up to the debt adjustment crisis in Brazil was triggered by the 1973 and 1979 OPEC oil price rise.
12 Limitations in domestic refinery capacity still mean that some lighter crude oil needs to be imported from the Middle East: partly as a result of repeated scandals at Petrobrás, the capability to process all the heavier Brazilian product is not yet fully in place.

13 Total Factor Productivity (TFP) represents the residual of overall output that is not accounted for by increases in the input of capital and labour. Accordingly, TFP can be thought of as a measure which captures the extent to which combined inputs into the production process are used more (or less) efficiently over time, within or between countries. TFP can also, in this sense, be thought of as a variety of index of technical progress.

14 For a comprehensive discussion of the nature and significance of national systems of innovation, see Nelson (1993).

15 For an account of the role of the state in building up Brazil's infrastructure and heavy industry-focused made-to-order capital goods sector, see Amann (2000).

16 For a good, comprehensive account of the issues affecting the sector, see Pompermayer (2018).

17 Resulting from the nature of regulation itself and Brazil's complex legal system.

18 See Chapter 5 for more details on this.

3

EDUCATION, SKILLS AND HUMAN CAPITAL

Of all the structural obstacles impeding the realisation of sustainable inclusive growth in Brazil, the question of human capital formation has proven perhaps the most ingrained and hard to overcome. In the previous chapter, it was observed that Brazil remains beset by low productivity performance, not least in relation to labour. It was also argued that over the long term, Brazil has encountered severe difficulties in trying to diversify its productive base and seize new market opportunities in emerging, dynamic sectors. Both of these issues are partly rooted in the challenges presented by an unevenly and, many would say, under-developed human capital stock. The implications of this challenge are not only felt on the productive plane: shortfalls in education and training also have helped to condition poverty and social exclusion over the years. In regard to the latter phenomena, important issues of equity arise, given the uneven access to quality education that characterises the Brazilian reality. In particular, there have been longstanding biases in provision that have mitigated against the life chances of individuals based on regional origin, ethnicity and gender. This has helped to facilitate intergenerational cycles of poverty and social exclusion which in turn have contributed to the emergence of Brazil as one of the world's most unequal societies.

Despite the pessimistic tone of much of the public discourse surrounding the issue of human capital in Brazil, there has in fact been commendable progress over the past couple of decades. Enrolment rates at both primary and secondary school levels have risen, decent advances in basic literacy and numeracy has been achieved, while, at the other end of the educational spectrum, leading Brazilian universities have been edging upwards in the global rankings. As indicated in the previous chapter, in some cases, human capital accumulation and knowledge acquisition have reached the point where Brazil has emerged as a world leader. This is certainly the instance in such areas as oil exploration and production, agricultural technology and aerospace (Amann & Cantwell, 2012).

What these admittedly special cases suggest is that where the policy and institutional conditions are right, Brazil is capable of developing a human capital base to match with the very best around the world. The challenge, which this chapter will later contemplate, concerns how such excellence can become more representative of the overall reality. Primarily, however, this chapter attempts to diagnose the current challenges surrounding education, skills and human capital development in Brazil. As in Chapter 2, this is accomplished, where possible, in international comparative context. Part of the idea here is that, from the standpoint of the issue of global competitiveness, a purely domestically focused approach would not be meaningful. At the same time, a comparative approach helps to shed light on the common challenges faced by Brazil and peer group countries as they attempt to break out of what many see as a middle-income trap.

To achieve its objectives, the structure of this chapter is as follows. First, a very brief overview of the evolution and institutional character of Brazil's educational and training system is presented. Next, the focus turns to a consideration of Brazil's school system and its performance in international comparative context both in terms of resources deployed and outcomes achieved. Attention is also paid to regional variations in school performance within Brazil, since it turns out that significant – and troubling – differences continue to exist in respect both of educational opportunities and outcomes. These, of course, help to explain yawning spatial disparities in economic and social development. Consideration is also given to aspects relating to gender and ethnicity. Following this discussion, the chapter then turns towards the issue of training and tertiary education. As the analysis will make clear, Brazil, by emerging market standards, has developed a sophisticated and comprehensive network of institutions aimed at developing vocational skills. The Brazilian "model" of vocational training has even been exported globally as part of development assistance programs signed with African economies during the PT administrations (2002–16) (Villalobos & Klasen, 2016). However, despite the pockets of excellence that exist, severe skills deficits exist, and there is an ongoing national debate concerning ways in which existing modalities of vocational training might be successfully reformed. This chapter analyses the current situation with a view to highlighting areas for improvement as well as assessing the undoubted achievements realised.

In many respects, Brazilian universities represent the jewel in the crown of the country's educational system. A very wide array of institutions has developed over the decades comprising universities rooted in the private sector, a network of federally funded universities and a significant grouping of universities financed by state governments (Neves, 2017). Brazil's leading universities, such as the University of São Paulo, the Getúlio Vargas Foundation business school (FGV), rank among the best in Latin America and have become serious international players, attracting research collaborators from around the world. This achievement is all the more remarkable given that Brazil's first fully fledged university opened its doors only as recently as 1932. Reviewing the evolution of Brazil's university system, this chapter will examine its performance according to widely deployed international metrics and will also consider the extent to which it has proven effective at translating knowledge generation into technical change, productivity and output growth.

Brazil's education system in brief historical and institutional context

The evolution of Brazil's educational system has been a long process, dating back to the colonial era. However, the sector's most significant reforms and expansion have been associated with the rise of the state from the mid-20th century onwards (Ferreira, 2010). Prior to its independence, education in colonial Brazil was at first strongly associated with the Jesuit order. Following the reforms of the Marquis of Pombal in the late 18th century, the colonial administration seized control, assigning to the state far greater responsibility for regulating education and its administrative structures (ibid.). The role of the state was only to further expand during the transition to a republic in the late 19th century and following the advent of the Vargas administration and the Estado Novo (or New State) in the 1930s. In the 1940s, as one of the lasting legacies of the corporatist era, the national industrial confederation (CNI), an umbrella trade association, took the lead in establishing the SENAI network of vocational training institutions, designed to develop the skills needed by a fast-expanding industrial sector. By 1950, Brazil had developed a sizeable, publicly funded primary education network. However, enrolment of primary-aged children at this point stood at only around 50% (De Moura Castro, 2018) with rates still lower at secondary level. The university and vocational educational systems were, at this stage, still at a comparatively early stage of development. The decades after World War II were to see a rapid change in this landscape, however.

A pivotal moment in the evolution of Brazil's educational system came in 1961, when, following years of debate a new federal legislative framework for the regulation and development of the sector was finally approved by congress (Ferreira, 2010). The years to follow saw the federal Ministry of Education assert more systematic control over matters concerning the nature of the school curriculum. The growing federal involvement in the development of the nation's educational provision was also cemented by accelerated investment in universities. During the first four decades of the post-World War II period, the federal administration sponsored the creation of a national network of universities financed from federal funds (Neves, 2017). As part of a national development strategy, begun during the 1950s and continuing under the military into the 1980s, federal universities were established in traditionally peripheral regions (e.g. the North East) as well as in the established urban centres of the South and South East. In tandem with this development, individual Brazilian states stepped up their investment in universities, resulting in the development of the extensive parallel network of nationally and locally funded institutions that can be seen today (ibid.). This public sector dual network was supplemented by the rise of private universities which tended both to have a more vocational bent and to be located in larger urban centres.

While the debt adjustment crisis and the end of military rule in the 1980s had long-lasting political and economic effects, the institutional basis of Brazil's educational and vocational training system was comparatively little affected. The biggest changes to impact the educational landscape were to arise in the 2000s following the election of President Lula in 2002. The most celebrated development cantered on the *Bolsa Família* (Family Grant) program. This program, discussed in more detail in Chapter 7, incentivised school attendance through linking it to payment of benefits for participating households. Partly as a result, the proportion of those between 6 and 14 attending school in 2015 had reached 97.7%, up from around 80% in 1980 (Pieri, 2018, p. 12).

The Lula administration and its successor under President Rousseff also stepped up participation rates in higher education. This was achieved through multiple means, which included a surge of investment in universities. Increased funding allocation to the federal universities sector allowed for an increase in student numbers, as well as, in several cases, the creation of entirely new institutions. As part of the Lula and Rousseff government's commitment to developing Brazil's more deprived regions, over the 2002–16 period, new federal universities were created in the North and North Eastern states of Para, Bahia and Pernambuco as well as in traditionally more affluent Minas Gerais. Another key objective of these administrations was to internationalise Brazilian higher education and provide enhanced learning and research opportunities for students in high-quality foreign institutions. This especially applied in scientific and technical subject areas, where a well-funded scholarship program entitled Ciência Sem Fronteiras (Science Without Borders) was founded in 2011. The program – which fell victim to budget cuts in 2017 under President Michel Temer – had granted just over 100,000 scholarships by 2016. Another notable aspect of Brazilian higher educational policy in recent years was the adoption of racial quotas. Legislation adopted in 2010 and 2012 allocated places at federal institutions to those from historically disadvantaged ethnic groups, notably those of African descent.

Vocational training also saw significant investment throughout the 2000s and into the present decade. Between 2003 and 2013, federal spending on vocational training rose from 0.04% of GDP to 0.2% (Souza et al., 2015). In 2011 a fresh initiative, PRONATEC (Programa Nacional de Acesso ao Ensino Técnico e Emprego – National Program of Access to Technical Training and Employment) was launched, aimed at substantially ramping up vocational training and labour market access opportunities. By 2014, accumulated enrolments on the approximately 900 courses operated by PRONATEC had risen to just over one million (ibid.).

Unlike its predecessors, the administration of Jair Bolsonaro, on taking office at the start of 2019, has adopted a sceptical, if not hostile tone towards Brazil's educational establishment. Part of the administration's attitude towards the sector is coloured by its positioning in the "culture wars" and its opposition to the social liberalism of the PT years. Thus, there has been a focus on issues such as educational policy around same-sex relationships and the maintenance of ethnically based quotas. The administration's first minister of education also made clear his wish to see history textbooks amended so as to give students a more favourable view of the 1964–85 military dictatorship. The administration's need to pursue fiscal adjustment has rendered many areas of discretionary expenditure vulnerable to cutbacks. The educational sector – perhaps especially given that it has been viewed as a pole of dissent – has been no exception. In mid-2019 spending cuts of 30% in the discretionary budget of federal universities were announced. Meanwhile, the National Educational Development Fund (FNDE) had 21% of its budget frozen for 2019 (BBC Brasil, 30 June 2019). Simultaneously. CAPES, the federal postgraduate student funding agency, has been forced by fiscal stringency to cut almost 3,500 grants. So far, Brazil's vocational training institutions appear to have avoided significant cutbacks. In this sector at least, the political temperature surrounding the debate is notably cooler than elsewhere.

The performance of the school system in international comparative context

Despite Brazil's reputation for lack of priority accorded to human capital formation, by OECD standards the country invests a reasonable portion of GDP in education. Summing together expenditure on primary, secondary and tertiary education,[1] Brazil in 2015 invested 5.5% of GDP in this area compared to an average of 4.5% for the OECD overall (OECD, 2018, p. 4). The accentuated share of national output devoted to education in Brazil reflects a considerable ramping up of public spending under the administrations of Presidents Lula and Rousseff: between 2005 and 2011 direct public spending on educational institutions rose by almost 70% (ibid.). This illustrated the determination of these administrations to implement a radical social reform agenda in which education would play a central role. Part of this, of course, was connected with the expansion of primary education as a necessary accompaniment to the *Bolsa Família* conditional cash transfer program. However, additional resources were also channelled into more advanced education, with expansion of the university system, both in terms of student numbers and quantity of institutions.

In terms of the sources of spending on education, it should be evident from the preceding discussion that these stem not from a single origin but, given Brazil's federative character, from three levels of government. Cumulatively, between 2000 and 2013, 28.8% of expenditures derived from the federal government with 33.9% arising from the states and the remaining 37.4% from municipalities (World Bank, 2017). Of federal expenditures, the largest share (31%) was destined for higher education, while the spending of sub-national levels of government was more biased towards expenditure on primary and secondary education.

While Brazil's overall expenditure on education is quite impressive in international terms, when more disaggregated data on spending are examined, it becomes apparent that investment in primary and secondary education is comparatively restricted compared to the global average. Table 3.1 makes this point all too clearly.

TABLE 3.1 Total expenditures (US$) on educational institutions per full-time equivalent student (2015)

	Primary	Secondary	Tertiary
Brazil	3,762	3,872	14,261
Chile	5,064	4,930	8,406
Colombia	3,178	2,817	6,369
France	7,395	11,747	16,145
Germany	8,619	11,791	17,036
Italy	8,426	9,079	11,257
S Korea	11,047	12,202	10,109
Japan	9,105	11,147	19,289
Mexico	2,874	3,129	8,170
United Kingdom	11,630	10,569	26,320
United States	11,727	13,084	30,003
OECD average	8,631	10,010	15,656
EU22 average	8,656	10,105	15,998

Source: Adapted from Table C1.1 Education at a glance 2018: OECD indicators.

As can be seen, while Brazil spends surprisingly generously on university and vocational level education (i.e. the tertiary level) by OECD standards, at least its spending on the primary and secondary levels is far more modest. In particular, the relative gap in spending per student between the primary/secondary and tertiary levels is greater in Brazil than in the other countries featuring in the table. This hints at an important facet of the way in which Brazil's educational policy structure has developed over time; the patterns of spending which it has generated have tended to lavish resources on comparatively few students.

Examining national data over time, it becomes clear that education in Brazil has been afforded a higher degree of priority in public spending over the past two decades. In 2001, total public spending on pre-tertiary and pre-university education stood at 3.8% of GDP. By 2015 this had risen to 4.8% of GDP, although the year on year increases realised to get to this point were concentrated in the 2001–11 period (Anuário Brasileiro de Educação Básica 2019, p. 121). By contrast, over the same period, public expenditure on tertiary and university education rose from 0.9% to 1.3% of GDP (ibid.).

Moving away from data on total expenditures, another important metric useful for international comparative purposes centres on teachers' salaries. As will be seen, despite increasing school enrolment – linked in part to the deployment of conditional cash transfer programs – students' attainment remains a key area for concern in Brazil. Undoubtedly part of the issue here centres on the quality and motivation of teachers in primary and secondary education (De Moura Castro, 2018). Considering the skill and effort required, Brazil's teachers are hardly among the country's best remunerated public servants. Data from the OECD (OECD, 2019a,b) points to the significant extent to which Brazilian teachers lag their international peers in salary terms. In 2017 average statutory minimum teachers' salaries in Brazil stood at US$14,000 compared with US$30,000 across the OECD, US$24,000 in Chile, US$24,900 in Costa Rica and US$20,000 in Mexico (ibid., p. 5). The OECD report makes a further interesting point which ties into a broader set of concerns surrounding patterns of spending on primary and secondary education in Brazil: the extent to which strong regional disparities exist. Thus, in Pará, the state with the highest level of salaries, average salaries are 5.6 times those of Mato Grosso, the region with the lowest. The report concludes that "the coefficient of variation between (Brazilian) subnational regions is higher than the coefficient of variation between countries in the OECD" (ibid., p. 5).

The theme of spatial disparity emerges once more when regional expenditures on basic education (as opposed to teachers' salaries alone) are considered. A recent World Bank report[2] compares expenditure by municipalities and states against average attainment in the IDEB (Índice de Desenvolvimento da Educação Básica – Index of Basic Education Development) (World Bank, 2017, p. 128). The latter is an index which reflects performance in exams set by the National Institute of Education Studies (INEP). From the data presented there appears some association between higher expenditures and higher attainments. In particular, states and municipalities in the North and North East (traditionally Brazil's least affluent regions) both tend to spend less on average and experience poorer attainment outcomes than those located in the more affluent South and South East. The study concludes that variations in expenditure between states and municipalities explain 11% of the variations in IDEB attainment outcomes (World Bank, 2017). Two inferences can be drawn from this. The first is that a failure to level up expenditures on educational provision in the traditionally poorer North and North East is likely a factor impeding the accumulation of human capital – and thus economic and social progress – in these regions. Second, while expenditure levels do appear to have an impact on outcomes, it is clear other factors must also be at work. Thus, there is every reason to believe performance improvements that do not require increases in resource input are both desirable and potentially achievable.

Moving away from quantitative expenditure-based input measures, what of the quality of these inputs? Brazilian national data indicate that the rise in overall expenditures indicated above has been accompanied by increasing professionalisation and formal qualification of the teaching workforce. Across all elementary school teachers, the proportion with a higher education qualification rose from 67% in 2008 to 79.9% in 2018 while the proportion of those with a postgraduate qualification increased from 28.3% in 2012 to 36.9% in 2018 (ABEB, 2019, p. 107). Again, however, there are notable regional disparities. While over 80% of elementary school teaching staff possess higher education qualifications in the South, South East and Centre West, in the North and North East only 75.2% and 68.2% did so in 2018. Thus, these traditionally disadvantaged regions suffer from both a relative lack of resources as well as a comparatively less qualified workforce.

The issue of educational outcomes, as opposed to inputs, has become one of the highest profile public policy matters in Brazil, and certainly among the most controversial. In overall terms, while Brazil has improved its performance – at least relative to its own past – by international standards it lags well behind. The most widely cited international survey of student attainment – the OECD Pisa rankings – provides interesting evidence both of Brazil's current relative standing and also of how this has evolved over time. Tables 3.2–3.4 summarise the main findings across performance in science, mathematics and reading.

The first and obvious point to note from the tables centres on Brazil's performance in international comparative terms. The latest (2018) data indicate that for reading, mathematics and science Brazil lags well below the OECD international average. It is also the case that, in relation to its own recent past (2009), Brazil

TABLE 3.2 Averages for age 15 years PISA reading scale: overall reading, 2018 and 2009

		All students	
Year/study	Jurisdiction	Average	Standard error
2018	**Selected countries and jurisdictions**	**453**	**(0.3)**
	International average (OECD)	**487**	**(0.4)**
	Chile	452	(2.6)
	Colombia	412	(3.3)
	Korea	514	(2.9)
	Mexico	420	(2.7)
	United Kingdom	504	(2.6)
	United States	505	(3.6)
	Argentina	402	(3.0)
	Brazil	**413**	**(2.1)**
	B-S-J-Z (China)	555	(2.7)
	Peru	401	(3.0)
	Russia	479	(3.1)
2009	**Selected countries and jurisdictions**	**469**	**(0.4)**
	International average (OECD)	**490**	**(0.5)**
	Chile	449	(3.1)
	Colombia	413	(3.7)
	Korea	539	(3.5)
	Mexico	425	(2.0)
	United Kingdom	494	(2.3)
	United States	500	(3.7)
	Argentina	398	(4.6)
	Brazil	**412**	**(2.7)**
	Peru	370	(4.0)
	Russia	459	(3.3)

Source: Adapted by author from Organization for Economic Cooperation and Development (OECD), Program for International Student Assessment (PISA), 2009 and 2018 reading, mathematics and science assessments.

TABLE 3.3 Averages for age 15 years PISA: mathematics scale, 2018 and 2009

Year/study	Jurisdiction	All students	
		Average	*Standard error*
2018	**Selected countries and jurisdictions**	**459**	**(0.3)**
	International average (OECD)	**489**	**(0.4)**
	Chile	417	(2.4)
	Colombia	391	(3.0)
	Korea	526	(3.1)
	Mexico	409	(2.5)
	United Kingdom	502	(2.6)
	United States	478	(3.2)
	Argentina	379	(2.8)
	Brazil	**384**	**(2.0)**
	B-S-J-Z (China)	591	(2.5)
	Peru	400	(2.6)
	Russia	488	(3.0)
2009	**Selected countries and jurisdictions**	**470**	**(0.4)**
	International average (OECD)	**492**	**(0.5)**
	Chile	421	(3.1)
	Colombia	381	(3.2)
	Korea	546	(4.0)
	Mexico	419	(1.8)
	United Kingdom	492	(2.4)
	United States	487	(3.6)
	Argentina	388	(4.1)
	Brazil	**386**	**(2.4)**
	Peru	365	(4.0)
	Russia	468	(3.3)

Source: Adapted by author from Organization for Economic Cooperation and Development (OECD), Program for International Student Assessment (PISA), 2009 and 2018 reading, mathematics and science assessments.

has seen little progress in the case of absolute scores. While scores advanced marginally in the case of reading, in the case of mathematics and science actually declined. However, if data from earlier periods are examined, evidence of sharper improvements becomes clear: between 2000 and 2009 scores for reading improved from 396 to 412, for mathematics from 356 to 386 and for science from 390 to 402. Hence, the picture that emerges for the first two decades of the 21st century is one of two halves: sharp improvements over the first ten years followed by far more modest progress in the second.

However, there are a couple of points which need to be made in mitigation here. In the first place, the average scores for all OECD nations retreated over the second decade of the 20th century (2009–18) and indeed by a greater amount than experienced by Brazil. Second, lack of progress in raising Brazil's average scores needs to be seen against a background of rising enrolment rates.

TABLE 3.4 Averages for age 15 years PISA science scale: overall science, 2018 and 2009

Year/study	Jurisdiction	All students	
		Average	Standard error
2018	**Selected countries and jurisdictions**	**458**	**(0.3)**
	International average (OECD)	**489**	**(0.4)**
	Chile	444	(2.4)
	Colombia	413	(3.1)
	Korea	519	(2.8)
	Mexico	419	(2.6)
	United Kingdom	505	(2.6)
	United States	502	(3.3)
	Argentina	404	(2.9)
	Brazil	**404**	**(2.1)**
	B-S-J-Z (China)	590	(2.7)
	Peru	404	(2.7)
	Russia	478	(2.9)
2009	**Selected countries and jurisdictions**	**475**	**(0.4)**
	International average (OECD)	**498**	**(0.5)**
	Chile	447	(2.9)
	Colombia	402	(3.6)
	Korea	538	(3.4)
	Mexico	416	(1.8)
	United Kingdom	514	(2.5)
	United States	502	(3.6)
	Argentina	401	(4.6)
	Brazil	**405**	**(2.4)**
	Peru	369	(3.5)
	Russia	478	(3.3)

Source: Adapted by author from Organization for Economic Cooperation and Development (OECD), Program for International Student Assessment (PISA), 2009 and 2018 reading, mathematics and science assessments.

As the OECD's own commentary on the 2018 results highlights, Brazil, along with five other countries (Albania, Indonesia, Mexico, Turkey and Uruguay) has been able to broadly maintain or slightly enhance average scores over a period when rates of participation have sharply increased (OECD, 2019a,b). This development can be seen as a significant achievement for two reasons. In the first place, a greater proportion of the relevant age group can be said to be achieving the declared scores. Between 2003 and 2015, the proportion of 15-year-olds in full-time education (the age at which students are assessed for the PISA rankings) rose steeply from 56% to 71%, an extraordinarily steep increase by national or international standards. The rise in enrolment rates stems at least in part from the introduction of the *Bolsa Família* conditional cash transfer program in 2004 which provides financial incentives to send and keep children in school. Second, to maintain or even enhance standards when student numbers and enrolment rates are increasing so fast is no small achievement. That this is so stems from the obvious resource and organisational challenges, but also from the issues of successful integration that may be encountered in attempting to educate students from marginalised communities and social backgrounds.

An important and increasingly politically salient theme across the world – and in Brazil itself – concerns variations in educational outcomes between genders. Mirroring a pattern commonly encountered elsewhere, data for 2018 show girls outperforming boys comfortably in reading (by 26 points compared to an OECD average of 30 points) while in mathematics the position is somewhat reversed with boys outperforming girls by nine points compared to an OECD average of three points. In science, performance is even between genders, representing the conclusion of a period where girls have rapidly closed the gap with boys (with the mean science score for girls increasing by no fewer than 13 points between 2006 and 2015). In addition to gender, concern also surrounds issues of equity relating to socio-economic status. In the case of reading, in the 2018 Pisa survey, more socio-economically advantaged groups of students outperformed disadvantaged students in reading by 97 score points compared with a gap of 89 score points across OECD countries. By comparison, in 2009 the score gap between socio-economically advantaged and disadvantaged students in Brazil stood at 84 points compared to 87 points across the OECD on average. In mathematics and science, socio-economic status was a strong predictor of performance accounting for 16% of the variation in scores, compared to 14% for the OECD on average. In the case of science, social advantage also accounted for 16% of the variation (with the equivalent figure for the OECD being 13%).

Despite the progress made in some areas, especially in the first decade of this century, further exploration of the data reveals some major causes for concern. These tie in with broader issues about the state of human capital formation in Brazil. In particular, in international comparative terms, there appear to exist a number of issues around performance in mathematics. According to the 2018 OECD Pisa survey, in this subject area, Brazil ranks especially unfavourably in relation to mean scores (69 out of 77) and the percentage of low performers (below proficiency level 2) (9th out of 77) (OECD, 2019). Across all subjects, the percentage of low performers is one of the highest among all participating countries (10th out of 76) while the disciplinary climate, ranked 75th out of 76, is just about the worst captured by the survey (ibid.). Of further concern, the proportion of students reporting always feeling sad was the fifth highest recorded in the survey while the percentage of students without clear ideas about their future career prospects ranked tenth among the 78 countries analysed.

Domestically commissioned and generated data also provide rich insights into school performance and educational outcomes. The Brazilian education foundation, Todos Para Educação in its *Annual Brazilian Basic Education Report* (Anuário Brasileiro de Educação Básica – ABEB) provides a wealth of data on educational investment and attainment. Some of the most interesting and significant data concern the evolution of basic literacy skills. Regarding the evolution of functional literacy among the 15–64 age group, the statistics[3] point to reasonable progress. Between 2001–2 and 2018, the proportion of the age group assessed as either illiterate or only in possession of rudimentary literacy declined from 39% to 30%. By contrast, the proportion of the 15–64 age group considered to be proficiently literate or of intermediate literacy rose from 32% to 37% (ABEB, 2019, p. 87). Those displaying basic literacy skills rose from 28% to 34% of the relevant age group (ibid.). Tying in with the results from the PISA studies, the ABEB data on literacy indicate that most of the progress realised since the start of the century was concentrated in the 2000s, rather than the 2010s. The former decade was, of course, the period in which the *Bolsa Família* was introduced and when investment in education was sharply ramped up. Since 2009, there has been very little change in the proportions of the population according to degree of literacy.

Although there has been significant progress in reducing the incidence of illiteracy over the past two decades, data provided by the Brazilian Geographical and Statistical Institute (IBGE), a government body, provide cause for concern in relation to social equity. According to the IBGE's own measure of literacy, there remain significant differences as between ethnic groups and regions of the country. Thus, for example, in 2018 the literacy rate for those 15 and over in the population stood at 96.1% of those classified as "white," but this falls to 91% for those termed "black" and 90.9% for those of "mixed" ethnic origin (ABEB, 2019, p. 86). Regarding the regional picture, the same dataset reveals notable disparities between the poor North and North East (where literacy rates stood at 92% and 86.2%, respectively, in 2018) and the more affluent South and Southeast where literacy rates were appreciably higher at 96.4% and 96.5%, respectively. Fortunately, there is some evidence that the regional literacy gap may be narrowing over time. Between 2012 and 2018, the proportion of the population in the North East considered literate by the IBGE survey rose from 82.9% to 86.2%, a far greater rate of change than for the country as a whole over the same period where the increase overall stood at 1.8 percentage points.

As should be evident by now, there is no doubt that the Brazilian school system has made significant progress since the start of the 21st century. The data reveal that both expenditures and average qualifications of staff have risen as the system has had to cope with rising student numbers, propelled by increasing enrolment rates and the impacts of conditional cash transfer programs. In the light of these developments it is impressive that progress has been made in respect to basic student attainment, and that Brazil, at points in time, has managed to improve its standing in the international Pisa rankings. However, it is equally clear that challenges remain. In international comparative terms, the evidence provided by the Pisa data would indicate that Brazil's relative advance has slowed significantly over the 2010s. This is a conclusion only reinforced when one examines relevant national datasets. At the same time, very clear evidence emerges of spatial, gender and ethnic disparities with regard to attainment. Thus, for example, girls continue to significantly outperform boys in the Pisa reading assessments while national data reveal non-trivial differences in literacy levels between those of white and non-white ethnic origin. Added to this, it is also clear that, compared to the North and North East, educational inputs and outcomes are significantly elevated in the traditionally more affluent South and South East of the country.

Improvements in educational investment and attainment are usually considered essential in tackling poverty and inequality, hence the priority ascribed to them, especially by the governments of Presidents Lula and Rousseff (2002–16). But, empirically, just how significant might they be? An interesting study by Madeiros et al. (2018) offers a note of caution. The study, a simulation exercise using a multivariate model, attempts to assess the degree to which rises in educational attainment might impact Brazil's still accentuated levels of income inequality. The authors conclude that considerable improvements would in fact be necessary to generate significant impacts on equity. Even with a doubling of the proportion of workers who had completed secondary education, the Gini coefficient would fall only by 7 percentage points in relation to its 2010 value (ibid., p. 45).

What are the reasons for this? Besides obvious factors such as the concentrated distribution of factors of production other than human capital, the authors point to influences such as the declining returns to primary and secondary education, the inertial impacts of demographic change and the continuing existence of labour market skills mismatches. The same factors, so the authors argue, also determine that improvements in educational outcomes might only be expected to have a more modest than anticipated impact on the evolution of poverty. One of the most important features of this study is that it draws our attention to the importance of labour market dynamics, in particular, the importance of ensuring that those entering the market have the skills necessary to match its evolving demands. Accordingly, the chapter now turns to examine the evolution and effectiveness of Brazil's vocational education and training (VET) system.

Vocational education and training in Brazil

As indicated earlier in this chapter, vocational education and training has a relatively long history in Brazil with the foundation of the first apprentice schools created by the Federal Government in 1909. As time went on, the federal system of apprentice schools, known as the Federal Institutes of Technological Education (IFET) expanded and by the 1970s, provided their students with general education alongside more technical training. Alongside the federal network of vocational training institutions, a parallel private system also evolved, sometimes termed the "S" system. This draws together private foundations such as SENAI, a national technical training and apprenticeship body and SEBRAE, an institution focused on promoting entrepreneurship and learning among small and medium enterprises. While these and similar institutions receive private subventions from business, they are also financed from payroll taxes. In this sense, they embody the close coordination between the state and industry that has characterised the corporatist evolution of Brazil following the emergence of the *Estado Novo* in the 1930s.

With respect to both public and private VET provision, it is fair to say that investment and throughput of students has notably increased in recent years. Between 2003 and 2013 alone, federal investment in VET rose from 0.04% of GDP to 0.2%. The most important development in this respect was the creation of PRONATEC (Programa Nacional de Acesso ao Ensino Técnico e Emprego – National Program for Access to Technical Training and Employment) in 2011 under the administration of President Lula. Besides increasing the number of institutions and training places, the PRONATEC program – which embraces both public and private sector providers – also offers financial assistance to students. The launch of PRONATEC was accompanied by a surge in those graduating from both public and private sector VET programs. Data from the Brazilian Ministry of Education and Culture (MEC) show that in 1999, 716,652 students graduated from such programs, compared with 1,251,720 in 2011 (the year PRONATEC launched) and 1,775,078 in 2016. However, there is evidence to suggest a fall-off in enrolments between 2016 and 2018 connected with fiscal retrenchment and the effects of economic recession.

In the light of the general expansion of VET provision in recent years, does Brazil compare favourably in international comparative terms when it comes to participation rates in vocational education? The OECD's 2019 *Education at a Glance* sounds a note of caution. According to the data revealed in this document, just 8% of Brazilian students at upper secondary level, compared to an OECD average of 40%, graduated with a vocational qualification in 2017. This proportion was in fact the second lowest among the OECD and partner countries included in the survey (OECD, 2019 p. 5). Regarding the participation of older groups (25 years and up) in vocational education, the proportion of this section of the Brazilian population so engaged (at 0.5%) also lies some way below the OECD average of 0.8%. Interestingly, in terms of gender, Brazil demonstrates a relatively strong bias towards female participation: compared with the OECD average of 46%, 57% of Brazilian upper secondary graduates are female. In terms of field of specialisation, the study reveals that, compared with their peers elsewhere, Brazilians undertaking VET courses tend to specialise to a significantly greater extent in education and information and communications technology (ICT) courses.

Given the policy priority that has been attached to VET provision in recent years, is it possible to come to any conclusions surrounding the effectiveness of such education? Portela de Souza et al. (2015) draw attention to one commonly deployed means of evaluation: the impact on earnings. In the studies reviewed, the returns on VET education (in terms of earnings differentials compared with general educational qualifications) ranged from 5.9 to 13.5% (ibid., pp. 13–14). A particularly interesting finding emerging from one of the studies (Gonzaga and Assunção, 2010) concerns the significantly higher earnings returns to "S" system programs compared to other private and public sector equivalents. These studies all tend to suggest that that VET programs are broadly successful in meeting labour market demands. There is also some evidence contained within them that they can be of special value (in terms of boosting earnings and labour force participation) for female students.

However, the expansion of VET provision in recent years has not been without its critics. In particular, a recent study by Magalhães and Castioni (2019) draws attention to what they regard as a major shortcoming of the Federal government's directly controlled programs in this sphere. In their analysis, which amounts to a reasonably comprehensive survey of the relevant empirical literature, the authors argue that, to an increasing extent, Brazil's vocational training programs have been emulating the more generalist, academically orientated courses of study offered by the universities. This apparent convergence on the university model may not prove in Brazil's long-term economic interests.(ibid., p. 1). This concern surrounding an apparent merging of academic and more vocationally orientated provision has strong echoes with the policy debate in the United Kingdom. Following their conversion into universities in 1992, the United Kingdom's former more technically and vocationally inclined polytechnics have encroached rapidly – and in some cases very successfully – onto the academic terrain occupied by the traditional universities. This has led to concern that, in this new setting, it may be more difficult to address successfully vocational skills gaps.

Universities: expansion and its challenges

The expansion of Brazil's network of universities and higher education institutions represents the most dramatic development in the country's education sector since the 1980s. Between 1991 and 2016, according to INEP data, the total number of those enrolled in Brazil's higher education institutions rose from 1,377,286 to 6,739,689, with the bulk of the growth occurring after the turn of the millennium. In GDP terms, spending on higher education has also risen significantly. Between 2010 and 2016, public spending in this area rose by 16% in real terms reaching 1.0% of GDP.

This is, in fact, slightly higher than the OECD average (0.9%). It is important to bear in mind that, as already stated, the structure of the sector is relatively complex in Brazil, consisting of federal government funded, state government funded and privately financed institutions. Thus, the overall spending on higher education on a national basis is higher than the OECD figures would suggest. Across all segments, but especially in regard to the federal component, growth of higher education and enhancement of access to it were key policy priorities for both the Lula and Rousseff administrations (2002–16). The objectives here were several. On the one hand, and perhaps most significantly, the expansion of higher education was seen by PT administrations as a key driver of social mobility, especially in terms of disadvantaged groups. This was particularly true when considering the efforts made to offer places in higher education to students of African descent and/or those from traditionally marginalised regions.

On the one hand, and in keeping with the structuralist analysis which dominated the economic thinking during the Lula and Rousseff years, investment in higher education, not least in STEM subject areas, was seen as a way of assisting the building of indigenous technological capabilities and what Nelson (1993) would term, Brazil's National System of Innovation. As a result, it was hoped that Brazil would sequentially and advantageously redefine its place in the global division of labour, placing the growth and development process onto a more resilient and sustainable footing. At the same time, the expansion of higher education also offered a means to pursue regional policy objectives, by facilitating public investment in economically peripheral but politically salient regions such as the North and North East. Finally, and towards the end of the PT years, the internationalisation of higher education – thanks largely to the Science Without Borders Program – served as a medium for enhancing Brazil's image abroad, a classic example of the deft soft power projection that flourished during this period.

At the time of writing, the Brazilian higher education system is in the midst of public funding cutbacks. These have been partly prompted by general fiscal exigencies. However, according to some, they also motivated by ideological opposition to the leftist or progressive social and political agenda which parts of the higher education sector embody. Thus, it would appear that the sector finds itself at the end of an expansionary cycle. In what follows an attempt is made – within the constraints of the space available – to evaluate the achievements and still unresolved difficulties associated with Brazilian higher education. To this end, the chapter focuses on the not unrelated issues of research performance in international comparative terms, social inclusion and contribution to innovation in the productive sector.

The expansion of investment in Brazilian higher education might have been expected to generate an improvement in research performance and in very general terms this is what we find. A recent report by the Ministry of Education and Culture (MEC, 2018) gives some idea of the increasing weight of Brazil as a global centre for academic research production. Between 1985 and 2012, the percentage of Brazilian scientific academic papers published as a proportion of the global total rose from approximately 0.5% to 2.8% (ibid., p. 17). While Brazil has significantly increased its output share, the country remains some way behind some of the leading industrialised economies, but ahead of many of its emerging market peers. According to data prepared by the Brazilian postgraduate funding agency, CAPES, between 2011 and 2016 Brazilian authors added 250,680 papers to the Web of Science, compared with, for example, 166,708 from Turkey and 194,126 from Russia. However, output from India, at 347,293 remained comfortably ahead in relation to Brazil, while the two leading countries featured, the United States and China, were, respectively, responsible for 2,521,998 and 1,402,689 papers. In terms of citation impact, Brazil has been performing increasingly favourably: this rose from 0.73 in 2011 to 0.86 in 2016. If this trend is maintained then by 2021 Brazil will have converged with the global average of 1.0 (MEC, 2018, p. 9). The MEC report also establishes that at the very top end – the top 1% of most cited papers globally – output from Brazil has already converged with the world average, though it still lags this average in relation to the broader, top 10%, category.

As part of the quest to raise the quality of Brazilian higher educational institutions in global terms, the administration of President Rousseff (2010–16) launched a program known as Science Without Borders (Ciência Sem Fronteiras) in 2011. This program was designed to increase access to international higher education opportunities by Brazilian students with the focus on STEM subjects. Over its duration, just over 100,000 students participated in the program, although by 2017 it had been wound down because of funding cuts. Unlike previous funding initiatives, Science Without Borders focused on undergraduate provision with students typically taking some credits abroad before returning home (a sandwich program). The program came in for some criticism, in particular, around a supposedly ill-designed articulation between students' courses at home and abroad, and the fact that competency in English presented more of a challenge than the program's designers had anticipated (Sá, 2016)

How have these efforts to achieve international research excellence been reflected in the ranking of Brazilian institutions among the world's leading universities? The results have not been startlingly encouraging, although Brazil performs well against its regional peers. Brazil's top ranked university in 2019, according to the Times Higher Education World Rankings data, is the University of São Paulo, which lies between the 251st and 300th places globally. In the second place lies the State University of Campinas (Unicamp) (which lies between the 501st and 600th places globally), while a series of high-profile institutions including the Federal Universities of Minas Gerais and São Paulo share third place in the national rankings, occupying between the 600th and 800th places globally. According to a table of Latin America's top ten universities, again deriving from the Times Higher Education rankings, Brazilian institutions account for half of those featuring. Once again, the University of São Paulo and Unicamp occupy, respectively, numbers one and two on this list. Despite this favourable showing, there is little evidence that in global terms, that Brazilian institutions are closing the gap with their world leading counterparts in North America and Europe. Indeed, according to research carried out by the World Economic Forum in 2017, it may prove very difficult for this to happen given the scale of the spending cutbacks since the onset of economic crisis in 2015 (WEF, 2018b).

One area of traditional strength for Brazil's leading research-focused universities, especially in the South and South East, has been their vital participation in the country's elaborate national system of innovation. Mazzucato and Penna

(2016, pp. 38–50) highlight the significance of these (especially the University of São Paulo and Unicamp) but also draw attention to a parallel network of public research institutions, which have close ties with universities or are higher educational institutions in their own right. Thus, for example, the publicly funded Fiocruz (Oswaldo Cruz Foundation) and INPE (National Space Research Institute) both carry out academic research and engage with postgraduate education while at the same time actively carrying out work directly bearing on real world applications. INPE has carried out extensive satellite-based research into the issue of deforestation, for example, while Fiocruz is a global centre of excellence in the fight against tropical diseases, Brazil's relatively successful record of public health improvements in this area can in no small part be credited to the efforts of Fiocruz-based researchers.

The ITA (Technical Institute of Aeronautics), another publicly funded research institute, provided the intellectual foundations of what became Embraer, one of the world's largest and most successful aerospace companies (Amann & Figueiredo, 2012). The telecommunications and oil and gas sectors also benefit from such publicly funded institutes (Mazzucato & Penna, 2016, pp. 41–2). The innovation studies literature is replete with rich case studies analysing the ways in which close interactions between higher education institutions, publicly funded research centres and enterprises (both private and SOE) have driven forward the building up of technological capabilities (Amann & Figueiredo, 2012). Despite the successes – which were discussed in Chapter 2 – the reality is that innovative activity and close interaction between higher education institutions, research institutions and the productive sector remain the exception rather than the rule. Looking ahead, there is an urgent need to ensure that such fruitful interactions become more widespread across Brazil's supply side.

The broader societal effects of research and higher education in Brazil proved a focal point for policy innovation in the first half of the 2010s. In particular, there arose a concern that historically, those from disadvantaged ethnic backgrounds, especially those of African descent had been underrepresented among the student body, notably in higher ranked institutions in the public sector. Prior to 2012, individual institutions were responsible for implementing any quotas they felt desirable (Barros, 2015). However, the Rousseff administration succeeded in passing the "Law of Quotas" in 2012. This law applied to federally run higher and technical education institutes. According to the law, 50% of places at these institutions are required to be allocated to those from the public school system and, of this 50%, the proportions of student admitted by ethnic group must reflect the local ethnic composition of the area in which the institution is located. The effect of the law is to open up higher education as never before to those from less privileged backgrounds since, as in the United Kingdom, the state-financed school system (as opposed to its privately financed counterpart) tends to be patronised by poorer families, those of African descent often ranking amongst the least affluent. The policy proved politically quite controversial as the prestigious federal higher education institutes had long featured among the bastions of Brazil's élite. Arguably, the law was among the measures which contributed to the growing unpopularity of the Rousseff administration among the middle and upper classes. However, the law and a related expansion of federally funded higher education institutions in economically depressed parts of the country, certainly did increase participation of disadvantaged groups. According to data provided by MEC, between 2013 (the year after the Law was passed) and 2014 the proportion of students admitted as part of the quota rose from 33% to 40% while the proportion of black students in the overall total increased from 17.25% to 21.5%.

Conclusions

The Brazilian education and training system has witnessed significant evolution since the end of the last millennium. This reflects the greater ambition of policymakers to effect positive social change and to improve the stock of human capital in an increasingly competitive global economy. In particular, investment in the publicly funded school system has risen sharply as, in partial response to conditional cash transfer programs, the authorities have had to respond to increasing enrolment rates. Encouragingly, the sharp increase in quantitative provision does not seem to have come at the cost of a reduction in quality: Brazil's position in the global educational rankings as evidenced by the Pisa scores has remained broadly static. There is also strong evidence that the teaching workforce is becoming better qualified and professionalised. On the other hand, compared with some of its emerging market counterparts, let alone the advanced industrial economies, Brazil has a long way to go if it is to begin to match their levels of educational attainment at primary and secondary levels.

The vocational education and training system has experienced rather less dramatic change. Yet again, however, a clear gap remains between performance in Brazil and that achieved among the OECD nations. Given the need to seize new windows of opportunity in the global division of labour and to manage structural change, further attention to this aspect of human capital formation seems more than opportune. In relation to the universities and higher education institutes, the past two decades have in overall terms seen rapid expansion, although, since the mid-2010s there have been resource cutbacks. While universities and higher education institutions have undoubtedly become more socially inclusive and internationalised, there is scant evidence that they are rapidly climbing the ladder of world rankings. That said, Brazil still leads Latin America as a whole in terms of higher education excellence whether evidenced by the rankings themselves, published output or the effectiveness with which institutions engage with the productive sector. Looking ahead, it will be important to build on these strengths if Brazil is to enhance its competitiveness and develop new sources of sustainable wealth generation.

Notes

1 For fuller definitions of these see the OECD's Glossary of Statistical Terms. Primary education relates to the initial phase of education starting at the age of five, six, or seven and lasting five or six years. Tertiary education refers to degree level or vocational education at age 16–17+ while secondary education relates to the phase between the two (normally education realised between 10–11 and 16–18 years old).
2 Um Ajuste Justo, Analise da Eficiência e Equidade do Gasto Público no Brasil (World Bank, 2017).
3 The statistics referred to here comprise the Indicador de Alfebetismo Funcional prepared by the Instituto Paulo Montenegro.

4

STATE-BUSINESS RELATIONS

The development of Brazil's economy has, from the Vargas era onwards, been closely conditioned, if not at times constrained by complex interactions between business and the state. Any consideration of the economic challenges now faced by Brazil would be fundamentally lacking if it did not take on board the nature of these interactions, their evolution and the ways in which they collectively shape the options for constructive reform and positive change. While field of state-business relations in Brazil has long provided an important subject for academic research, until quite recently, it did not feature heavily in the political debate or in popular discourse. Since the unfolding of the Lava Jato (Car Wash) scandal from 2014 onwards, this has changed, possibly irrevocably. As will be seen, the scandal revealed as never before the corrupt and economically deleterious practices that have characterised relationships between some elements of the state and leading business enterprises. Popular anger surrounding these revelations proved an important catalyst for political change, propelling the impeachment of President Dilma Rousseff in 2016. Two years later, the desire to sweep away corrupt networks binding state, business and leading political parties fuelled the accession of right-wing populist Jair Bolsonaro to the presidency.

Popular disdain for the corruption of the *ancien régime* has resulted in a political shift. Stemming from this, the paradigm of developmentalism and the long-established close business-state interactions which it fostered have increasingly been identified as fetters on economic and social progress. This helps to explain why the administration of President Bolsonaro, especially his Finance Minister, Paulo Guedes, has been so keen to embrace a reduced role for the state and to accelerate Brazil's integration into the global economy.

Thus, the current salience of business-state relations in the national policy debate cannot be denied. Not only this: a recasting of this relationship forms an indispensable component among the range of structural reforms necessary to underpin sustainable and inclusive growth in the future. As can be readily ascertained from among the chapters in this book, from issues such as the development of technological capabilities, to human capital formation, to the development of the financial sector, it is the manner in which the state has intervened that has played a critical role in determining the success – or otherwise – of the outcomes.

Against this background, this chapter seeks to highlight the evolution and key features surrounding the evolution of state-business relations in Brazil. The structure of the chapter is as follows. To begin with, the chapter presents a very brief overview of the key theoretical issues surrounding the analysis of state-business relations. The theoretical context and justification for state interventionism and, more specifically, the pursuit of a developmentalist approach (as long practiced in Brazil) are reviewed. In this connection, important theoretical contributions such as Evans' notion of embedded autonomy and Olson's logic of collective action are considered. Our brief theoretical overview also includes discussion of some of the hazards which may flow from state-business interactions, especially as concerns issues of rent seeking, capture and moral hazard.

Following this, the chapter turns to a consideration of the evolution of state-business relations over time. In this connection, four key epochs are identified and discussed. These comprise the era of corporatism, developmentalism and state-directed industrialisation (which stretched from the 1930s through to the mid-1980s), the period of hesitant globalisation (1985–2002), the cautious return of developmentalism (2002–16) and the advent of liberal reform (2016 to the present). In reviewing these periods, the changing character and institutional form of state-business relations is emphasised. Particular emphasis is placed on issues such as the emergence of state-owned enterprises, the privatisation process, the role of the state as a provider of source of capital for the private sector and the role of industry associations. The key achievements and shortcomings of each era are noted, specifically in terms of instances where state-business interactions produced developmentally constructive or counter-productive outcomes.

Finally, and very much informed by recent events, the chapter moves on to focus on the issue of corruption. The emphasis here is on the Car Wash corruption scandal of the late 2010s, what it can teach us about the character of state-business interactions in Brazil and the ways in which such relations may have exercised a baleful influence on the pursuit of sustainable and inclusive growth and development.

Business-state relations in Brazil: some theoretical context

As will be seen, as they have evolved over time, business-state relations in Brazil have come to comprise a dense network of connections between government and the private sector. Within this, extensive direct public sector participation in the productive sector and a political culture in which the representation of business interests (legitimately or otherwise) has long played a critical role. The model of state intervention that has emerged and its related patterns of business-government engagement extend well beyond the minimalist schema envisaged or advocated by basic neo-classical analysis. According to the latter, the involvement of the state in economic life should be optimally determined by the existence of market failures and the need to correct them, whether through regulation, the development of competition and antitrust policy or the direct provision of public goods. Such an analytical framework would clearly struggle to explain or account for the manner in which the Brazilian state – or that of many other emerging economies – has, for the most part of the last nine decades, extended its economic reach.

Against this background, it is not surprising that an extensive literature has grown up around the need to capture analytically the emergence of economies whose development does not always accord with a liberal capitalist model. This literature has come to be termed the "varieties of capitalism" literature[1] and has spawned theoretical studies of development experiences from around the world, but especially in relation to East and South East Asia and Latin America (Kohli, 2004). In their seminal original contribution, Hall and Soskice (2001) distinguish between liberal and coordinated market economies. In the latter category, which would arguably better accommodate Brazil, firms are more likely to coordinate with one another and with other key actors (e.g. the state) through non-market mechanisms. Such economies are more likely to witness attempts at strategic or dynamic orchestration by the state and close articulation between public and private sectors. Schneider (2009) builds upon this framework and argues that most Latin American economies in fact correspond to what he terms a Hierarchical Market Economy (HME). Such an economy would embrace four key features: "diversified business groups, multinational corporations, low-skilled labour and atomistic labour business relations" (ibid., p. 553). Schneider argues that "overall non-market, hierarchical relations in business groups and MNCs are central in organising capital and technology in Latin America, and are also pervasive in labour market regulation, union representation and employment relations" (ibid.).

A sense of the subordination of liberal market processes in constructing Brazilian capitalism is heightened when one considers the longer-established literature on corporatism. This literature, in contrast to its varieties of capitalism counterpart, devotes more attention to analysing the role of the state in economies which have departed from liberal capitalist modes of development. Important references in the corporatist literature such as Schmitter (1974) provide a useful means of analysing economies (and indeed societies) where relations between participants are mediated by political, social and institutional forces, rather than purely on the basis of abstract market relationships.

The corporatist literature grew up in response to the emergence in the early to mid-20th century of overt attempts to orchestrate societal and economic actors to generate mutually beneficial outcomes. Typically, and as demonstrated by experiences in Europe and Asia, efforts were made to forge a tripartite consensus around political and economic reform, binding together organised labour, business and the state. Examples of the various schemas realised here range from Mussolini's Italy to the post-war *wirtschaftwunder* in the Federal Republic of Germany. The Estado Novo (New State) of Brazil, initiated in the 1930s, provides yet another example. The corporatist literature arguably comprises an effective framework for analysing the bargaining relationships between major interest groups, not least the state and business enterprises. It can certainly help to account for how the Brazilian state has at times co-opted business in pursuit of national development objectives. However, given the contingencies and institutional and historical specificities at the heart of the corporatist literature's method, its analytical framework lacks predictive power, still less any internally coherent rigorous model. Schneider (2004) takes aim at the corporatist literature repeating the accusation that it contains "too much architecture and not enough engineering" (ibid., p. 11).

Perhaps in response to the perceived limitations of the corporatist literature, other literatures have grown up which specifically address business-government relations and the roles of the state in fostering the development process. Again, they do not lack relevance to the Brazilian case. A long-established contribution in this area has centred on the emergence of developmental states. Such states preside over extensive trade and industrial policy interventions aimed at improving the competitiveness of economies and repositioning them in the global division of labour. The classic study in this area is Alice Amsden's Asia's Next Giant (Amsden, 1992) which focuses on the experience of South Korea. This volume has been heavily influential in the Brazilian policy debate alongside a not-dissimilar Korea-focused study entitled *Kicking Away the Ladder* (Chang, 2002).[2] Perhaps the most important and certainly Brazil-relevant contribution in the recent era has been that of Peter Evans (1995) in his now classic study *Embedded Autonomy: States and Industrial Transformation*. Evans' volume focuses on the role of the state in promoting high technology industries (in this case the information technology sector), taking as its three case studies the experiences of Brazil, India and (once again) South Korea. In the theoretical exposition prior to the case studies themselves, Evans draws a distinction between predatory and developmental states, a categorisation that finds some analogue in Acemoglu and Robinson's (2012) contrast between inclusive and extractive economic and political institutions. Whereas "predatory states extract at the expense of society, undercutting development even in the narrow sense of capital accumulation...developmental states not only presided over industrial transformation but can plausibly be argued to have played a role in making it happen" (Evans, 1995, p. 12).

Evans suggests that effective developmental states embody two characteristics simultaneously, attributes that have often proved hard to reconcile in practice. On the one hand, such states are autonomous in the sense that they approximate to a Weberian bureaucracy and are organised along meritocratic lines. On the other hand, this autonomy co-exists with an embeddedness of the state in the market structures and environment which it seeks to influence. This "provides institutionalized channels for the continual negotiation and renegotiation of goals and policies" (ibid.). Such an idealised embedded and autonomous state would be able to function effectively as a policymaker, in the national interest, and without being captured by private interests. Such a state would prove highly effective in the context of, for example, a Nelson-style National System of Innovation (Nelson, 1993) where the ability to operate technically competently and participate in information flows form essential ingredients for success. Interestingly, in his analysis, Evans does not characterise the Brazilian state as precisely corresponding to either the predatory or developmental archetype. Instead, he considers Brazil's experience, alongside India's, as something of an intermediate case "exhibiting partial and imperfect approximations of embedded autonomy" (ibid., p. 13).

As we will see, there remains a lot of mileage in Evans' assessment even a quarter century after his landmark book's publication. While the Lava Jato case calls our attention to the predatory character of some of the Brazilian state's engagement with the economy, there are unquestionably other instances where government agencies and corporations have worked constructively alongside the private sector. This has enabled real developmental progress, whether in terms of technological capability building, the emergence of new export sectors or the strengthening of the financial sector. Within the innovation studies literature especially, numerous studies (see, for example, Amann & Figueiredo, 2012; Arbix, 2019) have been elaborated pointing to the emergence of a constructive interface between the state and the private sector. This has enabled Brazil to arrive at the global technological frontier in such diverse fields as biofuels, civil aerospace and oil exploration and production.

A notable feature of business-state interactions in Brazil, at least since the middle of the 20th century has been the prominence of industry associations and trade bodies. Such organisations may represent particular sectors (for example, ANFAVEA in the case of the automotive sector) or they may resemble broader associations, speaking for an entire range of sectors. Prominent examples of the latter would include the São Paulo state industry federation, FIESP and the national industrial confederation, CNI. The emergence of such industry associations accompanied the rise of corporatism from the 1930s onwards and has provided an important channel for information flows, policy debate and lobbying between private enterprise and the state. In the case of the CNI, the umbrella national organisation representing industry, its role extends beyond representation of interests and also embraces vocational training. As may be recalled, the SENAI industrial training programme is administered by the CNI. Given the high-profile nature and proliferation of such organisations, a considerable literature has grown up to analyse their role and contribution to the Brazilian development process (see, for example, Schneider, 2004; Doctor, 2016).

From a theoretical perspective, there remains some controversy as to how to interpret the rise of industry associations in Brazil or, indeed elsewhere in the region. One interpretation centres on the logic of collective action and is based on the insights of Olson (1965). According to this, industrial associations can come into being as the result of a calculus among individual enterprises. Such a calculus would involve participants arriving at the conclusion that their individual interests would be better served through collective action and representation. In this sense, business associations and lobby groups may spontaneously form. However, such an analysis arguably lacks grounding in the political and institutional specificities of a developing economy setting, and cannot readily account for the sudden wave of the formation of industry associations in the mid-20th century. Schneider (2004) advances an alternative explanation, arguing that, in fact, it was the state itself, wishing to engage more effectively with the private sector, that instigated the creation of these associations. However, while sector-level associations proliferated in Brazil, unlike in other countries in the region (especially Mexico) no powerful, peak and economy-wide representative body formed. For Schneider, the explanation here lies once more at the door of the state and its lack of support for any such initiative (ibid., p. 16).

Just as a substantial literature has grown up theorising state-business interactions in developing and emerging economies, so has another highly influential body of work has developed specifically focusing on the potential economic and social costs of such engagements. The principal contributions here centre on issues of rent seeking, inefficiency and corruption. The concept of rent seeking gained considerable policy traction – not least among the international financial institutions – following the publication in the *American Economic Review* of Anne Krueger's seminal 1974 paper entitled "The political economy of the rent seeking society" (Krueger, 1974). In essence the argument, which emerged in Krueger's and subsequent papers, was that in certain circumstances private agents actively seek to shape the economic environment around them in such a way that they can capture rents. These rents represent the excess payment to productive factors over and above what would otherwise be required to employ them. The pursuit of such rents creates no new value for society but may result in large private gains for the economic agent concerned.

How might rent seeking gain form in practice? One obvious example here is regulatory capture whereby powerful incumbent firms influence government agencies to restrict market entry or participation on the basis of rules which serve little or no wider public purpose. An extension of this argument is when firms influence regulators (in this case the competition authorities) to permit mergers which result in higher industrial concentration and associated rents. This issue has recently gained renewed traction with the publication in 2019 of Thomas Phlippon's celebrated volume *The Great Reversal: How America Gave up on Free Markets* (Philippon, 2019). As will be seen, over the past two decades in Brazil, rising concern has accompanied increasing industrial concentration in key sectors and supposed collusion between the state and the private sector in achieving this. Such concerns centre especially on the highly concentrated – and profitable – banking sector. Interestingly, concerns over the alleged "cartelization" of the economy lay among the motives underpinning rioting and social unrest in Chile in 2019. So far, however, in Brazil, the issue, while politically salient, has yet to catalyse the same degree of public disquiet.

This is demonstrably not the case with a second – and far more high profile – area of concern around state-business relations in Brazil: corruption. Corruption may be defined succinctly as the misuse of public power for private benefit but this belies a complex issue with multifaceted manifestations and numerous causal mechanisms. Corruption as an activity embodies such socially and economically undesirable behaviours as "bribery, extortion, collusion, nepotism, clientelism, fraud and embezzlement" (Prado & Carson, 2018, p. 741). As will be seen, Brazil has been wracked in recent years with the world's largest corruption scandal but, for now, in theoretical terms how might we understand its presence or growth? De Graaf (2007) presents a useful summary categorisation of theoretical approaches to the analysis of corrupt processes in society.

One commonly used approach centres on the application of Public Choice theory. According to this, corrupt acts can be understood as a consequence of rational actors seeking to maximise gains. The likelihood of corruption occurring would depend on the situational context. If this provides opportunities for the misuse of public power, there is lack of effective monitoring of officials, and there exists tacit public tolerance for malfeasance, then it is more likely that corrupt activities will flourish. De Graaf also highlights more sociological explanations, for example, so-called "Bad Apple" and organisational culture theories (ibid.), whereby we can understand the emergence of corruption as the result of the development of new social norms propelled, in some cases, by bad actors. Lastly, Ethos of Public Administration Theories conceptualise the emergence of corruption as the result of systemic pressures to perform on officials mingled with a lack of attention to integrity issues (ibid.). While these theories represent contrasting analytical frameworks – with some emphasising individual agency over organisational characteristics – all require there to be potential scope for corrupt activity in order for it to take place. In a context, such as that of Brazil, where, for many years the functions of the state were ever extending and the web of interconnections between the public and private sectors increasingly complex, there is no doubt that such scope expanded exponentially. The experience of the Car Wash scandal, explored in more detail later in this chapter, provides the most dramatic example of the risks to public probity that may arise in the context of extensive industrial interventionism.

Leaving aside issues of corruption and rent seeking behaviour, there lies a considerable and influential body of work, highlighting the potential damage which may be inflicted by ill-considered state interventionism in developing economies. The basis of this literature – which is heavily influenced by neo-classical theory – stretches back considerable time and embraces some of the most important work of Bela Belassa, and Little Scitovsky and Scott's landmark 1970 volume *Industry and Trade in Some Developing Countries: A Comparative Study*. These and subsequent contributions laid the ground for the design of World Bank structural adjustment policies from the 1980s onwards and continue to influence liberal economic policy design to this day.

The essence of this literature is that, in trying to shift the basis of comparative advantage, and in shielding strategic industries from global competition, product and factor market price distortions are introduced. These allow domestic prices to deviate from world prices and permit inefficiencies to develop, rendering economies increasingly unable to compete effectively in global markets. From the perspective of the advocates of this approach, the remedy is to "get the prices right" through trade and market liberalisation which, indeed were precisely the policy sets implemented in Brazil between the mid-1980s and the beginning of the 2000s. Subsequently, and up until 2016, some attempts were made to "bring the state back in," leading to a renewal of the neo-classical critique from among free market advocates, including the current Finance Minister, Paulo Guedes.

The evolution of state-business relations over time

Developmentalism and the activist state: 1930–85

Prior to the Wall Street crash of 1929 and the international depression it wrought, the economic functions of the Brazilian state were quite restricted, predominantly centring on its roles as a monetary authority and an enforcer of property rights. As for trade policy, Brazil's stance was comparatively liberal, as it had been since the later 19th century. The country engaged with the global economy based on its natural comparative advantage in natural resource-based product areas and was heavily reliant on imports of manufactured products (Abreu, 1990). This being said, it is important to note that, following the coffee boom of the last quarter of the 19th century, domestic industrial capacity and the technological capability that went with it had begun to emerge. This development centred on São Paulo and Rio de Janeiro states and was assisted by large-scale immigration from Europe during the period. However, such early industrialisation cannot be considered as part of a premeditated strategy of national economic development, nor was it the result of explicit public policy directed at the purpose. Instead, it may be seen as a function of growing local demand, the arrival of skilled entrepreneurs and workers from Europe, and rising urbanisation, especially in relation to the city of São Paulo.

As in so many countries across the globe, the stimulus for a step change in the role of the state centred on the Wall Street Crash of 1929 and the global depression which followed it. These critical events forced a reassessment of the liberal economic model which Brazil had broadly adhered to since independence from Portugal more than a century earlier. The perception that the established role of the state in the economy required urgent reassessment was certainly met with credulity by the recently appointed administration of Getúlio Vargas. President Vargas had come to power in 1930 following a disputed presidential election and subsequent bloodless military coup. In contrast to his predecessors who traced their roots to São Paulo and Minas Gerais states,[3] President Vargas hailed from the southern border state of Rio Grande do Sul. This state had long possessed a strong radical and secessionist tradition (Love, 1971). Unlike previous presidents, Vargas was far less beholden to traditional agricultural interests; instead he was more aligned with the concerns of the growing class of industrial entrepreneurs and managers who had felt themselves underrepresented by previous administrations.

As the 1930s wore on Vargas, responding to the interests of the industrial sector, and facing the need to contend with the challenges imposed by the global depression, forged a radically new role for the state in Brazil's economy. This development occurred in lockstep with the creation of the Estado Novo or "New State" and laid the foundations upon which the Brazilian economy would develop for the first four decades after World War II. The set of policies that emerged during the 1930s and 1940s were essentially designed to alter the position of Brazil in the global division of labour. This would involve the establishment of new enterprises and industrial sectors which, if successful, would reduce Brazil's industrial import coefficient. This in turn would help counter the effects of the global depression by reducing the external constraint. The latter had significantly increased between 1929 and 1931 as a result in the slump in demand for Brazilian exports (Abreu, 1989). While the strategy was more reactive than the planned industrialisation that would occur in the 1950s under President Kubitschek, it nevertheless represented a form of import substitution. This was an approach which would endure right up to the 1980s (Baer, 2013). Central to it was a preparedness to depart from the previously liberal trade policy regime by raising tariff and non-tariff barriers so as to restrict imports and favour domestic production of goods previously imported. Perhaps more significantly, from the point of view of this chapter, the Vargas era of the 1930s and early 1940s saw the forging of much closer business-state relations and, moreover, the advent of the state as a direct producer.

Regarding the increasing proximity of business-state relations, this was itself a product of the corporatist approach adopted by Vargas and which had echoes of Mussolini's Italy. Closer relations between business and government were of central importance, not only in facilitating economic navigation through the Great Depression but also, later in the 1930s, for heading off poles of opposition around communism and the crypto-fascist Integralist movement. Reflecting the contemporary corporatist ethos, the Vargas administration was keen to foster the organisation of industry into representative groups. According to Schneider (2004), this was achieved through "institutionalized access to policymaking, compulsory membership and financing, and representational monopolies" (p. 99). The result was the creation of high profile and, for a while, industry bodies, notably FIESP (the Industrial Federation of São Paulo) and the CNI (the National Industrial Confederation). The highly organised mode of industrial representation established under Vargas provided valuable channels for consultation and influence around such vital topics as tariff protection levels and the development of a comprehensive labour code. The latter was to play a vital role in the post-war development of Brazil and has, moreover, proven very difficult to reform in recent years.

Perhaps the most striking development under the Vargas administration during the 1930s and 1940s was the development of state-owned industries (SOEs). These were typically characterised by their capital intensity and strategic importance as suppliers of key inputs for emerging industries. The two outstanding examples here are Companhia Siderúgica Nacional (National Steel Company) founded in 1941 in Volta Redonda, Rio de Janeiro State, and the Companhia Vale do Rio Doce or CVRD. The latter was and remains under its new name, Vale, a major mining enterprise specialising in the extraction of metal ores. The coffee sector, Brazil's export mainstay, also witnessed a step change in state participation. In 1930, the National Coffee Council was created with the aim of facilitating greater price stability through market intervention. This followed more sporadic attempts earlier in the century of "coffee valorization." At this stage in Brazil's development process, state-driven attempts to stabilise the evolution of prices were assisted by the fact that Brazil was by far and away the world's largest producer. After World War II, Brazil's pre-eminence as a coffee producer was to be challenged, not least by the rise of Vietnam.

The outbreak of World War II in 1939, and the disruption to international trade that was to follow, provided the Vargas administration with further justification for the national developmentalist path that it had begun to follow. Moreover, the ability of the President to achieve policy objectives with minimal opposition had substantially increased following his dissolution of the legislature and his assumption of dictatorial powers in 1937. Consequently, the scope of the state's presence in the economy expanded further. Besides the passage of labour laws and the creation of the SOEs mentioned above, the Estado Novo under Vargas made the first move towards the creation of a state presence in the oil sector with the formation of the Conselho Nacional de Petróleo (National Oil Council). Also during this period, the state commenced its (still ongoing) direct involvement in the electricity sector with the foundation of the Companhia Hidro Elétrica de São Francisco (São Francisco Electric Company or CHESF). Hitherto this sector had been the province of private capital, especially that of foreign origin. Seeking to establish domestically owned capacity in transportation manufacturing, the Vargas administration took the unusual step[4] of founding the Fábrica Nacional de Motores (National Motor Works or FNM) in 1942. Initially producing aircraft engines, a decade later, it would engage in automotive production thanks to a technology transfer agreement with Alfa Romeo of Italy.

The aftermath of World War II did not see a re-evaluation of the developmentalist and corporatist approach to economic management despite the fact that its principal author, Getúlio Vargas, was deposed in a coup in 1945. Instead, as Brazil moved into the late 1940s and 1950s, there was a recommitment to the developmentalist path with the emphasis switching increasingly in the direction of state-driven industrialisation. This period has come to be seen as one in which Brazil embraced formalised import substitution industrialisation (ISI). Rather than a reactive stratagem borne of a seismic external economic shock (the Great Depression), Brazil in the 1950s implemented a sequenced and measured approach to structural change heavily influenced by the structuralist-influenced Economic Commission for Latin America (ECLA) (Bielschowsky, 1988). This strategy reached its apogee under the administration of President Juscelino Kubitschek (1956–60).

The pursuit of formal ISI spanned the period between the end of World War II and the late 1960s and had much in common with similar strategies pursued in other parts of the region, Argentina, Mexico and Peru being noteworthy exponents (Thorp, 1998). As Amsden (1992) and Kohli (2004) indicate in their studies, such an approach to facilitating structural change also found favour in South, East and South East Asia during the same period. In Brazil, as elsewhere, the objectives of formal ISI centred on the state identifying industrial sectors ripe for local development and the rapid replacement of imported products by those domestically produced. The question was, which sectors to prioritise and which to continue relying on imported production to meet local demand? Brazil chose, as so many other countries did, to focus on the creation of local industrial capacity in the consumer goods sector. As Colman and Nixson (1994) point out, the selection of this sector had certain advantages. These include the fact that consumer local needs would be promptly met and also that the financial and technological requirement were less burdensome than would the case had a more Soviet style quest to develop a capital goods sector been adopted. Thus it was that Kubitschek's famous Plano de Metas (Plan of Targets) of 1956–60 set great store by its objective of further developing a local automotive sector, alongside the creation of capacities in other consumer durables industries. This was achieved by a combination of protectionist trade measures and a policy of welcoming inward direct foreign investment.

The case of the ultimately successful attempt to meet home demand with domestically produced automobiles involved close articulation between the state, the national industrial confederation (the CNI), domestic capital and, increasingly, foreign automotive producers including Volkswagen, Ford and General Motors (Addis, 1999). Of course, the emergence of domestic (if not domestically owned) capacity, rather like the creation of industry associations under Vargas, needs to be seen as the product of purposeful state directed activity. Still, as the industry developed, so emerged a very high-profile representative association, ANFAVEA. This proved quite effective in advocating the sector's interests to the state and other relevant actors to[5] the extent that, during the liberal reform period of the 1990s, the automotive industry remained comparatively protected and, indeed benefitted from specific managed trade provisions within the framework of Mercosul (Özden & Parodi, 2004).

The 1950s were to see another development which would draw the private sector close to the state and ultimately result in the development of a financial institution with annual disbursements exceeding those of the World Bank. This, of course, was the creation of the Banco Nacional de Desenvolvimento Economico (BNDE – National Economic Development Bank) in 1952 (Paiva, 2012) during the final term of President Getúlio Vargas.[6] As will be explained in further detail in Chapter 6, the function of the BNDE, later the BNDES, was to facilitate investment in emerging and strategic sectors, especially, during the formal ISI period, in favoured industries. Given thin and risk averse private capital markets, such a lending institution had a vital role to play, disbursing loans at comparatively low interest rates (Torres & Zeidan, 2016). Its ability to do so rested on the Bank's status as a federal entity. This permitted it to borrow cost effectively on domestic and international markets and pass on this "saving" to its corporate clients. Such became the extent of the BNDES' lending activity that it arguably formed – and still forms – the most critical economic linkage between the state and the private sector. With its genesis under the *ne plus ultra* of Brazilian corporatism, President Vargas, the BNDES manifests in institutional form the idea that national development objectives are best served through close engagement with the private sector. As we will see, this fundamental tenet has come under severe scrutiny during the presidency of Jair Bolsonaro.

Another standout feature of the formal ISI period was the creation of myriad state-owned enterprises (SOEs), these being in some cases the result of nationalisation of formerly private ventures. Nationalisation or the creation of SOEs from scratch was especially prevalent in the public utility sector, notably in electricity generation and transmission (Gomes & Vieira, 2009). The 1950s and 1960s were to see a significant ramping up of public investment across network industries and indeed across infrastructure in general as railways, ports and airports fell under state ownership and control. Reflecting Brazil's federal character, there emerged during this period both municipal, state and federally run SOEs. Of significance to the fiscal adjustment process analysed in Chapter 5, state government owned banking institutions, alongside their federal counterparts such as the BNDE, and the Banco do Brasil (a commercial bank) expanded their activities.

In 1953, months before his departure from office for the final time,[7] President Vargas launched the highest profile, most technically capable and intensely politically controversial SOE of all, Petróleo Brasileiro S. A. (Petrobrás) (Quaglino & Dias, 1993). Petrobrás would go on to become the largest enterprise by sales in Brazil and, alongside similarly state-owned PDVSA of Venezuela and Pemex in Mexico, one of the three largest oil corporations in Latin America. The creation of Petrobrás and its technologically ambitious programme of international exploration and production that was to follow in later decades opened up yet further channels for close engagement between the private sector and the state. As Petrobrás ramped up fixed capital investments in refineries, pipelines, oil tankers and eventually drilling platforms, so developed an ecosystem of specialised contractors and large construction companies heavily dependent on Brazil's largest enterprise for orders and technical input (Morais, 2013).

Regarding the establishment of channels for innovation support, technology transfer and learning between the state and the private sectors, the period of formal ISI witnessed the development of elaborate mechanisms to support this endeavour. Schwartzman et al. (1995) and Frischtak (1993) in their seminal contributions to the debate surrounding Brazil's national system of innovation highlight the creation of incentives for private sector innovation. Of particular note was the establishment of FINEP (Financiadora dos Estudos e Projetos – Financing Agency for Studies and Projects) which provides for grants to support innovation within enterprises. Similarly, during this period, the large SOEs (in particular, Telebrás, Eletrobrás and Petrobrás) each established in-house research institutes, all of which ultimately enabled technology to be transferred elsewhere in the productive sector. The creation of a research institute in the aerospace field, the ITA (Instituto Tecnológico de Aeronáutica) by the state in 1950 ultimately provided the basis on which domestic aircraft production could begin (Amann & Figueiredo, 2012). Similarly, the Brazilian agricultural sector benefitted from innovation stemming from EMBRAPA, a research institute founded by the state some two decades later.

As is well documented in the literature (see, for example, Velloso et al., 2008; Baer, 2013), by the late 1960s Brazil's strategy of formal ISI required some modification as the economy faced challenges of faltering growth, issues of trade imbalance and higher than desired inflation. The result of this was the emergence of a "Post-ISI" strategy which combined a degree of capital market liberalisation, selective trade reform and sequenced currency devaluation. In response to the new strategy, enacted between 1966 and 1974, Brazil's economy reacted quite favourably with record rates of growth and the advent of what many have termed an "economic miracle" (ibid.).

However, as far as the nature of state-business relations was concerned, comparatively little changed: there was no systematic effort to reduce the scope of state intervention. In fact, once the Post-ISI strategy was abandoned in 1974 in the wake of the OPEC I oil crisis, its successor, the Second National Development Plan, doubled down on ISI (Amann, 2000). The Plan sought to extend the ISI process to the capital goods sector and used public sector procurement, especially from the energy and network industries, to support the creation of domestic capacity (ibid.). There was also a significant increase in the scale of public investment in infrastructure, the most iconic project in this regard being the Itaipú dam on the Brazil-Paraguay border. At the same time, Petrobrás stepped up its offshore oil exploration efforts. As these programmes unfolded, so were created enormous publicly financed opportunities for large construction companies, notably Odebrecht and Camargo Correâ and, in the capital goods sector, major industrial concerns such as Villares, Siemens and Verolme (ibid.).

Hesitant globalisation: 1985–2002

By the dawn of the 1980s, a half century after the inauguration of the Vargas era, an extensive, complex and multifaceted developmental state had been built up. This reflected the national consensus at the time that a combination of import substitution and state initiative were indispensable if Brazil were to re-order its position in the global division of labour and overcome structural obstacles to accelerated growth. Yet, as contemporary events showed, such a framing of the role for the state – and indeed the functioning of ISI itself – no longer appeared compatible with macroeconomic stability. The adoption of the Second National Development Plan and its intensified, state-driven programme of inward-orientated industrialisation had resulted in accelerated accumulation of international debt as current account pressures built up through the late 1970s and into the 1980s (Abreu, 1990). At the same time, the growth rates realised under the plan were disappointing compared with the miracle years of the late 1960s and early 1970s. The second OPEC oil price rise in 1979 followed by global monetary tightening intensified external balance pressures and made debt servicing yet more costly. Against this background, Brazil entered the 1980s debt adjustment crisis and by the middle of the decade was forced to seek assistance from the IMF (Cline, 1985).

What was to emerge from this episode and, around the same time, Brazil's transition to democracy, would recast the role of the state. However, the extent of this transformation would not prove as fundamental as that which would occur in Argentina and Chile. Even so, with Brazil in receipt of World Bank and IMF assistance, there was forced reassessment of its development model which the country had pursued since the days of Vargas. This would involve two main related axes – privatisation and trade liberalisation – which, as in the case of other Latin American economies mirrored key tenets of the policy set termed the Washington Consensus (Williamson, 1990).

The initial trade reforms in Brazil were initiated during the Sarney administration in 1985–87 and were very modest. Far more ambitious was the Abertura Comercial or "Trade Opening" programme which launched in 1990 and ran until 1995. This programme was promoted by the newly elected President Collor de Melo, Brazil's first directly elected president since the military coup in 1964. Its principal components centred on a progressive elimination of non-tariff barriers and a rolling timetable of tariff reductions (Kume, 1996). By 1995 compared with the start of the reform process in 1987, the effect of this programme was to have reduced simple average tariffs from 77.1% to 17.1%. For tariffs weighted by value added the reduction was from 67.8% to 10.4% (Abreu, 2004). It is worth noting that the Abertura also involved a significant reduction in tariff dispersal. This process of economic opening was accompanied by the establishment by the Treaty of Ascunción in 1991 of Mercosul, a customs union embracing initially Argentina, Brazil, Paraguay and Uruguay.

Given the scale of the trade reform programme and its obvious challenge to the interests of incumbent enterprises who had benefitted under ISI, it may seem strange that there was not more effective resistance to it from within the ranks of business. That this is the case reflects in part the resolve of the Sarney, Collor and then Franco administrations to recover favour with global investors, the IFIs (International Financial Institutions) and escape from the debt crisis.[8] However, declines in the cohesion and political salience of industry associations must have played a role, in as much as they offered much less political resistance than would have been the case two or three decades previously. Schneider (2004) forcefully makes the point that, by the 1980s and 1990s, the strength of business associations founded in the Vargas era had abated, while new organisations lacked the coherence and strength to plug the gap in effective representation. The result was a fragmentation and disjointedness which clearly hindered the ability of business to represent its interests to policymakers and state entities. Perhaps one partial exception here is ANFAVEA, the automotive trade association. Supported by its foreign multinational corporation-dominated membership, this proved relatively effective in maintaining elevated levels of protection (at least for assembled products). As already stated, it also supported the creation of a special trade regime within the newly created Mercosul customs union. Other sectors, however, were faced with a significant challenge as they witnessed a sharp scaling down of the protective arrangements they had benefitted from for decades.[9]

As the 1990s wore on, though, progress on trade reform certainly slowed and, if anything, went into partial reverse. Between 1995 and 1999 average tariffs weighted by value added actually rose from 10.4 to 15.4 percentage points (Abreu, 2004). Abreu links this modest elevation in protection to the need to respond to balance of payments difficulties experienced in the wake of the Mexican financial crisis of 1994 (ibid.); there is certainly no compelling evidence that the reversal of policy direction was motivated strongly by the voiced concerns of business. By 1998, Brazil's current account difficulties were severe enough to spur a further financing agreement with the IMF. This was followed by a maxi-devaluation of the Real at the beginning of 1999.

The stalled nature of trade reform reflects something profoundly ingrained in Brazil's political economy. Abreu (2004, p. 1) characterises Brazil as having "a strong inertial tradition of lack of commitment to trade liberalization" and considers the reform that did in fact take place as very modest compared to that experienced in other parts of the region, especially Chile (ibid.). Once macroeconomic difficulties were encountered, it proved comparatively straightforward and politically costless for the Cardoso administrations (1995–2002) to revert to a national default position and adopt more restrictive trade policy. It is noteworthy that the PT administrations which were to follow for the next 13 years, though quite enthusiastic in their embrace of inward foreign direct investment, made little or no effort to recommence trade reform. In this sense at least, the developmentalist project never really entirely disappeared.

One area where a more profound break was made with developmentalist traditions centres on the experience of Brazil's numerous SOEs. Starting in the late 1980s but accelerating rapidly in the 1990s Brazil played host to what was at the time the world's largest privatisation programme. Pinheiro (1999) provides interesting insights into the motivations surrounding the programme and argues, as he would subsequently (Pinheiro, 2018) that it was driven by the need to raise public revenue as much as by any concern over excessive direct state participation in the economy. The scale of the programme expanded considerably after 1995[10] as constitutional reforms led to an end to state monopolies in infrastructure and network industries. Between 1995 and 1998 alone, privatisation generated total revenues of US$ 60.1bn. This critical period saw Brazil's telecommunications network (comprising both federal and sub-national government-owned enterprises) transferred to the private sector. Other noteworthy privatisations to occur during the 1990s included those of publicly owned railway assets, utilities in the electricity distribution and generation sector such as Eletropaulo and Brazil's leading aircraft producer, Embraer. In addition to privatisation itself, constitutional changes allowed for an increase in the granting of concessions in fields previously off-limits to private capital. Following a constitutional amendment in 1995 private enterprises – including foreign concerns – were permitted to bid for exploration and development concessions in the oil and gas sector. The concession model was also used to stimulate private investment in highways and water and sanitation.

The privatisation and market opening processes had a significant impact upon Brazil's business landscape and its interactions with the state. In the first place, there was a strong surge in the entry of foreign multinational corporations as major enterprises such as AES, Telefónica and BP entered the Brazilian market for the first time. The 1990s and the two decades that followed were to see the presence of foreign capital spread from its traditional ISI redoubt of manufacturing into public utilities, energy and sundry network industries. To this process of internationalisation was added a fresh mode of interaction between state and business in many sectors, especially those which had been subject to intensive privatisation. This centred on the rise of the state as a regulator. Amann and Baer (2005) indicate how, as the privatisation process unfolded, the state, recognising monopoly and competition concerns inherent in network industries, launched a series of new regulatory bodies. The latter covered a range of sectors, for example, electricity (ANEEL), oil & gas (ANP), telecommunications (ANATEL) and water (ANA). At the same time, seeking to address competition concerns in non-regulated sectors, the national competition authority, CADE, saw its authority and autonomy enhanced: in 1994 it ceased being part of the Ministry of Justice and instead became an independent agency.

The cautious return of developmentalism: 2003–16

The election of President Luiz Inácio Lula da Silva in late 2002 opened up a fresh era for Brazil as the scope of social policy expanded and, buoyed by high commodity prices and strong initial growth, the new government sought to address long-standing structural weaknesses. However, the approach adopted by the new administration contrasted with that of its predecessor in some respects and was quite strongly influenced by structuralist insights. In particular, the new era of PT (Workers' Party) government saw something of a return for the state after the modest retreat experienced during the 1990s under Presidents Collor, Franco and Cardoso. What were the principal axes of this new, more ostensibly developmentalist epoch? In the first place, as Abreu (2004) notes, the new administration did not attempt to further progress the trade reforms begun more than a decade earlier. Instead, with the principal exception of the expansion of Mercosul (to include Chile and Venezuela), the PT years saw established protective structures retained in place and, in some cases (in the fields of oil and gas-related capital goods) expanded.

As the 2000s wore on and growth performance remained credible, there emerged a "new economic matrix" comprising a set of interventionist industrial policies strongly reminiscent of the pre-debt adjustment crisis era. Fonseca et al. (2013) documents some of these developments but the authors consider that while they represented a move towards the developmentalism of the past, it could not be stated categorically that a fully developmentalist programme had reasserted itself. What then were the specific policies involved? They included an ambitious multi-billion Real infrastructure development programme (the PAC or Programa Acelercação de Crescimento/Growth Acceleration Program), the promotion of national champion home-based multinational corporations, the stepping up of investment in research and development and a more active role for the BNDES in supporting strategic and technologically intensive sectors (Rufín & Manzetti, 2019).

The rise in industrial interventionism had particular repercussions for the oil and gas sector, where, as this chapter will shortly reveal, large-scale corruption became endemic. With the backing of the Lula and then Rousseff governments, Petrobrás began a rapid process of expansion, investing in new refineries at home and purchasing others abroad while building up exploration and development capability to capitalise on the discovery of "pre salt" hydrocarbons depositions off the South Eastern coast. Particular emphasis was placed on increasing the domestic content of the capital goods employed in these ventures and there emerged, de facto, a programme of import substitution in the oil and gas sector sustained by public investment and restrictive trade measures. As this process unfolded, so emerged a dense eco-system of domestic and foreign-owned enterprises in the engineering and construction sectors, heavily reliant on Petrobrás orders.

Also notable during the PT era was a deceleration in the pace of privatisation though not, as Rufín and Manzetti (2019) point out, its outright reversal. While Brazil avoided the full renationalisation promoted by other New Left administrations in Argentina, Bolivia and Venezuela, further sales of major public assets in electricity and network industries virtually ground to a halt. It is also important to note that the state retained a surprising grip over privatised corporations: the BNDES took substantial stakes in these enterprises through its investment banking division, BNDESpar, while public sector pension funds also accumulated large shareholdings (ibid.).

2016 and beyond: the end of developmentalism?

The impeachment of President Dilma Rousseff in August 2016 and her replacement by Vice President Michel Temer brought to an end more than 13 years of rule by the PT. With this development, and the subsequent election of Jair

Bolsonaro as President in 2018, there has been a pronounced change in approach to the management and development of Brazil's economy. Whereas the PT years had seen the adoption of a "new economic matrix" and developmentalist attempts to support strategic sectors and boost infrastructure spending, the new era would see the unfolding of liberal reforms on a scale unseen since the 1990s.

Oreiro and De Paula (2019) concisely summarise the key elements in this new policy landscape. They include labour market reforms (enacted in late 2016) aimed at tackling what many see as the inflexibilities of Vargas-era regulations, pensions reform (enacted in 2019),[11] tax reform (still to be legislated on),[12] a recommencement of the privatisation programme, the initiation of a new round of trade reform and the completion of a trade accord between the European Union and Mercosul[13] (ibid., p. 23). Beyond all of this, the Temer administration (2016–18) committed the federal government to a 20-year real terms spending freeze. This act alone severely limits the scope for public investment in PT-style developmentalist projects even if policymakers were so inclined. However, there is no indication that the current administration has any such yearning; quite the contrary in fact. Paulo Guedes, the current Finance Minister, has long been a firm advocate of liberal reform (Irajá, 2019) and is steeped in the Chicago School tradition of primacy for the private sector and limited state interventionism.[14]

Taking two of these recent developments – trade reforms and privatisation – as examples, there is no doubt that they point firmly towards a more restricted role for the state alongside greater exposure of the Brazilian productive sector to the forces of international competition. The trade reforms, the most ambitious in more than 20 years, will, if fully implemented, expose Brazil's long heavily protected industrial sectors to European exports. These will enjoy tariff-free access to Mercosul markets, presuming the agreement is finally ratified. In the longer term, the administration of President Bolsonaro has expressed its willingness to negotiate a free trade accord with the United States, a development which, if it ever reaches fruition, would provide a further competitive challenge to the industrial structures built up over more than half a century of developmentalism. The calculation of proponents of such reform in Brazil would be that, while elements of industry might struggle to compete in this new environment, other industrial sectors would be able to rise to the challenge. At the same time, Brazil's highly competitive, world class mining and agricultural sectors would be fully able to capitalise on their strength in key Western markets. Ahead of more ambitious multilateral agreements, the Bolsonaro administration in 2019 initiated a more modest unilateral trade reform reducing from 16% and 14% to zero tariffs on 260 categories of machinery equipment and telecommunications and computer hardware. The reform also renewed the zero tariff on 21 categories of capital good (Oreria & De Paula, 2019).

The clear intention here centres on reducing the costs of critical inputs which, in turn, might be expected to boost export performance in the longer run. The fact that such reforms could be implemented indicates that the new administration has been able to overcome protectionist opposition among some industrial associations. This reinforces the view taken by Schneider (2004) that these bodies, once powerful, have lost influence and purchase on the state. By contrast, mining and especially the agricultural lobbies have become important pillars of the President's support base.[15] The interests of these groups together with the avowed economic liberalism of the Finance Minister, help to explain why the nationalism of the Bolsonaro administration has not yet extended to the economic sphere. This presents something of a contrast with the more economically nationalist US administration of President Trump.

Taking the other key element of the current recasting of the role of the state, privatisation, the scope of proposed sales exceeds anything attempted since the late 1990s. In mid-2019, the Bolsonaro administration announced an ambitious programme for privatisation which envisages the sale of the postal service (Correios), the National Mint (Casa de Moeda), Eletrobrás,[16] Sepro, Dataprev,[17] port holding companies in São Paulo and Espírito Santo states and Trensurb and CBTU (urban train operators) (*El Pais*, 22 August 2019). Perhaps more strikingly, the authorities are preparing to grant private sector concessions to operate three national parks. In addition, in what would be a landmark development, consideration is being given to placing the remaining public holding of shares of Petrobrás in the hands of private investors (ibid.). If realised, the full transfer of Petrobrás to the private sector would represent a highly symbolic break with the state-driven industrialisation developmentalist model. It would also help draw a line under the all-encompassing Car Wash scandal (to be discussed shortly).

All, in all, policy events since 2016 appear to point to a definitive shift away from developmentalism and its binding together of business and state. However, as previous experience has shown, Brazil has partially retreated from this model before, only to return to it when impelled by crisis or changes in the political complexion of the administration. Whether such a "reversion to the mean" could take place at some point in the future is a matter of debate. In contemplating such a return to the past, beyond acknowledging the genuine economic achievements realised, it is important to recognise the deep-seated problems which have been bequeathed by Brazil's long embrace of developmentalism. Partly with this in mind, the next section provides overall assessment of the contribution of evolving state-business relations to Brazil's development process.

State-business relations and Brazil's development process: an assessment

Stretching right back to the *Estado Novo* in the 1930s, a complex set of interlinkages binding together state and business have formed an integral feature of Brazil's economic landscape. This close interplay between state and business characterises a defining attribute of the developmentalism that has long framed the country's policy and business environments. Considered in the light of the varieties of capitalism literature it is clear that Brazil corresponds less to a liberal market economy than one in which non-market mechanisms, hierarchical processes and active state interventionism have exercised critical influences. As successive administrations sought to reduce vulnerability to external shocks and carve out a new role for Brazil in the global division of labour, enterprises, both public and private, were intimately co-opted into the process. Targeted industrial policies, the incentivisation of collective action through the formation of business associations, protectionist trade policy, public sector procurement and the provision of subsidised credit for fixed capital investment were among the levers employed by the state to induce firms to behave in ways that served the collective national development interest.

Perhaps the most remarkable feature of this "model" has been its resilience in the face of wrenching economic and political challenges over the years. Thus, for example, the military coup in 1964 only resulted in modest adjustments[18] in development strategy, and even such reform as took place was reversed soon after the oil price shock of 1973. This stands in sharp contrast to the consequences of the Chilean military coup of 1973. This led to the dismantling of import substitution and set the country on a radically liberal economic course, reformulating established business-state relations.

The decade of liberal reform in Brazil that followed the debt adjustment crisis of the 1980s would, of course, see meaningful trade reform as well as the unfolding of the world's largest privatisation programme. However, as already noted, the momentum of trade reform dissipated before the end of the 1990s, while the BNDES national development bank and public sector pension funds ended up taking significant stakes in privatised companies.

In a fundamental sense, the supposed 1990s break with the developmentalism of the past was more apparent than real. In any case, the era of PT administrations which ran from 2003 to 2016 saw a clear reversion to the statist development strategies that defined the pre 1990, pre-liberal reform period. The debut of the PT's "new economic matrix" saw public and private enterprises bound more closely to state developmental objectives. BNDES lending rose, a programme of infrastructure building was launched, and Petrobrás embarked on an unprecedented investment spree designed to unleash the potential of recently discovered oil reserves. The impeachment of President Rousseff in 2016 saw the unravelling of this matrix. At the time of writing, Brazil is four years into a renewed push at liberal reform. However, whether this can be sustained or will ultimately expire, as in the past, remains a matter for debate. Certainly, one should never underestimate the hardiness of Brazilian developmentalism and, to coin a modish phrase, the economic "deep state" which nourishes it.

Resilient though Brazil's developmentalism has been, have the patterns of business-state interactions which have characterised it genuinely served Brazil's long-term economic interests? The answer here must be "only partially" and echoes Evans' conclusions a quarter of a century ago (Evans, 1995). Evans, it will be recalled, characterised the Brazilian state, in its attempts to induce industrial and competitive change among enterprises as occupying the middle ground between an "extractive" and an "embedded autonomous" state.[19] On the credit side of the ledger we can point to significant instances where the state and public and private enterprises have interacted in fruitful and productive ways, policy design has been careful, and inefficiencies minimised. This has been the case in celebrated cases, among them civil aerospace, life sciences, banking automation, flex fuel vehicles, hydro-electric power and offshore oil exploration (Schneider, 2015; Paduan, 2016). However, on the debit side of the ledger, there have been notably less successful cases – nuclear energy and informatics, for example – where attempts to seek new competitive advantages and build new capabilities have proven more frustrated. In such cases misjudged strategies, lack of alignment with market demand, poor management, bad policy design and inconsistency have been among factors responsible for the less positive outcomes.

Discussion of such high profile, high technology cases, occupies perhaps an unduly prominent place in the literature. This can blind us to more general systemic problems of competitiveness which, of course, were the focal point of Chapter 2. These concerns have demonstrably not been effectively addressed by the developmentalist model and its established patterns of state-business interactions. Indeed, it is argued by many businesses that the state itself is the problem, with what they claim to be its burdensome bureaucratic procedures and high taxes.

Moreover, at a global level, it is noteworthy that pockets of innovation and excellence are, just that, pockets among Brazilian enterprises in general (Amann & Figueiredo, 2012). This helps to explain why the past 40 years have seen the movement of Brazil's economy back towards a more traditional, commodity-based role in the international division of labour. The co-existence of lack of competitiveness in many sectors and the persistence of high levels of protection also lends weight to the neo-classical critiques long levelled against developmentalism by leading authors such as Bela Belassa and Ian Little. These, it will be recalled, suggest that attempts to nurture favoured sectors with protectionist measures run the rise of fostering inefficiency and rent-seeking. However, it is in regard to the not-unrelated issue of corruption where the highest profile challenge lies. It is to this that the final section of this chapter now turns.

Corruption and state-business relations

The emergence in Brazil of a developmentalist, interventionist state over several decades was always going to present opportunities for corruption, given the close proximity of business and the state which was at its core. Of course, as advanced in the earlier theoretical discussion, the possibility exists that close interactions between the state and business can be realised without the manifestation of rent seeking or corrupt practices. This, after all, would form one of the attributes – and benefits – of an embedded, autonomous state (Evans, 1995). However, the reality of Brazil's developmental state has unfortunately been at variance with this idealised form. Indeed, in particular circumstances and periods it has more closely resembled the "extractive" state of the type conceived by Acemoglu and

Robinson (2012). The period since the return to democracy in the mid-1980s has witnessed a series of high-profile cases which have shed light on the depth of the corruption issues afflicting the contemporary Brazilian economy.

Less than a decade after the return to civilian rule and under Brazil's first directly elected President in more than a quarter of a century there erupted a major corruption scandal, the severity of which both posed a real challenge to democratisation and shed a powerful spotlight on the role of state-business relations in the political process (Weyland, 1993). The major scandal, subsequently termed "Collorgate," involved a cash for access scheme in which individuals and businesses would, via P.C. Farias, a middleman, be able to engage with newly elected President Collor de Melo. This influence peddling enabled preferential treatment which could, for example, extend to bidding for public contracts. What is surprising, beyond the sheer brazenness of the scheme, is that it unfolded under a President ostensibly committed to reform of Brazil's development model. The President's administration at the time was, of course, engaged in an attempt to scale back of the role of the state and to open up the economy to external competition. Yet, simultaneously, the operation of the P.C. Farias scheme suggested that those prepared to engage closely – and corruptly – with the state were able to advance their interests. In response to the scandal President Collor was formally impeached in 1992. A year later a Government Procurement Law was passed which set out new ground rules around bidding for public contracts (Prado & Carson, 2018).

Further minor scandals ensued over the course of the 1990s. However, it was under the PT administration of Presidents Lula and Rousseff that the most consequential and far-reaching corruption schemes would emerge. The mid-2000s saw the revelation of what became known as the Big Monthly Stipend (*Mensalão*) scandal. This involved systematic payments instigated by the PT to secure support from other parties in Congress for the government's programme of legislation (Power et al., 2008). The payments were channelled via advertising budgets for SOEs, once again drawing businesses in to the machinations of a corrupt administration. The pursuit of such a cash for votes scheme drew on features which had long characterised congressional politics in Brazil: the presence of biddable individuals, weak party discipline, lack of real programmatic or ideological distinction between many parties and a fragmentation of the party system itself (ibid.). A series of prosecutions followed the exposure of the *Mensalão* scandal, resulting in the conviction and imprisonment of President Lula's Chief of Staff, José Dirceu. The willingness of prosecutors to investigate wrongdoing at the summit of government demonstrated the considerable institutional strength, resolution and independence of the judicial branch. This would be displayed once more a decade later as the world's largest corruption scandal, the *Lava Jato*, or Car Wash Scandal, played itself out.

The *Lava Jato* scandal once again involved exploitation of the close links which had evolved over the years between leading politicians, organs of state and big business. The scandal, which emerged in 2014, centred on the funding of political parties. Complex mechanisms were employed to facilitate the transfer of resources from leading Petrobrás and other SOE contractors to political parties, using kickbacks channelled through party placement within the SOEs themselves, and, on the outside, a network of money launderers and middlemen (Netto, 2016). Prosecutors, including the celebrated Sergio Moro (until recently justice minister) engaged in an increasingly wide-ranging inquiry which had strong echoes of the "Clean Hands" corruption investigation in Italy in the 1990s (Kerche, 2018). What emerged was an unprecedented network of graft in which public sector entities, including Petrobrás and Eletronuclear, were systematically being deprived of resources which were desperately needed to fund capital investment. The resources were effectively privatised by the political parties. The latter extended beyond the PT to embrace a range of parties from across the political spectrum (Netto, 2016).

As the scandal deepened several major enterprises centred on the construction industry were implicated with their senior management prosecuted. Brazil's largest construction company, Odebrecht, saw its CEO, Marcelo Odbebrecht, jailed for 19 years in 2016, although this sentence was later reduced. The scandal eventually spread internationally as it was discovered that Odebrecht had paid bribes to secure contracts outside of Brazil. In the case of Peru, this revelation led to the resignation of its President, Pedro Pablo Kuczynski in 2018. Within Brazil, leading politicians including the President of the Chamber of Deputies, Eduardo Cunha and even former President of the Republic, Luiz Inácio Lula da Silva were indicted and convicted as the *Lava Jato* investigation proceeded. The economic consequences of the unfolding of the *Lava Jato* case were quite severe in the short term. Campos (2019) reveals how a combination of recession and *Lava Jato* induced paralysis at key SOEs and resulted in severe restructuring and bankruptcies among contractors in the construction and infrastructure sectors. Leading construction enterprises were themselves in any case under severe operational duress due to prosecutions and investigations of senior executives.

Conclusions and prospects for change

Looking ahead, the critical question is whether the *Lava Jato* scandal will really serve to reset state-business relations in Brazil, or whether the same ecosystem of middlemen, SOEs and unscrupulous politicians and businesses will once again reassert itself, generating more opportunities for corruption. The early evidence is broadly positive: legislation enacted after 2017 has effectively outlawed corporate funding of political parties, while prosecutors have continued to instigate new rounds of investigation into *Lava Jato*-related wrongdoing. However, lasting change is only likely to result from a more systemic reform of state-business relations. This would need to involve the fostering of relationships that are more arms-length and less politicised. They would need to be mediated by institutional and market-determined frameworks which are more formal, contractual and regulatory in character. Such a transformation, if accomplished, would represent a real break with the past and would involve a recasting of Brazil's developmental state. The liberal reforms so far enacted by the Bolsonaro administration appear to be a move in this direction. However, much remains to be done; the historical precedents surrounding the durability of such reform processes are not encouraging.

Notes

1 See Hall and Soskice (2001).
2 Interestingly, this book became compulsory reading in Brazil's foreign ministry during the era of the Lula presidency.
3 The control of Brazilian federal politics by oligarchical groups from these states prior to the Vargas era is known in Brazil as the "café com leite" arrangement.
4 Whereas public ownership of network industries and oil and gas producers has been commonplace among developmental states globally, this phenomenon is far less common in the case of manufacturing industry.
5 Later on, the Bank would be renamed the National Economic and Social Development Bank, hence its present name: the BNDES.
6 Who had been elected to office in 1950 after 5 years out of power following his ejection by the military.
7 The President shot and killed himself on 24 August 1954 following the eruption of a scandal surrounding an assassination attempt on a political rival.
8 Brazil had been forced to impose a moratorium on servicing international debt in early 1987.
9 See for example, the case of the capital goods sector (Amann, 2000).
10 Just at a time when trade reform was sliding into reverse.
11 To be discussed in detail in Chapter 5.
12 This issue will also be reviewed in Chapter 5.
13 The agreement awaits ratification by member states of both blocs.
14 He obtained his Doctorate from the University of Chicago.
15 President Bolsonaro's political support base in Congress has often been described as the "Bullets, Beef and Bible" lobby, these referring to coalitions of supporters grounded in the fields of law and order, agriculture and evangelical Christianity (Cowan, 2016).
16 The majority federally owned electricity generation and transmission utility.
17 Serpro and Dataprev are the largest technology providers in the public sector.
18 In the direction of incentivising exports.
19 A position Brazil occupied along with India. South Korea, by contrast, approximated more closely to the idealised embedded and autonomous state.

5

FISCAL POLICY CHALLENGES

The previous chapter made clear the extensive and pivotal role the state has played in Brazil's development process. From economic regulation, to the establishment of state-owned enterprises and the provision of infrastructure, the state has shaped the economic emergence of Brazil and conditioned its structural transformation over several decades. Yet, the increasingly ambitious functions of the state could not always be fulfilled without recurrent fiscal challenges. Although Brazil's tax base was to deepen substantially between the pre-war Vargas period and the early 21st century, this was not sufficient to forestall repeated and severe fiscal crises, a significant ramping up of public debt and the consequent need for harsh periods of readjustment. This pattern of alternate fiscal expansion, followed by crisis and retrenchment, represents one of the factors imparting marked volatility to the growth process. In the Brazilian economic debate, this volatility has even acquired a folkloric depiction, the vôo de galinha, or "flight of the chicken", in which the economy proceeds forward in fits and starts as fiscal and external constraints alternatively tighten and loosen their grip. A major policy issue (and one which stretches back decades) therefore centres around the means whereby the fiscal constraint might be alleviated and public finances placed upon a sustainable footing.

Since the start of the 2010s, the requirement to pursue such fiscal sustainability has become more acute than ever for two reasons. In the first place, a protracted period of softer global commodity prices has via direct and indirect effects, adversely impacted the tax base. Second, and of much longer-term consequence, the challenges of Brazil's ageing population are being more keenly felt. This has occurred as pension obligations have mounted while the ratio of retirees to those in employment has increased in favour of the former. Facing these challenges, the administration of President Temer (2016–18) and latterly that of President

Bolsonaro (2019–the present) embarked on the most radical fiscal reform agenda since the latter half of the 1990s.

As will be seen, the reforms so far implemented centre on far-reaching changes to public sector employee pension arrangements and a dramatic 20-year real terms expenditure freeze. In immediate prospect are further reforms which would significantly simplify and render more efficient Brazil's byzantine tax system. At the heart of the reform process lies more than the simple desire to prevent further fiscal crises with their consequent impacts on output and employment. Rather, the reforms, especially those advanced since 2018, seek to reprofile patterns of public expenditure, re-directing resources to areas most likely to promote accelerated growth and social development. This reprioritisation of public spending has long been called for by leading commentators[1] not least because it holds out the prospect of tackling the highly income-concentrating effects of many aspects of public sector activity, notably expenditure on corporate tax breaks and civil service pensions. However, precisely because the reform process impinges on the interests of such powerful groups as sub-national governments, public sector employees and major corporations, it has long faced, and will continue to face considerable resistance. Consequently, the pathway for future reforms is far from smooth.

Seeking to understand better the complex dynamics of Brazilian fiscal policy and the reform process surrounding it, this chapter adopts the following two section structure.

The first section reviews fiscal performance and the evolution of fiscal policy over the long term. The discussion here begins by reviewing the fiscal stabilisation efforts that accompanied the launch of the Real Plan in the 1990s before moving on to consider the emergence of imbalances which contributed towards the crisis of 1998–99. The chapter then moves on to analyse the apparently successful fiscal consolidation which then followed in the early to mid-2000s as the first PT administration under President Lula sought to win favour with sceptical investors both at home and abroad. Following this, the chapter then considers the expansionary fiscal phase that marked the run up to crisis in 2014–16. As part of this discussion, the chapter assesses the extent to which shortcomings regarding fiscal policy and performance might be responsible for the economic crisis and recession that overtook Brazil in the middle of the last decade.

With the recent evolution of fiscal policy and performance covered, the second section of this chapter fixes its attention on current reform efforts, most especially the 2016 spending cap and the pension reforms of 2019. Bearing in mind that much remains to be done if Brazil's fiscal posture is to be made more compatible with the realisation of equitable, inclusive growth, the discussion focuses on further priority areas for reform, notably around the restructuring of the taxation system. Particular attention is paid to the potential for measures which might serve to alleviate constraints to growth and mitigate the income-concentrating biases implicit in many of the activities of the Brazilian public sector.

Fiscal policy and performance over the long term

Cautious fiscal reform, 1985–99

Following the return to civilian rule in 1985 and the accompanying debt adjustment crisis, policymakers redoubled their efforts to bring inflation under control and to put public finances on a sustainable footing. A fundamental part of this effort and one which immediately preceded Brazil's famous Real Plan[2] was the implementation of the Programa Imediata de Ação – PAI (Immediate Action Plan) of 1992. The PAI embraced a range of measures designed to assist fiscal adjustment and included measures to reduce public expenditure through reducing, via privatisation and de-regulation, the scope of the state (Arantes & Cazeiro Lopreat, 2017, p. 11). The PAI also comprised initiatives to increase tax collection, reduce spending on social security and to better control transfers to states and municipalities (Afonso et al., 2016, p. 45).

Once the Real Plan was properly under way in February 1994, a second important fiscal measure, the Emergency Social Fund, was introduced. The Fund was financed by the allocation of 15% of all tax revenues and was designed to ensure that resources were ring-fenced so as to satisfy spending obligations specially mandated under the 1988 constitution. In effect, the objective was to limit the discretionary power of Congress in allocating public revenues. As far as the generation of resources for public spending, the authorities developed two new streams: a finance transactions tax (Imposto Provisório sobre Movimentações Financeiras –IPMF – Provisional Tax on Financial Transactions) introduced in 1994 (Giambiagi & Além, 2001) and the Programa Nacional de Desestatização – PND (National Privatization Program). The PND would go on to generate significant resources later in the decade, averaging 5.8% of GDP between 1995 and 1998 (Arantes & Lopreat, 2017, p. 12).

While the Real Plan proved highly successful in its anti-inflationary objectives, with inflation declining from quadruple to single digits between 1993 and 1997, fiscal performance was less impressive. Fiscal austerity, including the PAI, under the Collor administration (1990–92) saw a primary deficit[3] of 0.08% of GDP for the consolidated public sector in 1989 transformed into a surplus of 5.26% by 1994. This helped the operational balance (which also includes debt servicing) to move from a deficit of 6.9% of GDP to a surplus of 1.36% over the same period (Cysne, 2002, p. 61). However, once the Real Plan properly got underway, the key fiscal indicators rapidly deteriorated. By 1997 the primary and operational balances were, respectively, registering deficits of 0.68% and 4.07% of GDP. The fiscal deterioration, perhaps at first sight paradoxical against a background of price stabilisation, can be traced to three main factors. These were, respectively, sharp rises in payroll and associated expenses, increases in the social security deficit and, in relation to the operational balance, the impact of high real interest rates on debt servicing costs (ibid., p. 62).

Amann and Baer (2000) argue that pension costs especially placed great strain on the public finances: by the late 1990s they had reached 43% of total public sector personnel expenditure up from 35% at the end of 1992 (p. 1809). The authors also highlight the particular difficulties that the largest states – São Paulo, Minas Gerais and Rio de Janeiro – had in containing the expansion of personnel costs. This difficulty helped result in increasing transfers from the federal to the state governments. Between 1994 and 1998, these rose from 2.55% to 3.02% of GDP. In respect of debt servicing costs, the maintenance of high interest rates placed upward pressure on the operational deficit. Such monetary tightness was essential, however, for the maintenance of the exchange rate anchor. The latter saw the new currency, the Real, pegged against the US Dollar, initially in a target range close to parity.

By the end of the 1990s, thus, while Brazil had succeeded in taming hyperinflation there had been no accompanying fiscal adjustment. Instead, the primary and operational balances deteriorated markedly. With this, the public debt to GDP ratio shot upwards, from 31% to 41% between 1993 and 1998. This, in tandem with a rising trade deficit – also a partial consequence of the exchange rate anchor – prompted increasing investor concern both at home and abroad. The administration of President Cardoso clearly realised the need to maintain capital inflows in the face of an expanding current account deficit and the need to shore up the Real against the Dollar.

Against this background, it urgently sought to reassure investors through intensified efforts at fiscal reform. However, these were not successful. In particular, a landmark measure which would have set ceilings on personnel expenditures among state and municipal government public servant failed to pass through Congress in June 1997 (ibid., p. 1811). This obliged the administration to rely on piecemeal temporary fiscal measures enacted by presidential decree. The problem the Cardoso administration faced was not a failure to recognise the urgency or importance of fiscal reform. Rather, it was unable to muster the necessary support in Congress for measures which would have compromised the interests of powerful groups such as public employees and sub-national governments. The political capital which would have been needed to press forward against these headwinds was in short supply, much having been expended on the passage of a constitutional amendment allowing President Cardoso to run for a second term in 1998.[4]

Crisis and fiscal consolidation, 1999–2005

However, the context for fiscal reform was to change radically following the crisis of 1998–99 and the intervention of the IMF. The eruption of this crisis occurred as Brazil was drawn into broader international financial turmoil in the wake of the Asian financial crisis of 1997 and the subsequent Russian Ruble crisis of mid-1998. These events led to a sharp drop of confidence among global investors in emerging economy assets. With this, yield spreads on emerging market bonds rose sharply, presenting Brazil with yet higher borrowing costs and difficulties in rolling over debt. In the course of 1998 net portfolio flows registered a negative outflow (US$1.8 bn) for the first time since 1989. Desperate to staunch the flow, base interest rates were elevated to almost 50%. However, these measures failed to tackle the issues which had triggered investor concern and were ultimately unsuccessful in maintaining the *Real's* peg with the US Dollar. In mid-January 1999, bowing to the inevitable, the *Real* was allowed to float freely and subsequently devalued by 40% over the next two months (ibid., p. 1817). By this stage, however, the IMF had already begun to grant assistance and, from this, stemmed a period of genuine structural reforms, which Orair and Gobetti (2017) characterise as one of *fiscal consolidation* (ibid., p. 52).

The new macroeconomic environment which came into being in the wake of the 1998–99 crisis elevated the role of fiscal policy in the overall pursuit of price stability and consistent growth. According to the original schema of the Real Plan, control of inflation was largely vested in the maintenance of an exchange rate anchor. The latter, by moulding agents' expectations and compressing import prices, was intended to exercise restraint on domestic price formation. The new framework, agreed in conjunction with the IMF adopted an arguably more conventional dual approach. With no explicit target now set for the exchange rate, control over inflation was henceforward to be exercised through an inflation targeting regime. This embraced which periodic interest rate adjustments by the monetary policy committee (COPOM) of the Banco Central do Brasil (Brazilian Central Bank). The decision to alter rates or to leave them as before would depend on COPOM's reading of inflation trends and forecasts.

However, these monetary measures were to be bolstered by a heftier dose of fiscal orthodoxy. This was operationalised through the setting of demanding primary surplus targets. As part of the initial agreement with the IMF, signed in 1998, a primary target of no less than 3.1% of GDP was set, a highly ambitious goal which, at the time seemed far too optimistic. However, and perhaps surprisingly, the new and ambitious targets were achieved. Comparing the 1995–98 with the 1999–2005 periods, Orair and Gobetti (2017, p. 52) indicate that the average primary balance realised rose from a deficit of 0.2% of GDP to more than 4.0% of GDP. How was this striking fiscal turnaround achieved? In broad terms, the key drivers comprised a rise in public revenue over the period of no less than 6.6 percentage points of GDP, allied to a reduction in public investment amounting to 1.3 percentage points of GDP (ibid.). This rise in public revenues is all the more noteworthy given that the 1999–2005 period saw a deceleration in the privatisation programme following the sale of the most attractive assets (especially SOEs in the telecommunications sector) in the previous decade. Part of the explanation here is connected with the recovery in output that eventually followed the 1998–99 crisis. This would have raised the tax take in any circumstances, other things being equal. However, the fiscal adjustment package agreed with the IMF accomplished a more aggressive adjustment process than could be realised through fiscal drag alone. The centrepiece here was the imposition of higher tax rates on upper income brackets (Amann & Baer, 2000).

Perhaps of longer lasting structural impact, though was the passage of a critical reform measure in 2000 known as the *Lei de Responsibilidade Fiscal* (Law of Fiscal Responsibility or LRF). The LRF is arguably the most important structural measure surrounding Brazilian public finances to be implemented between the return to democracy in 1985 and the passage of the Bolsonaro administrations pension reforms in 2019. The motivation and necessity underpinning the LRF stems from Brazil's highly federative character. Central to the 1988 Constitution was the desire to cement democracy in place through explicit avoidance of an overly centralised state. Consequently, the Constitution granted considerable financial and administrative autonomy to Brazil's 26 states and more than 5,000 municipalities. The practical impact of this measure was for the federal government to cede much authority over these sub-national governments in critical fiscal matters relating to revenue raising, levels and patterns of spending and borrowing. States and municipalities were able to set their own budgets according to their own rules, which in turn would be monitored and implemented by their own institutions (Nunes, 2013). Not only this; state governments could also borrow funds from their very own banks which, in the 1990s, had only just begun to be privatised. Thus, not only was fiscal policy decentralised; so was an important facet of control over monetary policy.

A very important asymmetry in this decentralised system centred on the fact that the financial, constitutionally mandated obligation of the federal government to transfer resources to sub-national governments was not adequately matched by federal powers of intervention. Among other things, this meant that the federal government was neither able to withhold resources or properly sanction states and municipalities in the event of fiscal irresponsibility at local level. One consequence of the significant degree of budgetary autonomy granted by the 1988 Constitution was the outbreak of the so-called "Fiscal War" between states in the 1990s (Dulci, 2002). As Brazil's economy opened up, states and municipalities competed among themselves to attract inward investment, especially from abroad. This resulted in a proliferation of local level tax exemptions or reductions in addition to sub-national government-financed investment in relevant infrastructure. All of this served to exert added pressure on state and municipal finances which, as we have already seen, were under strain as a result of an upward spike in personnel costs.

For much of the 1990s, the potentially adverse fiscal consequences of the 1988 Constitution had been recognised. However, the administration of President Cardoso lacked the political capital to overcome staunch resistance to reform from sub-national governments and their powerful supporters in Congress. Only with crisis and IMF intervention in 1998–99 did the political climate change sufficiently for reform to proceed, with the LRF finally receiving assent in 2000. What then, were the mains dimensions of the Law and what were the key changes that it realised?

In contrast to the arrangements that preceded it, the LRF comprises unified mechanisms and rules for fiscal planning and monitoring across all levels of government. This means that federal governments and their officials are subject to the same procedures, norms and penalties as their counterparts at state and municipal level (Nunes, 2013). The legislation also covers other public bodies including public funds and State-Owned Enterprises. The LRF contains sanctions for breaches of rules and procedures, which extended beyond institutional level to include penalties for individual legislators and officials. The creation of individual liability for breaches of the LRF is highly reminiscent of the legal mechanisms introduced in the United Kingdom during the early 1980s by the government of Margaret Thatcher to control spending at local level. The legislation put in place made it possible for UK local authority councillors to be made jointly and severally liable for losses arising from fiscal breaches, such as failing to set property taxes (Russell, 2018). In the case of Brazil, a longstanding issue centred on legislators nearing the end of their term in office seeking to gain electoral favour by engaging in fiscally destabilising spending surges. The LRF adopted special mechanisms to discourage such behaviour which, again, included provision for individual sanctions.

One important feature of the LRF is that it introduced a unified fiscal planning procedure across all levels of government. Since the passage of the Law each fiscal authority is obliged to set budgetary targets within a multiyear framework entitled the PPA or *Plano Plurianual*. The PPA creates a four-year planning horizon for capital expenditure and related items. This is complemented by another compulsory planning framework known as the LDO or *Lei de Diretrizes Orçamentárias* (Budget Directives Law) which, over a three-year period, establishes targets for general spending, revenues and, relatedly, primary and nominal balances.

Finally, a third measure, termed the LOA or *Lei Orçamentária Anual* (Annual Budgets Law), provides a framework for annual budget setting consistent with the previously established targets under the PPA and LDO. The establishment of three complementary planning procedures has been designed to allow officials and legislators to mesh long-term, strategic planning and target acquisition with shorter-term budgetary management. From the perspective of the National Treasury, a key attribute of the LRF is that it permits detailed oversight of budget planning according to a uniform format throughout the public sector. This in turn has the potential to better facilitate the meeting of meta-level fiscal targets (such as the public sector primary surplus) whether these be individually determined or agreed in concert with the IMF. Before leaving the LRF it is worth highlighting one of its most noteworthy specific features: limits on personnel expenditures. As will be recalled from earlier in this chapter, a sharp rise in this expenditure category, especially at sub-national government level, was one of the main drivers of fiscal deterioration in the late 1990s. Seeking to tackle this issue the LRF mandates an expenditure cap on personnel of 50% of net current receipts for the federal government, and 60% for states and municipalities (Nunes, 2013).

The election of President Luiz Inácio Lula da Silva to office in 2002 initially provoked nervousness among both domestic and foreign investors. Specifically, there was concern that the broadly liberal economic reform agenda and commitment to macroeconomic prudence pursued by the Cardoso administration would be jettisoned in favour of a more radical approach. Eventually these fears would be partly confirmed as Brazil's economy entered the 2010s. Initially, however, the new administration was keen to build its credibility and to forge a reputation for economic competence and pragmatism. For this reason, there was no initial rollback on the liberal market reforms of the 1990s, especially those regarding privatisation and trade liberalisation. At the same time, the Lula administration was at pains to retain its commitment to the broad macroeconomic framework that had been developed by its predecessor in conjunction with the IMF. Thus, the inflation targeting mechanism was retained and so to was adherence to the fiscal reform agenda.

In concrete terms, the Lula administration's initial commitment to fiscal orthodoxy would see it intensify efforts at setting and attaining demanding targets for the overall public sector primary surplus. Thus, between 2003 and 2004 the primary surplus target was elevated from 3.75% of GDP to 4.25%. By 2004, the effects of the government's efforts were becoming apparent. Indeed, the authorities succeeded in overshooting their target, with the primary surplus attaining 4.7% in October of that year. The renewed push at fiscal adjustment was achieved through careful containment of expenditures alongside aggressive efforts of revenue raising. According to Amann and Baer (2006, p. 222) over the first two years of the Lula administration's initial term, the tax burden grew to reach 36% of GDP, a level equivalent to that which one might encounter among the advanced industrialised economies of Europe and North America. By contrast, the incidence of tax revenue to GDP in 2004 in Chile, Mexico and Argentina stood at just 17.3%, 18.3% and 17.4%, respectively (ibid.). Improved fiscal performance managed to win over the confidence of investors to the extent that some loosening of monetary policy could be contemplated without undermining the external valuation of the *Real*. Against this background, base interest rates were modestly lowered over the course of 2003–4. This was quite an achievement given the investor anxiety that had accompanied the election of Brazil's first PT administration only a few months before.

Perhaps the most significant fiscal reform of the years of PT administrations (2003–16) came in late 2003 with the passage of a controversial social security reform package. It will be recalled that the intervention of the IMF at the end of the 1990s had resulted in the passage of the Law of Fiscal Responsibility (LRF). While the LRF enhanced the federal authorities' ability to exercise financial control over sub-national governments, it was never intended to represent a definitive solution to Brazil's recurrent fiscal disequilibria and crises. Therefore, supplementary measures would be required to meet this objective and would need to do so by entering the politically contentious territory surrounding taxation, pensions and rules surrounding public sector employees (Giambiagi, 2007). With Brazil still in receipt of IMF assistance and a new administration anxious to enhance further its growing reputation for macroeconomic responsibility, there arose the necessary combination of political will and external institutional pressure to move forward on reform. The social security reform package that emerged from this backdrop proved more ambitious than many expected.

The measures eventually approved by Congress targeted the social security system applying to civil servants. At first sight, the selection of this aspect of public finance as the focal point for reform might seem strange since, in most advanced economies it would not exercise major fiscal implications compared with, say, expenditure on education, health or, indeed, general social security. However, in Brazil, thanks to an exceptionally generous range of benefits and an extensive federal workforce, the issue could not have been of greater salience. In 2002, one year prior to the reform, expenditure on civil service social security and pension benefits amounted to R$39bn. This compared with total federal expenditure on healthcare of R$30bn and disbursements by the INSS social security system (which covers private sector workers) of R$17bn (Amann & Baer, 2006, p. 231). An interesting feature of these expenditures concerns the number of individuals actually or potentially standing to benefit from them. Whereas the civil service social security and pensions scheme served 3.5m individuals and their dependents, its far less generously funded private sector employee counterpart, the INSS, had a client group of no fewer than 19m people. Thus, in reforming the civil service social security and pension system the issues at stake went beyond a mere calculus of impact on the primary balance; considerations of equity also pertained.

Against this background, the reforms adopted sought to contain the growth of spending on civil service employee benefits in an attempt to put fiscal policy onto a more sustainable footing while freeing up resources for pressing social priorities. Most controversially, the reform package increased the minimum retirement age for civil servants to 60 for men and 55 for women, while obliging those still active members of the scheme to begin making contributions if their income stood above R$1440 per month. The end of the non-contributory pensions for better paid individuals was accompanied by caps on their earnings and pension benefits. In addition, new restrictions were imposed on the benefits that could be paid to widows and orphans of members of the scheme (ibid.). In contrast to the decisive approach adopted towards the civil service social security system, measures which would have delivered savings – and arguably more equitable outcomes – in the private sector employee INSS scheme were not adopted (Giambiagi, 2007, p. 104). Thus, an important potential avenue of reform was not explored and would have to be left to future administrations.

Developmentalism and fiscal expansion, 2005–15

By 2005 the Lula administration appeared well set along the path of fiscal adjustment, having complemented emergency measures with politically contentious structural reforms. These, together with a rising tax take from a recovering economy had generated a series of healthy primary surpluses.[5] Sound performance on the primary balance had permitted the incidence of public sector debt in GDP to diminish. Between 2002 and 2005 Brazil's net public debt to GDP ratio had declined from 59.99% to 47.97%, a figure actually below the 52.21% average for the advanced countries. The improving fiscal position and recovering investor sentiment offered clear evidence that the macroeconomic crisis which had enveloped the late 1990s was at an end. The breathing space so provided allowed President Lula's economic team the opportunity to think more strategically about fiscal policy and how it might be adapted to suit Brazil's changing economic circumstances. What was to emerge from this deliberation was, according to Odair and Gobetti (2017), an expansionary phase of fiscal policy. This, ultimately, would contribute towards the disastrous economic depression which overtook Brazil in the middle of the following decade. With the benefit of hindsight, it is easy to be highly critical of the decision to loosen the reins of fiscal policy. However, at the time, convincing arguments could be made in favour of a more expansionist approach.

Central to the rethinking of fiscal policy was a concern that the setting of elevated targets for the primary surplus, while favourable to the erosion of public debt and the containment of inflation, were damaging to Brazil's growth prospects. Indeed, the danger arose that continued adherence to tight fiscal policy could leave the country trapped in a sort of low-growth steady state where the authorities were unable to carry out the strategic investments necessary to raise supply side capacity, productivity and innovative capability. Evidence that Brazil may have entered some sort of low growth trap was not hard to uncover at the time. Between 2001 and 2003, despite exiting the 1998–99 crisis, annual average GDP growth stood at well below 2%, with industrial (as opposed to agricultural) performance especially disappointing.

The detailed arguments surrounding the fiscal means of escape from this apparent trap here are summarised by Amann and Baer (2006). In their paper, the authors point out that high primary balance surpluses were required to sustain investor confidence, to keep inflation in check, and to eventually drive down interest rates. Given the partial completion of fiscal reform, to meet them there was little choice but to squeeze discretionary spending in key areas such as infrastructure, research support and human capital development. This was largely because of the elevated scope of non-discretionary expenditure items in the federal government budget, items over which the authorities had little to no effective control. The latter included amortisation refinancing (40.1% of total government spending in 2004) and debt servicing, constitutionally mandated transfers to sub-national governments, and social security payments (collectively 31.8% of total government spending in 2004). Thus, no less than 79.8% of overall federal government spending was non-discretionary. Thus was shifted the burden of adjustment (on the expenditure side) on to growth-promoting discretionary spending categories, especially fixed capital investment. One way of alleviating the fiscal constraint on such spending, would have been to boost government revenue. However, there were two obstacles here: slow progress on tax reform and the fact that the tax take as a proportion of national output had already risen sharply and was, as we have seen, well above the Latin American average.

When the administration of President Lula was emphatically returned to office in 2006, a key policy priority emerged centred on the need to reignite growth through alleviating structural constraints to accelerated development. A particular emphasis was to be placed on raising levels of public investment to overcome bottlenecks which, it was argued, were limiting Brazil's growth prospects. How could all of this be realised given the fiscal pressures on discretionary expenditures described above? The simple answer is that the administration began to progressively loosen fiscal policy, allowing the primary balance to deteriorate. That such a departure from demanding primary surplus targets could be implemented without triggering market anxiety reflects the strong credibility for macroeconomic management the Lula government had built up over its first term.

As Table 5.1 indicates, from 2006 to the dawn of economic crisis in 2013, there was a marked reduction in the consolidated public sector primary balance. There were a two key dimensions to the relaxation of fiscal policy that took place. Orair and Gobetti (2017) highlight the increasing use of special tax breaks and exemptions which were designed to stimulate the productive sector to invest. The impact of these was to stall growth in the tax to GDP ratio: whereas this had risen from 23.4% GDP in 1988 to 33.6% in 2005, over the course of the 2005–14 period the ratio remained around a third of annual GDP. Ayres et al. (2019) focus on the expenditure component of the fiscal loosening process. As the Lula administration moved in a more interventionist direction after re-election in 2006,

TABLE 5.1 Key fiscal indicators, 2006–19 (below the line, % of GDP)

Year	Nominal balance				Primary balance			
	Consolidated public sector	Federal	Subnational	SOEs	Consolidated public sector	Federal	Subnational	SOEs
2006	−3.6	−3.1	−0.7	0.2	3.2	2.1	0.8	0.2
2007	−2.7	−2.2	−0.5	−0.1	3.2	2.2	1.1	0.0
2008	−2.0	−0.8	−1.1	−0.1	3.3	2.3	1.0	0.1
2009	−3.2	−3.2	0.1	0.0	1.9	1.3	0.6	0.0
2010	−2.4	−1.2	−1.2	0.0	2.6	2.0	0.5	0.1
2011	−2.5	−2.0	−0.5	0.0	2.9	2.1	0.8	0.1
2012	−2.3	−1.3	−0.9	−0.1	2.2	1.8	0.4	−0.1
2013	−3.0	−2.1	−0.8	−0.1	1.7	1.4	0.3	0.0
2014	−6.0	−4.7	−1.1	−0.1	−0.6	−0.4	−0.1	0.1
2015	−10.2	−8.6	−1.5	−0.2	−1.9	−1.9	0.2	−0.1
2016	−9.0	−7.6	−1.3	−0.1	−2.5	−2.5	0.1	0.0
2017	−7.8	−7.0	−0.7	−0.1	−1.7	−1.8	0.1	0.0
2018	−7.1	−6.3	−0.9	0.0	−1.6	−1.7	0.1	0.1
2019	−6.4	−5.8	−0.6	0.0	−1.3	−1.5	0.2	0.0

Source: IPEA, 2019, p. 3; Banco Central do Brasil.

it began to promote increases in public investment, especially in infrastructure. The landmark policy here was the launch in 2007 of the Programa de Aceleração de Crescimento (Growth Acceleration Program) or PAC. The PAC, comprising two phases (the second begun under President Rousseff in 2011), envisaged approximately R$2 Trillion in investments across such diverse sectors as housing, energy, highways, ports and railways.

As this process unfolded the public investment expenditure component of the primary balance rose at a very rapid rate: whereas this aggregate shrank by an annual average of 7.7% between 1999 and 2004, between 2005 and 2010 it rose at an astonishing annual average of 21.2%. Even these figures may represent an understatement of the rise in public investment. There are two reasons for this. On the one hand, the BNDES, a public sector bank, lent heavily to enterprises to promote investment and this activity would not appear in the public sector fiscal balance. Similarly exempt from such inclusion were the expenditures of Petrobrás, the state-controlled oil company. The latter invested heavily in oil refining capacity as part of the PAC, while it was also spending billions of Reais developing the recently discovered pre-salt oil fields off Brazil's South Eastern coast.

Important though the rise in investment activity was as a component of fiscal loosening, it cannot be considered its principal driver. Orair and Gobetti (2017) argue that this, in fact, was constituted by social benefits: between 1998 and 2015 these expanded from 5.9% of GDP to 9.2%, an enormous increase. Part of the reason for this came not from an expansion in the scope of the Bolsa Familia or other anti-poverty measures but rather because of a more generous rule for setting the minimum salary adopted by President Lula in 2006. This adjustment had the effect of significantly ratcheting up pension payments and related public sector benefits since annual increases for these are constitutionally linked to the level of the minimum salary.

While the value of the primary surplus declined as fiscal policy loosened there was little if any adverse reaction on behalf of economic observers or investors. One reason for this was linked to the fact that the nominal deficit for the public sector was shrinking. As Table 5.1 indicates, between 2006 and 2012 it declined by an impressive 1.3% of GDP. This is attributable to the fact that a combination of lower interest rates and increased ability to borrow in local currency terms had served to contain the growth of debt servicing costs. Another factor at work was growing international regard for the performance of Brazil's economy which, riding a surge in commodity prices, was delivering average annual growth comfortably above 3% between 2006 and 2012.

The pro-growth orientation of fiscal policy during President Lula's second term (2006–10) was exemplified in the administration's response to the international financial crisis of 2008. Although the Brazilian economy was little exposed to the first-round financial effects of the crisis, partly due to a well-capitalised banking system (see Chapter 6), it nevertheless remained susceptible to external trade shocks. To offset this at the end of 2008 the authorities engineered an additional fiscal stimulus. According to Triches and Bertrussi (2017, p. 384), the relevant measures consisted of a reduction in the federal IPI sales tax on cars and trucks, new reduced rate bands for personal income tax and increased investment in Brazilian companies by the BNDES development bank. Partly as a result of this, the economy rebounded quickly and in 2010 delivered GDP growth of 7.5%, the highest in more than 20 years.

Given these developments, at the very start of the 2010s analysts could have been forgiven for expressing cautious approval at the track taken by fiscal policy in Brazil. Primary surpluses were still being generated, the nominal deficit was well under control (on average less than 3% of GDP) and the authorities appeared to have averted the steep recession witnessed in Europe and North America. Yet within four years a serious fiscal crisis would emerge which, as she tackled it, would lead to the impeachment of President Dilma Rousseff in 2016. What went wrong?

The general dimensions of the crisis are captured in Table 5.1 which illustrates the astonishingly rapid deterioration of the nominal and primary balances between 2013 and 2015. By 2015, the former balance was registering a deficit of 10.2% of GDP, having registered a much smaller 3% GDP gap as recently as two years earlier. Holland (2019, p. 94) draws attention to the impact on public debt which, as the primary balance turned negative, ballooned from 53.3% of GDP at the end of 2013 to 58.5% in December 2014 and 75% three years later.

At first sight, the timing of the crisis seems curious; after all the global recession which followed the failure of Lehmann Brothers in 2008 was receding. However, by the middle of the 2010s Brazil was faced with serious second round effects of the global financial crisis. These centred on declines in global commodity prices, triggered by a slowdown in China together with investor unwinding of long positions in key natural resource-based products such as oil and soya. The adverse commodity price shift hurt Brazilian growth intensely since the economy had become, as we saw in Chapter 2, much more reliant on exports of these products. Whereas growth peaked at 7.5% GDP p.a. in 2010, it had declined to around 3% p.a. between 2011 and 2013, before turning strongly negative between 2014 and 2016. As Holland (2019) suggests, the primary balance then became trapped in a pincer movement between diminishing revenues and stubbornly rising expenditures. Table 5.2 indicates the scale of this problem as it rapidly overtook the public sector accounts.

Considering the revenue side first, Table 5.2 indicates the considerable extent (2.6% of GDP) by which government receipts shrank in relative and indeed absolute terms between 2011 and 2015. Of course, a reduction in such revenue would be expected given a slowing, then contracting economy. However, the issue was made worse by the effects of two fiscal stimulus packages enacted, respectively, in 2008/9 and 2012 (ibid.). These granted tax exemptions and reductions but did not prove effective in sustaining high rates of growth beyond 2011. As GDP growth began to fall away these measures accelerated the decline in public sector revenues. On the expenditure side, government policy choices and the scale of non-discretionary spending made it hard to contain the damage to the primary

TABLE 5.2 Government revenue and expenditure by area (variation % GDP)

	1997–2015	2011–15
Primary spending	5.3	1.2
Payroll	−0.5	−0.3
Income transfer to households	4.0	1.0
Pension benefits	2.5	0.8
Bolsa Familia	0.5	0.1
Investment	0.6	0.13
Fixed gross capital formation	0.34	−0.11
Minha Casa Minha Vida Housing Programme	0.3	0.28
Health	0.4	0.1
Education	0.5	0.1
Subsidies	0.8	0.8
Net revenue	3.4	−2.6

Source: Adapted from Holland (2019, p.99)

balance engendered by the fall in revenues. Constitutional commitments to pensions, social benefits and income transfers meant spending on these items continued to rise between 2011 and 2015 (Table 5.2). At the same time, new spending programmes on housing (Minha Casa, Minha Vida) and conditional cash transfers (Bolsa Familía) could not be trimmed for obvious political and social reasons.

As the scale of the fiscal crisis grew worse around 2014–15, so the administration of Dilma Rousseff resorted to creative, not to say desperate, measures to mitigate it. The means employed centred on the use of public sector banks such as the Caixa Econômica Federal and the BNDES to front payments for regular expenditure items such as the Bolsa. This would temporarily flatter the primary balance account. However, the authorities would later be obliged, at a more financially convenient moment, to refund the banks in question. These manoeuvres came to be termed "Pedaladas Fiscais" or "fiscal pedaling" (Vallaverde, 2017). As, in effect, loans from public sector banks to the federal government, they were illegal under Brazilian law. It was for the commission of the Pedaladas, rather than any involvement in the Lava Jato scandal, that President Dilma Rousseff was impeached in the middle of 2016.

Contemporary fiscal adjustment and reform efforts

On removal from office, President Dilma Rousseff was replaced, as the constitution demanded, by her Vice President, Michel Temer. President Temer did not share his predecessor's affiliation with the PT (Workers' Party). Rather, he was a longstanding member and sometime President of the PMDB. This is a broad centrist party that can trace its roots to the official opposition that existed in Congress during the military era. On taking office in 2016 President Temer quickly set economic policy on an entirely new footing, dispensing with the "new economic matrix" and the state interventionism that had characterised the PT years. In its place, the new administration re-embraced market liberali-sation and macroeconomic orthodoxy. It did so under the guidance of Minister of Finance, Henrique Meirelles a prominent banker and former governor of the Brazilian Central Bank.

Among the most urgent tasks facing Mr Meirelles and his new economic team was the need to engineer macroeconomic stabilisation, with a particular focus on fiscal adjustment and reform. One obvious option to be pursued in this regard would have comprised a conventional package of spending cuts and tax increases. These would have been imposed on a temporary basis until the primary balance had begun to move back into surplus. To have followed this path would have been to replicate the policy response to fiscal disequilibrium adopted in previous crisis periods, notably in 1990–92 and 1998–99. However, the administration decided upon a much more radical and structurally based approach. To this end it sought to impose a new fiscal settlement that, in principle at least, would pre-vent the recurrence of crises. That this decision was made reflects a number of factors, not least the scale of the fiscal deterioration between 2010 and 2016; the fact that previous adjustment packages had only transient effects; and theoretical developments in the macroeconomics literature around the potential of fiscal rules (Giambiagi & Tinoco, 2019).

PEC 55 – a new fiscal rule

In recent years, a body of literature had emerged pointing to the benefits of adopting rules which set out transparent and predictable criteria for the for-mulation of public sector spending plans (ibid.). Such arrangements would bind legislators and policymakers to agreed spending limits for a determined period of time; they could thus potentially offer a more rigorous solution to the tackling of fiscal disequilibria than the pursuit of primary balance targets. The United King-dom, under Chancellor of the Exchequer Gordon Brown, was an early exponent of fiscal rule adoption.[6] However, in the British case the framework centred on a stipulation that, over the economic cycle, government borrowing could only be permitted if it were used to fund public investment. In the case of Brazil, the choice of rule instead veered towards one centred on expenditure-based curbs. This is not surprising given the dynamics leading up to the 2013–16 fiscal crisis in which relentless increases in expenditure played a primary role. For the new administration, a curbing of selected PT-era spending programmes would also be congruent with a desire to reshape the Brazilian state, and to reduce its participa-tion in economic output (Da Costa Oreiro & de Paula, 2019).

Against this background, the Temer administration at the end of 2016 se-cured passage of constitutional amendment PEC 55. This measure, the most dramatic fiscal reform in three decades, imposed a real terms federal govern-ment spending freeze to run for 20 years. Under the terms of this new, legally binding fiscal rule, expenditure would only be able to rise from 2016 levels to reflect the rise in prices, with the possibility of a review of the measure not possible until 2020. For Giambiagi (2019, p. 9) the legislation marked a watershed moment after a 25-year period in which federal government spending had relentlessly risen from 14% to 24% of GDP. According to a recent IMF research paper, the spending freeze over the 2019–24 period implies an average annual 0.5% percentage point reduction in federal government expenditure as a proportion of GDP (Flamini & Soto, 2019). So far, according to the authors, the burden of the adjustment has fallen on capital expenditure (ibid., p. 2) although there is evidence that, prior to the eruption of the COVID-19 pandemic the Bolsonaro administration was also actively targeting expenditures in the fields of social policy. Media reports suggest the authorities were attempting to contain spending on the Bolsa Família by holding up applications. According to news magazine *Exame* no fewer than 3.5 million people in early 2020 were waiting for the latter to be processed (Exame, February 19, 2020).

As far as the performance of the primary balance is concerned, the initial impact of the spending freeze measure appears to have been positive. Between 2016 and 2019 the consolidated public sector primary deficit shrank from 2.5% of GDP to 1.3%. This figure is especially impressive when one bears in mind the relatively weak recovery Brazil experienced from the depths of the 2013–16 recession.

However, the advent of the COVID-19 pandemic on Brazilian shores in the first half of 2020 as well as a contraction in the tax base brought with it a set of emergency tax and spending initiatives. These forced measures – amounting to 4.3% of GDP – represented a temporary departure from the fiscal rules adopted by the Bolsonaro administration. They included, principally, the payment of a basic emergency income for informal workers, the allowance of delays in paying tax bills, the bringing forward of an extra monthly payment for pensions, increased spending on health, extra resources to speed up Bolsa payments and increased transfers to states and municipalities (The Intercept Brasil, April 29, 2020). According to estimates by the Brazilian Central Bank, the unexpected fiscal shock will push the primary deficit up to 6.2% of GDP for 2020 (Exame, April 27, 2020).

Despite these sudden developments, the current administration is not disposed to permanently abandon its expenditure freeze-based fiscal strategy. As commentators such as Giambiagi (2019) and Flamini and Soto (2019) are well aware, there are significant potential costs to this adhesion. These centre on the fact that, as during previous adjustment episodes, the scope for growth and social development-promoting expenditures is being squeezed out by weak revenue growth, a binding global expenditure limit and the fact that the scope for limiting non-discretionary expenditures remains constrained by slow progress on fiscal reform. Is there any possibility of escaping such a potential low growth trap without discarding Brazil's recently adopted fiscal rule? Two by no means mutually exclusive solutions, present themselves.

The first, highlighted by Giambiagi (2019) centres on a more flexible approach towards, the interpretation of PEC 55. Giambiagi is especially concerned by the compression of public sector investment which has been engendered by current fiscal adjustment efforts. Between 2014 and 2019, he notes, federal investment as a proportion of GDP fell from 1.34% to 0.7% of GDP. Such as trajectory is clearly at odds with the desire to promote sustained and resilient growth in the future. In order to tackle this issue, one possibility suggested is, from 2021 onwards, to adopt two expenditure ceilings, one for current spending and the other for total spending (ibid., p. 23). The advantage here is that investment would be allowed to grow in relation to current expenditures while retaining clear and transparent global spending limits. Another possibility would be to launch a review of the operation of the PEC 55 after 2020, with a view to examine whether any of its growth-constraining features could be reformed.

A second potential solution is offered by Flamini and Soto (2019). As with Giambiagi (2019), the authors are preoccupied with the effects of PEC 55 on future growth and development prospects, especially in terms of restricted public infrastructure investment. The authors estimate the spending required to close Brazil's infrastructure gap at 3.5% of GDP per annum but suggest that efficiency savings of 3% are available from the health and education budgets could be feasible in meeting this requirement. If the authors are correct in their conclusions then it might be possible to enhance Brazil's growth prospects without any change to the formulation of the spending cap. However, both politically and managerially, unlocking the necessary savings is likely to prove very challenging.

Plausible or not, these attempts to create budgetary space for growth promoting spending do not really tackle the structural drivers of the fiscal constraint, especially those surrounding the rise in non-discretionary expenditures and the generation of stable public revenue streams. It is to these issues that the discussion now turns.

Pension, social security and tax reform efforts

The desire to curb spending on pensions and social security has been a long-standing objective of policymakers. Indeed, as we have seen, the most significant fiscal reform of the Lula administration, (implemented in 2003) centred on pensions and social security. However, this reform did not prove sufficient to contain the relentless rise in pension and social security expenditures. According to de Souza et al. (2018, p. 7) by 2016 these had reached 13% of GDP, exceeding combined spending on health and education. Worryingly, given the consequent burden on the taxpayer, employer and employee contributions stood that year at only 8.2% GDP.

Given the ageing population and in the absence of reform, de Souza et al. (2018) state that, up to 2060 an annual 0.2 percentage point in GDP rise in public sector financing requirement for pensions and social security would prove necessary. On a similar basis, pension payments alone, would increase from 8.6% of GDP in 2019 to 17% in 2060, according to official estimates. If these projections proved true, then an intolerable burden on public finances would result. Recent data shed further light on this issue. Federal budget estimates for 2019 show expenditure on pensions and social security reaching an astonishing 53.4% of total spending.[7]

Aside from the fiscal burden engendered by underfunded pension and social security liabilities, there are also questions of equity. As noted, Brazil spends approximately 13% of its annual national income on pensions and social security, exceeding the 12.4% average for the more advanced economies of the OECD. However, unlike the OECD where entitlement to receive state pensions and social security is near universal, in the case of Brazil, beneficiaries are restricted to public sector employees or those private sector employees enrolled in the INSS system. For the approximately 23% of workers in the Brazilian informal economy[8] there is no such entitlement,[9] yet such workers, at least through their payment of indirect taxation, fund the pensions of their formal sector counterparts.

Given the need to tackle issues of equity, to avoid future fiscal crises and to allow scope for discretionary expenditures, work began under the Temer administration on a new pension reform. The measures were subsequently developed under the Bolsonaro administration and received final congressional approval in October 2019. According to Senate estimates, they should result in accumulated savings of R$800.2 bn by 2030. By the end of the 2020s, the savings produced by the new measures should equate to 2% of GDP per annum. While this figure does not augur a definitive resolution of Brazil's structural fiscal challenges, the situation has certainly become less critical.

KEY MEASURES: OCTOBER 2019 PENSION REFORM

Urban, private sector workers – This employee category contributes to the government-run INSS pension and social security scheme. The retirement age for this group is lifted to 65 years for men and 62 for women up from 56 (men) and 53 (women). Rises in retirement ages were also planned for rural workers but this proposal was abandoned

Federal government employees – Minimum retirement age set as for urban INSS-enrolled employees. Minimum contribution for pension now set at 30 years

Unified and elevated contribution rates – INSS and lower paid Federal Government employees now to make contributions at the same rate. Those on minimum salary to pay at a rate of 7.5% of income as opposed to 8% currently. Those earning between R$998.01 and R$2,000 will pay 8.25% of their salary in contributions (up from 7.5%). Contribution rates for higher income public employees rise to 16.79%

Amended transitional arrangements – New arrangements introduced for the implementation of the pension changes on existing scheme members

Source: Agência Brasil, October 23, 2019

The main measures adopted by the latest pension and social security reform initiative are presented in the text box. As can be seen, the reforms centre on rule changes which seek to increase the scale of contributions while scaling back entitlements.

Although the pension reform eventually approved did not match the ambition of earlier proposals it nevertheless represents a significant political achievement for an administration which has eschewed the explicit coalition building of its predecessors. The passage of the reform sent an important signal to investors that the Bolsonaro government was serious about effecting structural change. However, as many observers noted, more reforms would need to be carried out before confidence could be fully won over (Financial Times, October 23, 2019).

One such critical area of reform surrounds taxes, a policy domain where re-markably little progress has been made so far. The Brazilian taxation system is one of the world's most complex with overlapping layers of taxes levied by different levels of government. Beyond Federal Income Tax, there exist a welter of sales taxes ranging from the IPI federally imposed industrial products tax, to the state level good and services ICMS tax and the municipal ISS tax on services. In addition to these, additional sales taxed are levied on selected goods and services while there also exists a complex system of payroll levies designed to fund social security, employee training, accident insurance and social assistance. These include but are not limited to the INSS, FGTS, PIS-PASEP and RAT levies.

On top of this, there is a social spending contribution tax levied on corporate profits (CSLL). In contrast to what is typically encountered in Europe, where sales taxes are generally combined in a single Value-Added Tax (VAT), and there are single income, capital gains and profits tax systems for individuals and companies, the Brazilian system is extraordinarily intricate. Compliance costs associated with such a complex system are naturally very high and represent a constant source of vexation for domestic and foreign investors alike (Machado et al., 2017). Moreover, in terms of sales tax, the lack of a unified VAT results in an overlapping system of taxes at state, municipal and federal level. These give rise to a cascading effect on tax liability as a product moves from one node on the production chain to the next (Orair & Gobetti, 2019). This creates a clear competitive disadvantage for exporters, especially manufacturers, who wish to add value locally.

The issues created by Brazil's byzantine tax system have long been recognised. Consequently, reform proposals have appeared (and then been withdrawn) under centre right, centrist, centre left and left-wing administrations. The absence of progress can mainly be traced to political opposition from states and municipalities who fear their tax raising powers being diluted. This is because most proposals so far have involved consolidating state, municipal and federal sales taxes into a unified federal value-added tax. Ceding tax raising authority to the centre, not only undermines the constitutionally-guaranteed autonomy of sub-national governments; it also threatens to create a situation that wealthier states fear would involve net losses in revenue. This is because, for reasons of regional equity, the federal government may not feel inclined to pass back to wealthier sub-national governments all the sales tax revenue generated in their jurisdictions.

Orair and Gobetti (2019) in a comprehensive study, set out the current options for tax reform. In general terms, the options presented centre on a long-established, but so far unrealised set of objectives. These consist of the creation of a simplified, consolidated value-added tax administered centrally which is both more straightforward to administer and far less costly in terms of compliance (ibid., pp. 11–12). The authors highlight two reform proposals which broadly meet these criteria and have been advanced, respectively, by the Federal Senate and the Chamber of Deputies.

According to the Chamber's proposal a current slew of sales and payroll taxes (PIS, Cofins and IPI on the federal side; ICMS on the state side and ISS on the municipal side) would be replaced by two taxes: a national goods and services tax (Imposto sobre Bens e Serviços – IBS) and a federal services tax (IS) (ibid., p. 12). For its part the Senate has suggested an alternative which folds nine federal and sub-national taxes (PIS, Cofins, IPI, Cide-combustíveis, IOF, Pasep and Salário Educação, ICMS and ISS) into two. The two new taxes would comprise a state level tax on goods and services (IBS) and a federal tax on services (IS). For his part, Finance Minister Paulo Guedes has set out a counter proposal which would replace three sales taxes (IPI, ICMS and ISS) with a single tax on goods and services (IBS). At the same time, the Guedes proposal would cut, rather than reform corporate payroll taxes. The resultant shortfall would be made up by the levying of a financial transactions tax and/or a tax on dividends (EIU, 2020, pp. 7–8).

Movement towards a conclusive tax reform appeared to be gaining ground by the middle of 2020, boosted by the government's recent success in securing passage of its pensions and social security reform. However, the history of tax reform, given its political and technical complexity, is peppered with false dawns and dashed hopes. Against this background, and with the eruption of the COVID-19 pandemic in mind, it would be wise to remain sceptical as to the prospect of rapid progress.

Another dimension of fiscal reform being pursued by the current administration centres on institutionalising and embedding fiscal responsibility. Under the label of Plano Mais Brasil, Menos Brasília (More Brazil, Less Brasília Plan), the current government is seeking to pass constitutional amendments which would enable the formation of a fiscal council (EIU, 2019). The council would comprise the President, the heads of both houses of Congress, the Chief Justice of the Supreme Court, the Head of the Federal Audit Court and an assemblage of governors and mayors. The body would have similar objectives to the UK's Office for Budget Responsibility (OBR) in that it would have oversight of fiscal affairs and aim to promote the pursuit of fiscal sustainability and responsibility. Other constitutional amendment proposals in the pipeline would reduce corporate tax breaks and prevent the federal government from bailing out the states and municipalities (ibid.)

Conclusions

Brazil's economic history has been littered with recurrent fiscal crises which, all too often, have required drastic measures to address them. Such crises have contributed to the volatile growth trajectory which has become a defining feature of the Brazilian economy over the past half century and more. Over the years, a number of attempts have been made to tackle the structural drivers of fiscal fragility which lie at the heart of the problem. However, these proved wholly insufficient in preventing the deep fiscal crisis which overtook Brazil between 2014 and 2016. While emergency measures – including a 20-year real terms spending freeze – subsequently helped strengthen Brazil's public finances, it remains the case that severe structural challenges remain. In particular, caught between the new spending cap and elevated non-discretionary spending obligations, the scope for discretionary, growth-promoting expenditure is now severely constrained. In the wake of the global COVID-19 pandemic, the situation has become much more challenging still.

Against this background, a new round of fiscal reforms are under consideration. These aim in the long term to expand the scope for discretionary spending while preventing the onset of a fresh crisis. In this connection, the passage of a comprehensive pension and social security reform in late 2019 represents a real step forward. However, as most, including the current administration would admit, much remains to be done. In particular, there is an urgent need to streamline Brazil's extremely complex tax system while institutionally embedding (at sub-national as well as at federal level) the imperative for fiscal responsibility. To address these and related issues, the reform process will need to continue apace in the years ahead.

Notes

1 See, for example, Giambiagi (2007).
2 The Real Plan launched in 1993.
3 The primary balance represents the net balance of revenues minus non-debt related expenditures. As will be seen later, the primary balance has been adopted as the key fiscal target measure.
4 This measure was in fact approved and the President went on to be re-elected.
5 The latter hovered around 4.3% of GDP between 2003 and 2005.
6 This fiscal rule, termed "the golden rule" was implemented in 1998 though had been abandoned a decade later in the wake of the international financial crisis.
7 This figure includes payments to those in both the public sector employee and private employee (INSS) schemes.
8 Estimate derived by Barbosa Filho and de Moura (2012).
9 Except for families eligible for the Bolsa Família.

6

UNLOCKING INVESTMENT

Monetary policy, the financial sector and the challenge of efficient intermediation

As underlined in Chapter 1, a recurrent issue surrounding Brazil's development process has centred on inadequate investment, whether in terms of fixed capital equipment, infrastructure, education or technology. The failure to invest consistently and sufficiently in these areas has, over the years, constrained economic growth and productivity. It has also rendered the Brazilian economy more vulnerable to internal and external shocks. The experience of Brazil stands in some contrast to other key countries and regions, whether these be classified as emerging or advanced industrialised economies. As Figure 6.1 demonstrates, as a proportion of GDP, Brazil invests significantly less in fixed capital formation than the OECD average. A particularly sobering contrast can be drawn with China. Whereas Brazil devoted 15.4% of its GDP to fixed capital investment in 2018, the equivalent figure for China was a remarkable 44.1%.

Against this background, it is not surprising that boosting investment in the Brazilian economy represents a long-cherished policy objective. For many countries, the realisation of such a goal might be partially achievable through the direct action of the state, most particularly through accelerated public sector infrastructure spending. This is indeed the path that was embarked on by China in response to the 2008–9 financial crisis. However, as Chapter 5 noted, Brazil has long remained bound by tight fiscal constraints. With the recent self-imposition of a 20-year real terms spending freeze, these constraints will place significant limits on public investment for the foreseeable future.

Consequently, the search for solutions to Brazil's chronic issue of underinvestment must involve greater emphasis on the private sector. However, in placing such reliance, it is vital to understand – and address – the challenges faced by the private sector in raising capital. Stemming from this, a key objective

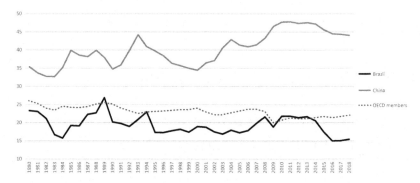

FIGURE 6.1 Capital formation % GDP, 1980–2018.
Source: Author elaboration based on World Bank Indicators.

of this chapter is to explore the roles of monetary policy, state development banks and private capital markets in relation to the evolution of capital formation throughout the Brazilian economy. A particular stress will be placed on recent financial market innovation and reform efforts aimed at improving access to cost-effective business financing.

Aside from the specific issue of capital formation, the motivation underpinning this chapter also stems from a recognition that the course of monetary policy and the state of financial sector development can have a critical impact on the development process more generally. Monetary policy, through its impact on interest rates and exchange rates, exercises clear influence on levels of economic activity, the price level and agents' expectations. It has long been recognised that an effective and credible monetary policy framework is essential for the realisation of sustainable and inclusive growth over the long term (Younsi & Nafla, 2019). In terms of financial sector development more specifically, the theoretical literature abounds with channels highlighting the constructive role that this can play in the economic development process. Soares da Silva (2015) draws attention to some of the main arguments here.

First, following Greenwood et al. (2010) effective financial systems can efficiently mobilise scarce savings resources "by choosing safe and profitable projects." Second, according to Soares da Silva (2015, p. 4) effective financial systems "can encourage an entrepreneurial response in (these) dynamic sectors," while "banks may contribute to reducing agency costs, encouraging innovation and diversification of economic activities" (after Aghion et al. (2005)). Soares da Silva (2015, p. 4) also draws our attention to the ability of "financial institutions (to) provide liquidity to households and enterprises, smoothing consumption cycles."

As this chapter will demonstrate, it is far from clear that the Brazilian financial system, despite progressive evolution over the years, is fully living up to the potential suggested here. A number of reasons exist for this and, perhaps unsurprisingly, they are related to a combination of policy missteps and ingrained structural challenges which have yet to be fully overcome. These include but are not limited to, abrupt changes in the monetary policy regime; legal complexity and its effects on interest rate spreads; crowding out effects engendered by fiscal profligacy; financial conservatism among many business enterprises, and excessive concentration in the banking sector. Such factors have contributed to a situation where, over the long run, the Brazilian economy has been hampered by high real base interest rates (by global standards), wide interest rate spreads, limited – and state-dominated – sources for long term business finance, thin domestic capital markets, a large unbanked population and limited consumer choice.

To tackle these issues and thus identify the key policy issues which need to be addressed around monetary policy and the financial sector, this chapter adopts the following approach. In the first place, the evolution of monetary policy over the past three decades is briefly reviewed with the aim of understanding why, until recently, high real base interest rates were such a constant feature of the Brazilian economic landscape. Over the past half-decade, however, rates have fallen considerably and this chapter considers the reasons underlying this and whether such monetary conditions are likely to persist over the longer term. It is argued that the sharp decline in real interest rates forms part of a monetary and financial transition in Brazil. Stemming from this transition, while restrictions undoubtedly still exist, broad and cost-effective access to capital is becoming increasingly widespread.

Moving on from the discussion around monetary policy the chapter next turns its attention to the functioning of the financial system itself. The evolution of Brazil's banking system is considered and, in highlighting issues around market concentration and the nature of the legal system, arguments are advanced as to why interest rate spreads, and commercial interest rates, have been so high. With this in mind, the prospects for market reform and de-concentration in the banking sector are considered. Given the historical realities of high real commercial interest rates and thin domestic capital markets, it is not surprising that the need has arisen to find alternative means of providing cost effective finance. For this reason, the state-owned BNDES development bank was established with the aim of providing economically strategic sectors access to subsidised credit. The chapter considers the role of this bank, one of the largest such institutions in the world. Its objectives and operational functions are analysed, together, briefly, with recent reforms which aim at reshaping its profile within the Brazilian financial system.

Chapter 2 in this volume argues that much of the Brazilian productive sector remains characterised by lack of dynamism and low levels of innovation. However, like a select few of its counterparts (e.g. aerospace, life sciences), the financial sector comprises a broad exception to this rule. The final section of this chapter examines recent and novel developments in Brazilian finance, ranging from the emergence of the Fintechs, to new investor platforms such as the renowned enterprise, XP. By way of a conclusion, the prospects for future structural shifts and reforms in financial markets are considered.

Monetary policy and its challenges

Surveying the economic development of Brazil since the return to civilian rule in the mid-1980s, it is hard not to be struck by the experimentation and abrupt regime change which has attended the implementation of monetary policy. This is most obviously reflected in the number of currencies which Brazil has spawned over this period, from the Cruzado to the Cruzado Novo, to the Cruzeiro, the Cruzeiro Real and latterly, the Real (Baer, 2013). Aside from the introduction of new currencies, monetary regimes themselves have varied. Accommodative, pro-growth approaches came to be supplanted by contractionary, shock therapy strategies which in turn gave way to exchange rate and ultimately inflation targeting frameworks. As this rapid sequence of monetary experiments unfolded the authorities frequently proved successful in containing inflation in the short term. However, until the adoption of the Real in 1993–94 these achievements were always short-lived, with inflation returning with a vengeance after a temporary dip.

Evidence presented in Ayres et al. (2019) suggests that, prior to the introduction of the Real monetary policy was either flawed in basic conception, or if better designed, hampered by misalignment of other counter-inflationary tools, notably fiscal policy. One example, in particular, stands out in this regard: the Collor Plan I, implemented in 1990 under Brazil's first directly elected President in almost 30 years. The Plan was based on the hypothesis that a sharp monetary shock would be able, in conjunction with limited fiscal contraction, to halt escalating hyperinflation. In practice, this expectation turned out to be unfounded. The monetary shock – a temporary freezing of 80% of bank deposits and financial investments – did produce a short-lived contraction in monetary aggregates, but proved so unpopular that it could not be sustained. The supplementary fiscal measures also failed to hold in place so hyperinflation returned (ibid., p. 16). Attempts were made, for example, under the 1989 Summer Plan and the Collor Plan II of 1991 to supplement monetary and fiscal counter inflationary measures with a price freeze. However, once the freeze was lifted inflation rebounded.

In reviewing the shortcomings of counter-inflationary efforts in the 1980s and early 1990s the most striking dimension of the experience surrounds the time inconsistency of monetary policy regimes. Attempts to build credibility among economic agents were hampered by constant switching between approaches founded on monetary aggregate targeting, the introduction of new currencies and the attempt to peg such currencies to the US dollar. Quite understandably, this contributed to considerable volatility of real interest rates over time, creating a highly uncertain environment for borrowers and lenders. During this period the state dominated the demand side of the domestic capital market, borrowing short term at high real interest rates (the so-called overnight market) to plug widening fiscal deficits. The returns on the overnight market were sufficiently attractive to offer lucrative investment opportunities for private individuals and, indeed, the private non-financial sector (Amann, 2000). As such, it often proved more lucrative to invest in government paper than in fixed capital formation, adding to the competitiveness issues facing industry and commerce (ibid.).

Brazil entered a new monetary era with the launch of the Real Plan in 1993. The broad details of the Plan have already been touched on in Chapter 1. It will be recalled that the Real Plan comprised a range of orthodox and heterodox measures and, as such, filled in many of the holes left unaddressed by previous stabilisation plans (Silva, 2002). The fiscal elements of the Plan have already been dealt with in Chapter 5, but of course these orthodox components were supplemented by a more heterodox-orientated progressive de-indexation. The objective here, deriving from the heterodox insights of former Finance Minister Luiz Carlos Bresser Perreira, was to tackle head-on the inertial dimension of inflation. However, the most high-profile element of the Real Plan centred on its distinctive and carefully thought out monetary approach. This focused on the creation of a new currency, the Real, which was pegged to the US dollar, initially at parity. Monetary policy was thus to be guided by an exchange rate target. What was the logic behind such an arrangement?

Svensson (1992) provides a very useful overview of the theoretical basis that guided the adoption of exchange rate targets by many economies in the 1980s and 1990s. The author highlights the contributions of Paul Krugman whose target zone model (Krugman & Rotemberg, 1991) stimulated much further research and policy innovation. In essence, this literature indicates that the adoption of an exchange rate targeting mechanism provides a transparent and verifiable means of the authorities demonstrating their commitment to the pursuit of a credible macroeconomic strategy. Monetary policy, specifically the setting of interest rates, is formulated with the objective of maintaining the exchange rate within given target bands, usually against a major currency such as the US dollar. Economic agents are able to observe in real time the success, or otherwise, encountered by the monetary authorities in achieving their core objective. If targets can be met, so credibility can be built, and agents can begin to factor in a stable exchange rate into their price setting behaviour. If the expectation is that the currency in question can hold its value in future periods against its foreign counterparts, then moderation in price and wage setting is more likely to prevail. Furthermore, depending on the level at which the target zone is set, success in meeting it will ensure that import prices on domestic currency terms will be held down. This, in turn, will exercise control over price formation in the tradables sector, especially when an economy is either open or, as in the case of Brazil during the early 1990s, in the throes of trade liberalisation.

The adoption of exchange rate targeting arrangements was common across Latin America in the 1990s, with countries adopting hard and soft pegs (Frenkel & Rapetti, 2010). In the case of Argentina, for example, the administration of President Carlos Menem adopted a convertibility plan in which the Peso was locked at parity with the US dollar. Other countries such as Brazil with the *Real* adopted a more flexible approach termed the asymmetric band in which there was scope for appreciation of a currency above a defined minimum floor (ibid., p. 20). The mechanism employed to implement Brazil's new currency, the *Real* was one of the most ingenious features of the entire counter-inflationary strategy. Instead of the sudden introduction of a new currency, as had typically characterised previous stabilisation plans, the *Real* in February 1994 began life as a shadow currency, the URV (*Unidade Real de Valor* or Real Unit of Value). The URV, like the *Real* which would follow it, was pegged at parity to the US dollar. Economic agents, in conducting transactions could observe the (stable) price in URVs while paying or setting prices and wages in the rapidly depreciating currency of the day, the *Cruzeiro Real*. Once they were able to make use of the *Real* in earnest, in July 1994 they were thus attuned to a more stable unit of account. As events proved, this contributed significantly to the ending of hyperinflation in Brazil inside a two-year period.

From 1994 until just before the end of the decade, Brazil's monetary regime centred on the maintenance of the external value of the *Real*. A major implication of this fact was that it would prove necessary to maintain comparatively tight monetary policy, both to manage demand in the economy but, more particularly to attract sufficient capital inflows to buoy up the level of the currency. The results of this were quite dramatic in terms of growth of the money supply. Ayres et al. (2019, p. 43) plot growth in the money supply against inflation. The plot indicates the rapid fall in money supply growth – and inflation – which followed the introduction of the *Real*. Annual growth in broad money of 6,000% immediately prior to the launch of the *Real* in 1994 was, over the next two years superseded by periods in which the money supply increased by less than 2% annually. Afonso et al. (2016) point out that, initially at least, the *Real* plan saw active monetary aggregate targeting in tandem with exchange rate targeting. Difficulties in successfully accomplishing the latter saw the emphasis switch to an exclusively exchange rate targeting approach which was to last up until early 1999.

A clear implication of the *Real* Plan's reliance on tight monetary policy to prop up the exchange rate was the existence of high nominal (and real) base interest rates. Table 6.1 indicates that the benchmark SELIC base interest rate averaged well over 20% p.a. in the second half of the 1990s. With inflation running at under half this value, real base rates of interest averaged well above 10%. Of course, as will be discussed in more detail later in this chapter, the actual real interest rates paid by borrowers could be considerably higher given the existence of wide spreads. Upward pressure on base rates became particularly acute in the 1997–98 period as the authorities fought to maintain the external value of the Real in the face of an investor selloff. The latter had been triggered, not by any resurgence in inflation but by deteriorating current account balance performance, caused in turn by what many investors perceived to be an overvalued exchange rate. Investor concerns around this deterioration in external performance were amplified by the broader emerging markets financial crisis of 1997–98. By 1998, and with an IMF assistance package signed off, the authorities in Brazil had already allowed the floor of the Real/US dollar band to decline. At year's end the Real, no longer at parity with the Dollar, was trading at US$1.20 (Afonso et al., 2016, p. 47).

TABLE 6.1 Gross capital formation (% of GDP)

Country name	1980	1981	1982	1983	1984	1985	1986	1987
Brazil	**23.35**	**23.08**	**21.09**	**16.68**	**15.74**	**19.20**	**19.09**	**22.30**
China	35.38	33.69	32.75	32.69	35.17	39.89	38.57	38.15
East Asia & Pacific	33.40	32.33	31.51	31.01	31.50	32.88	32.26	32.53
India	21.08	20.83	20.98	20.05	21.03	22.65	22.08	24.05
Latin America & Caribbean	24.32	24.15	21.82	17.97	17.65	19.01	18.69	20.91
OECD members	26.00	25.32	23.97	23.49	24.54	24.25	24.16	24.45
Sub-Saharan Africa		43.50	39.38	34.89	29.35	23.42	25.04	22.83
United States	23.31	24.28	22.07	22.25	25.10	24.19	23.74	23.62
European Union	25.69	23.37	23.02	22.45	22.58	22.47	22.44	22.67

Country name	1988	1989	1990	1991	1992	1993	1994	1995
Brazil	**22.72**	**26.90**	**20.17**	**19.77**	**18.93**	**20.85**	**17.29**	**17.29**
China	39.92	37.90	34.73	35.87	39.84	44.24	39.68	39.68
East Asia & Pacific	34.43	34.32	33.77	33.90	34.44	35.54	34.14	34.14
India	25.12	26.07	28.62	23.97	25.33	24.40	27.79	27.79
Latin America & Caribbean	22.41	22.85	19.71	19.82	20.20	21.21	19.42	19.42
OECD members	25.14	25.51	25.14	24.02	23.24	22.55	23.12	23.12
Sub-Saharan Africa	22.28	24.60	24.22	24.60	23.16	23.29	22.58	22.58
United States	22.83	22.51	21.53	20.11	20.08	20.39	21.27	21.27
European Union	24.04	24.85	24.64	23.62	22.65	20.94	21.65	21.65

(Continued)

Country name	1996	1997	1998	1999	2000	2001	2002	2003
Brazil	**17.27**	**17.76**	**18.16**	**17.39**	**18.90**	**18.74**	**17.45**	**16.86**
China	38.37	36.34	35.68	34.96	34.43	36.42	37.08	40.63
East Asia & Pacific	33.89	32.63	30.49	29.60	29.79	29.75	29.30	30.72
India	26.04	28.12	26.62	29.29	26.68	26.66	27.22	29.50
Latin America & Caribbean	19.37	20.78	21.44	19.56	20.17	19.62	18.20	17.83
OECD members	23.23	23.45	23.57	23.60	24.01	22.91	22.22	22.24
Sub-Saharan Africa	21.89	21.97	23.29	22.19	22.19	21.58	20.79	21.78
United States	21.70	22.41	22.96	23.42	23.68	22.18	21.71	21.74
European Union	21.35	21.46	22.17	22.37	22.99	22.45	21.63	21.51

Country name	2004	2005	2006	2007	2008	2009	2010	2011
Brazil	**17.91**	**17.20**	**17.82**	**19.82**	**21.62**	**18.80**	**21.80**	**21.83**
China	42.89	41.39	40.93	41.48	43.30	46.52	47.72	47.82
East Asia & Pacific	31.77	31.45	31.26	31.34	32.30	31.68	32.80	33.11
India	36.09	38.08	38.90	41.93	37.85	40.11	40.22	39.59
Latin America & Caribbean	19.13	19.43	20.34	21.73	22.87	20.20	21.54	21.96
OECD members	22.71	23.22	23.74	23.71	23.08	19.97	20.71	21.28
Sub-Saharan Africa	21.93	21.67	22.08	21.22	22.17	22.82	20.95	21.33
United States	22.66	23.38	23.54	22.59	21.12	17.80	18.74	19.10
European Union	21.67	21.85	22.76	23.55	23.03	19.80	20.44	20.87

Country name	2012	2013	2014	2015	2016	2017	2018
Brazil	**21.42**	**21.69**	**20.55**	**17.41**	**14.97**	**15.04**	**15.42**
China	47.39	47.57	47.21	45.60	44.47	44.34	44.06
East Asia & Pacific	33.22	33.33	33.33	32.61	31.99	32.19	32.32
India	38.35	34.02	34.27	32.12	30.21	30.94	31.31
Latin America & Caribbean	22.10	22.00	21.18	20.60	17.39	16.94	18.81
OECD members	21.12	21.13	21.48	21.72	21.42	21.81	22.08
Sub-Saharan Africa	21.63	22.30	22.75	22.96	21.91	20.53	20.51
United States	20.02	20.41	20.81	21.10	20.39	20.66	21.01
European Union	19.61	19.28	19.72	20.14	20.24	20.67	21.09

Source: World Bank World Development Indicators.

At the beginning of 1999, unable to defend the *Real* within established target bands, the authorities allowed the currency to float downwards[1]. Having abandoned the exchange rate targeting regime the stage was set for a new approach to monetary policy formation – inflation targeting. The switch to inflation targeting, which became increasingly the norm across Latin America, reflected inherent difficulties associated with the use of exchange rate anchors. In particular, as the case of Argentina in 2002 showed yet more dramatically than that of Brazil, it seemed impossible to reconcile the long run maintenance of a hard currency peg with external balance. Sooner or later, given competitiveness issues in the tradables sector, trade deficits would accumulate to the point where investor concern mounted. Interest rates would need to rise to unsustainable levels to attract capital inflows, restricting growth in investment and preventing supply side competitiveness from improving.

Therefore, a new approach to monetary policy was required which allowed for exchange rate flexibility to address external disequilibria while still permitting a measure of control over the price level. The adoption of inflation targeting, for many Latin American countries, from Chile, to Mexico to Brazil offered an attractive solution. Like exchange rate targeting, inflation targeting offered the benefit of a clear and readily observable and verifiable policy rule. In essence, monetary policy, as exercised through the setting of base interest rates, would be guided by an expert committee whose members would continually monitor target bands for inflation indicators. Base rates could be adjusted upwards or downwards depending on success encountered in remaining between the preset bounds.

In concrete terms, according to Souza Jr. (2014) the initial configuration of Brazil's inflation targeting arrangements took on the following form. In the first place, the chosen inflation measure for the target was the IPCA consumer price measure of inflation published by the government statistical agency, IBGE. Second, the bands would stretch 2% above and below the selected target IPCA inflation value. Third, targets would be set by the central government but monitored by the monetary policy committee of the Brazilian Central Bank (BCB). Finally, the BCB would produce a quarterly inflation report in which details would be set out concerning macroeconomic conditions and the configuration of monetary policy in response to the price level. For 2000 the central target for inflation as measured by the IPCA index was 6% with, of course a plus or minus 2% zone for allowed variation. By 2005 this central target had been reduced to 4.5%, a value it still held in 2018. The Temer administration, being further committed to price stability, introduced more demanding targets in mid-2018, setting values of 4.25%, 4.0% and 3.75% for 2019, 2020 and 2021, respectively (Reuters, 26 June 2018).

How successful have these targeting efforts proven? In general terms, as far as keeping inflation within the selected bounds, the framework has been remarkably successful. According to BCB data, since 2005, the upper bound of inflation was only breached between 2014 and 2016. This was a crisis period for the Brazilian economy in which the *Real* came under significant downward pressure.

Subsequently, as Table 6.1 attests, inflation has remained some way below the upper bound specified in the targeting framework. Of course, the penalty for this favourable inflationary performance came, for many years in the form of high base interest rates. As Table 6.1 shows, these hit double digit levels, especially during periods of heightened inflationary pressure, most recently during the 2014–16 crisis episode. Subsequently, with tightening fiscal policy (see Chapter 5) and the abatement of the 2014–16 economic crisis, inflation has fallen off. These developments have allowed the authorities to lower the benchmark SELIC interest rate to record low levels.

In the first half of 2020, the authorities were obliged to depart temporarily from their established monetary régime as an emergency response to the Coronavirus crisis. In order to shore up financial markets, stimulate the economy and inject liquidity, at the beginning of May, Congress approved a constitutional amendment which would allow the Brazilian Central Bank to engage in monetary financing (*Financial Times*, 8 May 2020). The new measure allows the Bank to engage in bond purchases which will permit a quantitative easing programme to commence, if deemed necessary. Private as well as public bond purchases are contemplated, with the value of potential corporate bonds to be acquired as high as R$ 1 trillion, according to the Central Bank President (ibid.). The extent to which the authorities will exploit this facility remains to be seen, but for the time being it is being viewed as a temporary emergency measure. It would appear that the official commitment to price stability remains undimmed.

The banking system, real interest rates and interest rate spreads

The previous section noted that, in very broad terms, success in countering inflation has allowed for a reduction in nominal base interest rates over the long term. Other things being equal, this must be regarded as a positive development as far as the necessity to increase the rate of investment in Brazil's structurally constrained economy. However, the evolution of base interest rates tells only half the story in terms of an understanding of how credit conditions have changed in recent years. More meaningful insight can be gleaned regarding this issue from an examination of data concerning the path of average real interest rates paid by borrowers in the Brazilian economy. In this connection, Figure 6.2 offers some interesting and internationally comparative data.

As will be readily observable from Figure 6.2, as in the case of the benchmark nominal SELIC rate (see Table 6.1), broadly speaking, Brazilian real interest rates have come down over time: between 1999 and 2018 they fell from 77.5% to 35% p.a. Of course, at points during this period – notably between 2014 and 2017 – real interest rates increased in response to monetary tightening aimed at arresting accelerating inflation. More striking than the trend of Brazilian real interest rates is how they compare with those elsewhere in Latin America and among major economies outside the region. As Figure 6.2 indicates, real interest rates in Brazil

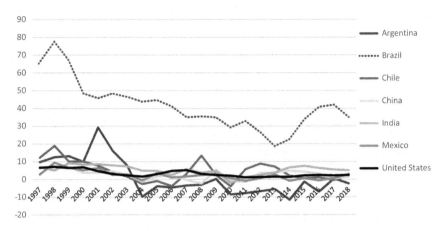

FIGURE 6.2 Real interest rates, 1997–2018, selected countries.
Source: Author Elaboration from World Bank World Development Indicators.

have consistently far outstripped those in Argentina, Chile, China, Mexico, India and the United States. For example, in 2018 real interest rates in Brazil stood at 35% p.a. whereas in the United States the equivalent value was just 2.4% p.a. The implications of this comparison are very stark: compared to their international peers Brazilian enterprises face considerably higher borrowing costs, at least in terms of accessing credit from non-public sector lenders. This fact alone goes some way to explaining, for example, why fixed capital investment in Brazil has been so compressed over the years compared with, say, China or even Chile. Addressing the issue of high real commercial interest rates has thus, unsurprisingly, become a major policy issue and one which has elicited a variety of responses over the years ranging from financial market reforms to the direct provision of credit by public sector lenders. Before turning to these, however, it is worth analysing the factors which have driven the formation of such high interest rates over the years. In particular, it worth delving into the issue of the wide interest rate spreads which have characterised the Brazilian financial landscape for a very long time.

The issue of interest rate spreads is central to any understanding of why it is the case that Brazilian real interest rates facing borrowers have been so persistently high. The interest rate spread in commercial banking terms represents the gap between the interest paid on deposits and that received from loans and other interest generating activities. For any bank to remain profitable over the longer term it is essential that spreads are positive. This is because, aside from fee income and proprietary trading, spreads are a bank's major source of revenue. This is especially the case for traditional commercial and retail banking activity. The interesting feature of spreads is their international variation. Figure 6.3 illustrates very starkly the extent to which Brazil's interest spreads vastly exceed those of selected key emerging market countries. For example, in 2018, interest rate spreads in Brazil stood at no less than 32.2 percentage points, compared with just

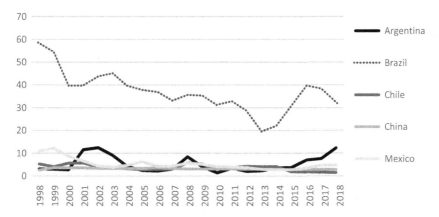

FIGURE 6.3   Interest rate spreads, 1998–2018 (lending rate minus deposit rate, %).
Source: Elaborated by Author from World Bank Data.

2.85 in China. However, while still elevated by global standards, Figure 6.3 also indicates another, more favourable feature: interest spreads in Brazil have been on a generally downward path over the past two decades. Between 1998 and 2018 they declined by approximately 26 percentage points.

Nevertheless, with high interest rate spreads still prevalent it is not hard to see why Brazilian commercial interest rates depicted in Figure 6.2 remain so high. What factors account for the persistence of high spreads? Determined to answer this question and to address what has become a major policy issue, the Brazilian Central Bank (Banco Central do Brasil – BCB) have begun to elaborate a series of statistics relating to the topic and, in their Relatório de Economia Bancária (Banking Economics Report), quantitatively decompose the spread into its constituent components (BCB, 2018). De Carvalho[2] (2019) summarises key elements of this report.

Most noteworthily, perhaps, the report estimates that, between 2015 and 2017 the single most important component of the spread (37.4% in fact) stems from the costs arising from debt default. Next to debt default, the next most important component (25%) arises from administrative expenses, with taxes on financial operations accounting for 22.8%. Lastly, just 14.9% of the overall spread is accounted for by the simple margin between the cost of capture of deposits and the interest charged to borrowers (ibid.). This represents, in effect, the net average margin the bank receives after allowing for the impacts of default, taxes and administration costs. Such a margin is still quite high, which may lead to suspicion that the Brazilian banking sector, able to lend at such net margins, is not operating as competitively as might be desired. This issue will be examined a little later in this chapter.

For the time being, it is worth focusing on the most important driver of high interest rates spreads, according to the BCB: financial default. Default and delinquency among borrowers are, of course, a fact of life across the financial sector worldwide. However, this appears to be an especially serious problem in Brazil given the low asset recovery rate compared with many countries. According to the World Bank's Doing Business Report 2019, in Brazil, on average just 14.6% of assets are recovered from bad loans. This compares with a rate of 30.9% for Latin America as a whole, 36.9% for China, 26.5% for India and 81.8% for the United States. Thus, there appears to be a significant problem in banks realising assets over which they may have taken security. De Carvalho (2019) plots spreads against asset loss rates across a range of countries. He finds a reasonable linear relationship. Interestingly, Brazil, Argentina and Paraguay cluster around each other on the plot, having both very low rates of asset recovery and high interest spreads. Conversely, economies such as Japan and the United Kingdom cluster together at the other end of the spectrum, enjoying both high asset recovery rates and low interest rate spreads.

Given the issues around default and low asset recovery rates, what steps have been taken to address them and have they worked? The key problems over the long term have been the legal complexities – and numerous avenues for appeal – facing creditors attempting to foreclose on borrowers in default. The single most important policy response so far to these issues emerged in 2005, with the passage of Brazil's new Bankruptcy Law. This made it easier than before for lenders to secure assets from borrowers in default. In this regard there were two key elements to the Law according to Ponticelli and Alencar (2016). First, the Law removed successor liability, enabling businesses in default to be sold as going concerns. This meant purchasers of these businesses no longer took on responsibility for credit, tax or labour law liabilities, increasing the value of the businesses they purchased, making them more attractive assets, and thus increasing the potential value recovered by creditors (ibid., p. 8). Second, the Law increased the rank priority of lenders in bankruptcy claims and capped the amount that could be recovered by the Labour Courts (ibid.). How effective were these measures?

The evidence, in fact indicates that the Bankruptcy Law of 2005 has played a constructive role in improving credit availability and in narrowing spreads. Looking at World Bank data from the Doing Business in Brazil publication, in São Paulo state, asset recovery rates stood at just 0.2% in 2005 (World Bank, 2018). Two years later and with the Law in force, the rate had risen to 12.1% and by 2019, for Brazil as a whole, stood at 14.6%. The data clearly indicate a break point after 2005 when the Law was introduced, with recovery rates permanently improving afterwards. As noted in Figure 6.3, interest rate spreads did decline notably between the passage of the Law (2005) and the onset of recession in 2014. The latter, in raising the overall likelihood of default, unsurprisingly pushed spreads up though they have unsurprisingly declined following the end of recession. Figure 6.4 shows that as a proportion of GDP, credit to the private sector rose quite strongly following the introduction of the Law, at least until the onset of recession around 2014.

Some interesting evidence concerning the links between the Law, ease of foreclosure, credit availability and firm investment is uncovered in an econometric study by Ponticelli and Alencar (2016). The authors find that in Brazilian

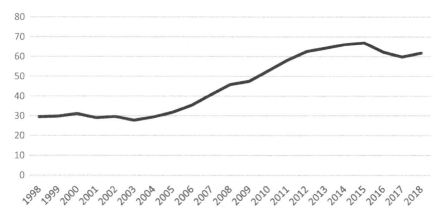

FIGURE 6.4 Credit as a proportion of GDP (%), Brazil, 1998–2018.
Source: Author Elaboration based on World Development Indicators.

municipalities with better quality court enforcement, credit availability, firm investment and output improves. The research suggests that, without introducing any new legal measures, it may be possible to tackle interest rate spreads and improve credit availability by reforming court processes at local level.

All in all, while interest rate spreads remain high by international standards, there is evidence that a considered legal response has been mounted to the issue and that this has been paying dividends. However, elevated spreads and high borrowing costs, as has been noted stem from more than the nature of legal measures and quality of enforcement. What of the role of market structures, specifically the relatively high degree of market concentration that surrounds the Brazilian banking sector?

In beginning to grapple with this topic it is worth noting the fact that, in international comparative terms, Brazilian financial institutions, despite the low asset recovery rate they face, enjoy a high degree of profitability. Data provided by the IMF's Financial Soundness Indicators publication indicates, that for 2017 – a year of very weak economic performance – Brazil's financial institutions enjoyed, on average, a 13.8% rate of return on net assets. This compares with equivalent figures of 3.4% for the United States, 3.2% for Switzerland and 4.9% for the UK. However, compared to some of its emerging market peers, the Brazilian rate of return seems less out of line. In China and Mexico, for example, financial institutions experienced an average rate of return on net assets of 14.5% and 19.6%, respectively. Nevertheless, the sense that the Brazilian financial sector may be earning excess returns, and that it does so on the basis of restricted competition, has long been a source of preoccupation in the economic policy debate and in broader political discourse.

In examining the evolution of Brazil's financial system since the inception of the Real Plan it becomes clear that, at the very least, a profound process of consolidation has been at work. Torres et al. (2014) point out that between 1994 (the year the *Real* launched) and 2000, the number of financial institutions in

Brazil declined from 893 to 551. Of these, the number of commercial banks in the market fell from 36 to 26. What factors account for the dramatic pace of sectoral consolidation? Torres et al. (2014) argue that two key drivers were at work. In the first place, regulatory reform in the mid-1990s sought to increase capital and reserve requirements pursuant to Brazil's accession to the Basel accord. In effect, this increased market participation costs and elevated barriers to entry in the banking sector.

In the second place, domestic macroeconomic developments after 1994 began to create a harsher environment for banking institutions. This may seem paradoxical in the face of a successful stabilisation programme. However, with lower inflation, came lower bond yields and fewer opportunities for banks to profit by the overnight and other short-term money markets. Weaker institutions were especially exposed to the diminution of the what had been a very lucrative and largely risk-free line of business. Hence, the mid to late 1990s saw the failure of some banks and a managed consolidation of the sector by two federal agencies: PROER for private sector institutions and PROES for sub-national or other public sector ones (ibid.). In some cases, the weak state of banks' balance sheets meant a formal rescue was required. This even happened in the case of Brazil's largest commercial bank, the publicly owned Banco do Brasil. In this connection, it is worth pointing out that the 1990s saw the unfolding of a privatisation process which embraced state banks considered healthy enough to be transferred out of the public sector. The best known of these banks, the State Bank of São Paulo, BANESPA, was sold to the Spanish bank, Santander in 2000. Another noteworthy development, which in the long run would aid the consolidation of institutions' balance sheets, was a ban on state bank lending to state governments. This was enacted under the Law of Fiscal Responsibility in the 1990s.

One initial feature of the consolidation process as it unfolded was the entry of large international groups into Brazilian commercial banking. Aside from the arrival of Santander via the Banespa privatisation, HSBC established a comprehensive nationwide presence following its purchase of Bamerindus in 1997. However, in the midst of recession, HSBC in 2016 sold most of its Brazilian operations to Bradesco, one of the leading domestic banking groups. Other foreign participants such as Bank of Boston and Lloyds Bank have recently withdrawn from the Brazilian market. This has left it in the hands of an increasingly concentrated group of domestic private sector and state-owned operators.

According to data elaborated by Torres et al. (2014), on the cusp of Brazil's recent recession, government-owned banks accounted for 33% of the market, as opposed to a share of just under 16% for foreign banks. Collectively, Brazil's largest five banks (Itaú-Unibanco, Banco do Brasil, Caixa Econômica Federal, Bradesco and Santander) accounted for no less than 80% of assets. Of these banks two – Banco do Brasil and Caixa – are majority owned by the federal government. Etchemendy and Puente (2017) draw quite a strong contrast between current banking market structures in Brazil and elsewhere in Latin America. Whereas

Brazil has developed a banking market dominated by a select few, predominantly domestic players, in Mexico, the key market participants are predominantly foreign institutions. Contrastingly, in Argentina, the market is divided more evenly between local private sector, public sector and foreign private sector banks. What might the implications of Brazil's distinctive pattern of banking sector consolidation and market concentration be from the perspective of spreads and patterns of lending? In an important Banco Central do Brasil study, Joaquim and Van Doornik (2019) provide some illuminating answers.

The study focuses on the impacts of bank mergers on the cost of credit and economic activity, drawing on municipal level data. The data employed are able to demonstrate the effects on credit conditions that a reduced number of lenders can have at a highly disaggregated local level. The results, spanning the 2010s, are quite stark. First, they indicate that a decline in bank competition increases lending spreads while reducing the volume of credit. The reduced volume of credit here is experienced through fewer loans being extended rather than a reduction in the average size of the loan (ibid., p. 4). Second, the study establishes a link between bank M&A activity, credit availability and firm output, both in the tradeable and non-tradeable sectors (ibid., p. 4). On this basis, the authors calculate that if bank competition increased enough for spreads to fall to global averages, total output would rise by 5% (ibid., p. 4). The implications of this study could not be clearer: though banks may derive private benefit through the enhanced returns available to them as a result of consolidation, there is a clear social cost in terms of foregone output. Since low investment rates are a binding constraint to accelerated, inclusive development, the pursuit of a more competitive banking market must surely be a top policy priority.

The role of the BNDES

The BNDES (Banco Nacional de Desenvolvimento Econômico e Social – National Social and Economic Development Bank) was created in 1952 during the second presidency of Getúlio Vargas. As in the case of many other Vargas era policy innovations, the launch of the BNDES represented an attempt, by direct state intervention, to reshape Brazilian economy and society. This would be achieved by tackling ingrained obstacles to economic progress, in particular, those created by lack of industrial and infrastructural investment. By providing a means of channelling public resources into these areas, the BNDES would be able to act as a kind of motor of development, facilitating the ambitious projects embraced by the prevailing strategy of Import Substitution Industrialization. The principal operational mode of the BNDES initially centred on the provision of credit at subsidised interest rates to facilitate long term fixed capital investment. The necessity of a public institution to perform what in many countries is a private sector function reflected both the thinness of Brazilian capital markets and the existence of high rate spreads, both of which generated very high commercial interest rates.

Torres and Zeidan (2016) in discussing what is termed the Life Cycle Hypothesis of development banks, suggest that over time, the functions of an institution such as the BNDES might change from these initial industrialisation promotion, direct credit provision functions. As private capital markets developed and alternative sources of finance multiplied, then the role of such a development bank would narrow in focus. Rather than direct origination of credit, such banks might be expected at a more advanced point in their life cycles to focus on the issue of credit guarantees and interest rate equalisation. These public interventions in credit markets aim at lowering effective interest rates facing favoured borrowers. However, the actual provision of loans would be facilitated by commercial banks. Moving beyond this stage, it is possible that with sufficiently deep and liquid capital markets, the need for such institutions might vanish altogether. It is noteworthy, for example, that neither the United States or the United Kingdom operates an official development bank, although some development bank-type functions, such as export credit guarantees, are exercised by public sector-linked agencies. To what extent has the role of the BNDES changed in recent years and, is it the case that its functions and operational scale have narrowed, as suggested by the life cycle hypothesis?

As Brazil embraced globalisation and limited liberal market reform in the 1990s and 2000s it might be expected that the role and scale of operation of the BNDES would have shrunk. This would result from presumed opportunities for expanded credit provision opened up by increased foreign participation in domestic capital markets. However, as has already been made clear in this chapter, spreads and base rates remained high in the face of banking sector consolidation. This maintained a real role for the BNDES, whether as a direct lender or a provider of rate subsidies to the private sector lenders. As Figure 6.5 shows, between 1995 and 2010, disbursements to all sectors by the BNDES quadrupled in scale, from 1.01% to 4.33% of GDP. By this stage annual disbursements of the BNDES far exceeded those of the World Bank. Thus, far from being an institution in

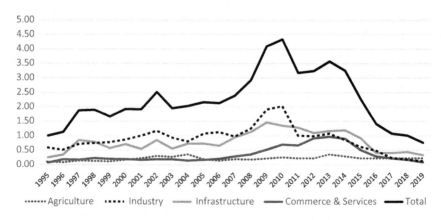

FIGURE 6.5 BNDES disbursements by sector (% GDP).
Source: Elaborated by author from BNDES data.

retreat, as market liberalisation and stabilisation gained ground, the role of the BNDES in Brazilian economic life actually increased. In functional terms, there were a number of dimensions to this.

In addition to its traditional direct lending functions, the BNDES, by the 1990s, had diversified into interest rate equalisation, the finance of machinery purchases (via the FINAME programme), the finance of exports (via the FINAMEX and PROEX programmes) and, most controversially, into a direct investor in industry (via the BNDESpar programme). The BNDESpar programme played a critical role in the privatisation process (Pinheiro, 1999). This was because it provided assurance to private sector investors that there would be a reliable market participant, perhaps prepared to prop up the share price when necessary. The critical role played by the BNDES as a purchaser of privatised assets gave rise to a critique at the time that the privatisation programme was more apparent than real. Certainly, it was the case that the state, through the BNDESpar programme, retained important stakes in the critical network and heavy industries that were the focus of the privatisation effort (ibid.).

By the 2010s, the BNDES, beyond its economic functions, had also become an important arm of Brazil's increasingly ambitious foreign policy strategy. In particular, a special directorate was established within the Bank to facilitate trade and investment with Africa, a foreign policy priority for Presidents Lula and Rousseff. To this end, a branch office was opened up in Johannesburg and, to facilitate the operation of Brazilian enterprises in Europe, another branch office was established in London.

An important question concerns the effectiveness of the BNDES of meeting its objectives in promoting the productive sector. In a key recent study, Silva & Saccaro (2019) examine the impact of access to BNDES credit for investment in fixed capital stock (via the FINAME programme) on the survivability of firms. The conclusions (based on an extensive sample of enterprises gleaned from relevant microdata over the 2002 to 2016 period) are very clear: firms with access to such credit tend to survive for longer than their counterparts without. The author finds that this effect is even greater for small firms than for larger ones (ibid.).

The question of firm size and its relationship with BNDES funding has become a highly important issue in recent years. For its critics, the BNDES unduly favours large, established enterprises looking to further cement their already strong positions in Brazilian domestic markets. The view here is that, the BNDES has become an instrument to channel subsidised credit to a favoured corporate oligarchy. Missing has been sufficient focus on promoting challenger enterprises or adequate support for small and medium firms (SMEs). Perhaps this critique is not quite fair. While it does remain the case that the bulk of disbursements (especially regarding export credit) is directed towards large MNCs, the BNDES has over the past decade and a half, opened up new credit lines for SMEs. It has also sought to amplify credit provision in emerging and technologically strategic sectors. Nevertheless, political pressure has mounted on the Bank[3] and, under Presidents Temer and Bolsonaro it has been obliged to trim back its lending activities following years of rapid expansion under the Lula and Rousseff administrations. This policy development, alongside the impacts of recession on demand for credit, has caused BNDES disbursements to fall rapidly since 2015 (Figure 6.5).

Financial innovation and emerging sources of capital

So far, this chapter has attempted to analyse the evolution of the traditional financial landscape and its constituent institutions. It has been noted that a recurring issue surrounding the Brazilian financial system has been the persistence of high real interest rates facing borrowers, both individual and commercial. While spreads and base rates have come down, conventional bank borrowing in Brazil remains expensive by global standards, especially if access to BNDES funding is not possible.

Targeting the market opportunities created by this breech have emerged a new generation of disruptive financial service providers, the Fintechs, which have drawn on internet-based technologies. Lisboa et al. (2018) in a comprehensive study, analyse the rise of this phenomenon. Between February and November 2017 alone the number of Fintechs rose from 264 to 369 according to data gleaned by the authors from Fintechlab Radar, an industry publication (ibid.). Of the Fintechs surveyed, 27% were located in payments, 18% were in financial management, 17% were in credit and loans, 9% were in investment, 8% were in insurance, 6% were in funding, 5% were in debt collection, 5% were in cryptocurrency, 3% were in foreign exchange and the final 3% were in multiservice functions.

Lisboa et al. (2018) note the growing extent to which fintechs are sharing the market space once exclusively served by conventional financial institutions. As a result, consumer and corporate customers now have a degree of choice which did not used to exist in the highly oligopolistic environment of traditional finance. Perhaps the most celebrated of the new financial sector challengers is XP Investimentos, a diversified financial services firm. Originally founded in the early 2000s to provide classes and learning materials for would-be investors, XP has subsequently expanded into "brokerage, asset management, investment banking and other services" and had some US$ 84bn of assets under its custody by September 2019 (*Financial Times*, 6 December 2019). XP, over the course of its meteoric rise, has performed two important functions. In the first place, it has broadened the investor base by drawing in small scale retail investors who, when real interest rates were higher, would have channelled their savings into bank deposits, the overnight market, or government bonds. Second, thanks to its expanding investor base, XP is able to assist corporate borrowers to issue bonds successfully onto an increasingly liquid market.

The XP phenomenon forms part of a larger picture of profound change affecting financial markets as innovation and lower real interest rate drive new patterns of capital raising. This is especially true regarding the corporate sector.

One of the most important features here has been something of a renaissance in Brazil's stock markets. The latter had already become more attractive to domestic and foreign investors alike as a result of corporate governance reforms passed by Congress in 2000. These protected the interests of smaller shareholders and improved transparency, leading to the creation of the *Novo Mercado*, a section of São Paulo stock exchange (Bovespa) listings devoted to enterprises who adopted the new corporate governance provisions and additional measures to improve transparency and investors' rights.

The result was a significant expansion of new listings from 2000 onwards, following a period in which the Bovespa had barely witnessed any (Santana et al., 2008). As the 2010s became the 2020s, these important developments, combined with less attractive interest rates, had increasingly lured small investors into the stock and bond markets, turning the latter into more appealing sources for enterprises in search of capital raising. According to a survey by the *Financial Times* (FT, February 20, 2020), the share of retail investors on the São Paulo stock market rose by 5 percentage points, from 14% to 18% between 2015 and 2019. According to the same survey, the boom in domestic retail investment has been associated with a relative decline in the importance in foreign investors: by the end of 2019 "the value of stocks owned by local investors overtook that of stocks held by foreign investors for the first time since 2014" (ibid.).

With these developments ongoing, it is not surprising that patterns of corporate funding are changing. Between 2016 and 2020, the amount of corporate bonds outstanding doubled and rose more than 35% in 2019 alone (ibid.). As Figure 6.6 indicates, this followed a sustained period in which the private corporate bond issuance to GDP ratio had already been rising quite steeply. These developments have unfolded just as BNDES lending has significantly retracted. Hence, there now appears to be a marked shift towards private domestic capital markets as a source of funding for Brazilian businesses.

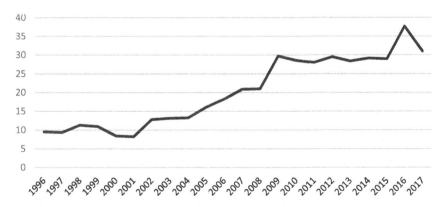

FIGURE 6.6   Corporate bond issuance volume to GDP, Brazil (%).
Source: Author Elaboration based on Central Bank of Brazil/World Bank data.

Conclusions

For much of the recent past, the configuration of monetary policy, together with structural features of the financial system, created unfavourable conditions for a much-needed surge in investment. In particular, growing concentration of the banking sector, tight, anti-inflationary monetary policy and legal obstacles to debt foreclosure kept base rates, interest rate spreads and, ultimately, real borrowing rates, very high. For large corporate organisations looking to raise fixed capital investment, few options existed beyond the usage of retained earnings or recourse to the national development bank, the BNDES.

However, this chapter argued that Brazil, for at least the past decade, has been in the throes of a monetary and financial sector transition. Thanks to effective counter-inflationary management, price pressures have abated and inflation in Brazil has remained in single digits. This has allowed base interest rates to fall to record low levels. In turn, this has forced many investors to search for alternative opportunities in the stock and bond markets. At the same time, legal reforms and emergence from recession have allowed interest rate spreads to decline, stimulating bank lending. Still, the most interesting part of the story lies well away from conventional commercial banking. Thanks to resurgent stock and bond markets and a new wave of insurgent Fintech financial service providers, those seeking to raise capital now face an unprecedentedly wide range of options. With the BNDES winding in the scope of its operations, the Brazilian financial market is increasingly driven by private sector participants, among them dynamic new players such as XP Investimentos.

If these developments are sustained, there is no doubt that the investment constraints that have been holding Brazil's economy back can be far more effectively tackled in the future. Whether this will prove to be the case will depend in part on the prospective track of monetary policy, and also whether regulatory developments continue to favour financial market innovation and the entry of new participants. On both counts, the long term monetary and financial history of Brazil would certainly counsel us to caution.

Notes

1 The Real fell from R$1.20 to R$1.98 between December 1998 and January 1999.
2 Carlos Viana de Carvalho was Director of Economic Policy of the BCB at the time of this publication.
3 A Congressional committee of inquiry (CPI) was even launched into its activities.

7

SECURING INCLUSIVE GROWTH AND TACKLING POVERTY

Beyond *Bolsa Família*

For the majority of the post Vargas period, economic development strategy in Brazil has focused on effecting structural change. As Chapter 1 made clear, influenced by structuralist perspectives on development, the objective has been to sequentially shift Brazil's position in the global division of labour, enabling it to break from inherited circumstances and grow at an accelerated rate. This has seen the transformation of both Brazil's economy and society. An agriculturally rooted and predominantly rural economy has become one characterised by industrialisation, urbanisation and increasing technological capability. In many senses Brazil has undergone a technocratically inspired revolution which, it must be acknowledged, has not been without its successes. From aerospace, to agribusiness, to life sciences, to its home-grown multinationals Brazil has developed pockets of world class excellence. As domestic and global market conditions permitted, this allowed for phases of rapid growth which, while they endured, facilitated the national build-up of wealth and assets.

Far too often missing from this episodic development process, however, has been commensurate social progress. As Brazil modernised, urbanised and industrialised from the 1930s through to the 1980s, attempts to tackle ingrained poverty and income inequality took a back seat to structuralist-inspired, supply side-focused development strategy. Not only did poverty linger, its character morphed. From being predominantly a rurally based phenomenon centred on economically peripheral regions, conspicuous poverty also became a defining characteristic of Brazil's booming cities. Indeed, urban marginalisation with its shanty towns and crime-infested neighbourhoods came to represent Brazil to the outside world just as much as the beaches of Rio de Janeiro or the Amazonian forest. At the same time, the entrenchment of poverty co-evolved with an increasingly skewed distribution of income. As Brazilian post war society and economy developed, income concentration grew as land reform failed to materialise, returns to the owners of industrial assets rose and hyperinflation ate away at the purchasing power of the labour force.

The co-existence of economic progress alongside arrested social development was to endure until the 1990s. Then, the counter-inflationary success of the Real stabilisation plan was to lay the foundations for a partly successful and reasonably sustained assault on poverty and inequality. This featured, in the 2000s the launch of conditional cash transfer together with other lower profile, targeted social programmes. Still, even as their advocates would admit, the social development policy initiatives of the past two decades were never going to represent a definitive solution to Brazil's deep-rooted problems of poverty and inequality. For this, further reform, possibly embracing asset redistribution, would have been required. Whatever the hopes for progress here, they have been checked by the economic crisis of 2013–17 and the subsequent election of an administration committed to orthodox economic management.

Thus, as Brazil enters the third decade of the millennium, the attainment of a level of social development fully commensurate with the country's economic achievements remains a great and unmet challenge. The purpose of this chapter is to delve into the nature of this challenge in some detail. In order to do this the chapter is organised as follows. First, long-term trends in poverty and inequality are reviewed including, where appropriate, relevant international comparisons. The data informing this discussion include poverty line derived measures, Gini and Theil indices of interpersonal income distribution and social development measures of the variety included in the United Nations Development Program (UNDP) Human Development Index. Given that poverty and income inequality in Brazil have strong regional and ethnic dimensions, an effort is made to illustrate how these factors play out according to relevant indicators.

Following this quantitative overview, the discussion then turns to the policy domain. Specifically, the chapter breaks down policy responses to poverty and skewed income distribution into three eras: the pre-stabilisation period (c. 1980–94), the epoch of stabilisation and pro-poor development strategy (1994–2013) and the contemporary period of crisis, retrenchment and adjustment (2013–). For each era, the attempts of policymakers to promote social development are outlined and their successes (or otherwise) evaluated.

From this discussion, it becomes readily apparent that the policy response thus far has only proved partially effective. The chapter concludes by arguing that serious structural impediments to accelerated progress on social development have remained in place and that these require addressing as a matter of priority. In this connection likelihood of further policy initiatives to tackle these obstacles is briefly considered.

Key trends in poverty and income distribution

The challenges Brazil currently faces around social development have roots which extend back for a considerable period of time; they are also intimately connected with the way Brazil's economy has long evolved. From natural resources extractivism under colonial rule, to economic liberalism in the 19th century and, on to the state-driven developmentalism of Vargas and beyond, for much of its history, there was little, if any, real attempt to confront the social deficits left unchecked by economic progress. That this was the case is especially concerning given the nature of the Brazilian economy's early emergence, rooted as it was in slavery, and characterised by a highly skewed distribution of land in favour of a privileged colonial elite (Versiani, 2018). With these features as starting points, consistent and determined efforts would have been needed to ensure that the fruits of economic growth were widely enjoyed. Such initiatives would have needed to be of sufficient weight to ensure that path dependent processes of asset deprivation, intergenerational poverty and exclusion were halted in their tracks. Unfortunately, as many authors make clear,[1] this was not to be the case; poverty and inequality persisted on a grand scale despite undoubted economic progress.

Since the 1980s, however, there appears to have been something of a sea change in the relationship between economic development and social progress in Brazil. Figure 7.1 indicates that very real strides have been made in driving down the incidence of poverty, though not in eliminating it altogether.

The data in Figure 7.1 indicate that, using a World Bank, headcount ratio measure, based on a threshold of US$1.90 a day (adjusted for purchasing power parity) poverty in Brazil declined sharply between 1990 and 2014. Between these two years, the percentage of the population living in poverty according to the relevant measure fell from 21.6% to 2.7%. Subsequently, associated with economic crisis, the incidence of poverty began to rise again, with the share of the population living in poverty defined by the $US1.90 PPP-adjusted measure rising to 4.5% by 2018. In terms of the generalised decline in the incidence of poverty since 1990, particularly strong progress was made during the first decade of the millennium when, as will be discussed, explicit anti-poverty measures were rolled out on an unprecedented scale. A global comparison provides broader perspective on Brazil's achievements here. For Latin America as a whole, the

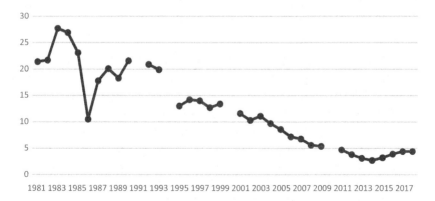

FIGURE 7.1 Brazil: poverty headcount ratio at $1.90 a day (2011 PPP) (% of population).
Source: Author Elaboration from World Bank Data.

post 1990 period has roughly paralleled that of Brazil with those considered poor according to the World Bank's headcount measure of poverty falling from 15.2% of the population in 1990 to 4.4% in 2018. This followed a period – the 1980s – where, like Brazil, the region as a whole saw the incidence of poverty rise as it experienced the so-called "lost decade" of declining output and rising inflation.

Far more dramatic, however, compared with Brazil or Latin America in general has been the vertiginous fall in poverty in the East Asian & Pacific region: between 1990 and 2018 the incidence of poverty according to the World Bank headcount measure fell from 61.3% to 1.3%. This astonishing achievement was strongly driven by developments in China, as market liberalisation and the adoption of an economic reform progress propelled growth and prosperity, if not a more even distribution of income. On a less dramatic scale, but still impressive in historical terms, was the drop in poverty experienced in Sub-Saharan Africa, a region where Brazil itself for a period made an increasingly relevant contribution in promoting social development (IPEA/World Bank, 2011). Between 1990 and 2015, the incidence of poverty in this region declined from 54.9% to 42.3%

Perhaps for more than the presence of accentuated poverty *per se*, Brazil has long been renowned as one of the most unequal societies on earth. Anyone first setting foot in the country cannot but be startled by the co-existence, often in very close physical proximity, of conspicuous wealth and grinding poverty. Has it been the case that inequality has declined in lockstep with poverty in recent years? The answer, according to Tables 7.1 and 7.2 is a cautious "yes".

As indicated in the tables, over the course of the 1990s and into the 2010s, income inequality declined noticeably in Brazil. In the case of the Gini coefficient, between 1990 and 2014, this index of income inequality fell from 60.5 to 52.1. For the alternative Theil index, a sharp decline was also witnessed with its value falling from 0.773 to 0.541 between the same two years. However, as in the case of poverty, the economic crisis of 2014–18 appears to have reversed a longstanding, favourable trend: between these two years the Gini index rose by 1.8 points.

In international comparative terms, where does Brazil stand in regard to its performance on income distribution? The available – and somewhat incomplete – World Bank data do not allow for regional comparisons, but do enable inter-country assessments to be made. As far as the Gini coefficient-based measure is concerned, Brazil fared quite favourably over the 1990 to 2018 period when set beside major extra-regional economies (Table 7.1). While, like Brazil, inequality tended to decline in Argentina, Chile and Mexico, this was not the case in China or India where the evidence is that despite (or because of) their growth dynamism and rapid reform, inequality actually rose. In the United States, too, over the period, the data point to a failure for inequality to fall.

Of course, the aggregate poverty and distribution data, however striking, only allow for a partial view of the progress on social development made in recent years, or indeed the scale of the challenges that remain to be addressed. To gain greater insight here it is worth focusing on indicators of human well-being that are not all necessarily derived from income-based data. In this regard, some

TABLE 7.1 Income inequality, GINI index (World Bank estimate), 1982–2018

	1982	1983	1984	1985	1986	1987	1988	1989	1990	1991	1992	1993
Brazil	**58.4**	**59**	**58.4**	**55.6**	**58.5**	**59.7**	**61.4**	**63.3**	**60.5**		**53.2**	**60.1**
Argentina				42.8	45.3				46.8	45.5	44.9	45.9
Chile						56.2			57.2		54.8	
Mexico								54.3			53.7	
India		32.1				32.6						32.7
South Africa												59.3
China									32.2			
United States					37.5					38.2		

	1994	1995	1996	1997	1998	1999	2000	2001	2002	2003	2004	2005
Brazil		**59.6**	**59.9**	**59.8**	**59.6**	**59**		**58.4**	**58.1**	**57.6**	**56.5**	**56.3**
Argentina	48.9	49.5	49.1	50.7	49.8	51.1	53.3	53.8	51.2	48.6	48	46.7
Chile	56.4		54.9		55.5		52.8			51.5		
Mexico	54.3		54.8		53.4		52.6		50.1		50	50.1
India											36.8	
South Africa			60.7				57.8					64.8
China			35.2			38.7			42			40.9
United States	40.2			40.7			40.3				40.5	

(Continued)

	2006	2007	2008	2009	2010	2011	2012	2013	2014	2015	2016	2017	2018
Brazil	**55.6**	**54.9**	**54**	**53.7**		**52.9**	**53.5**	**52.8**	**52.1**	**51.9**	**53.3**	**53.3**	**53.9**
Argentina	46.6	45.3	44.1	44.5	42.7	41.4	41	41.7		42	41.2	41.4	
Chile	47.3			47		46		45.8		44.4		44.4	
Mexico	48.9		49.9		47.2		48.7		48.7		46.3		45.4
India				37.5		37.8							
South Africa			63		63.4				63				
China			43		43.7		42.2	39.7	39.2	38.6	38.5		
United States		41			40.3			41			41.4		

Source: Author elaboration from World Bank data.

TABLE 7.2 Income distribution, Brazil – Theil index

1982	0.705
1983	0.721
1984	0.702
1985	0.727
1986	0.717
1987	0.741
1988	0.779
1989	0.889
1990	0.773
1991	
1992	0.695
1993	0.772
1994	
1995	0.733
1996	0.732
1997	0.738
1998	0.734
1999	0.711
2000	
2001	0.726
2002	0.710
2003	0.685
2004	0.665
2005	0.660
2006	0.644
2007	0.624
2008	0.602
2009	0.597
2010	
2011	0.569
2012	0.598
2013	0.562
2014	0.541

Source: Author elaboration from IPEA data.

very useful – and internationally comparable – data are offered by the United Nations Development Program's Human Development Index (HDI).

The HDI index attempts to overcome some of the limitations of purely income-based poverty measures by factoring in indicators of other basic building blocks of human development – education and life expectancy – alongside standard of living. How have these indicators evolved over time and has Brazil's overall HDI score improved? The evidence is clear on this point: between 1990 and 2018, the country's HDI score rose from 0.613 to 0.761, placing it by 2018 joint 79th (alongside Colombia) out of 189 countries (UNCTAD, 2019). Over this period average life expectancy rose from 66.3 to 75.7, expected years of schooling from 12.2 to 15.4, mean years of schooling from 3.8 to 7.8 and Gross National Income per capita in 2011 PPP-adjusted US dollars from $10,082 to $14,068. Examining the evolution of these data between the start and end years it is noticeable, and perhaps somewhat surprising that the HDI indicator itself has risen at a comparatively constant rate, alongside life expectancy and years of schooling. However, it is evident that the contribution imparted by growth in income has slacked off noticeably since 2010, reflecting the onset of economic crisis. It is also the case that since 2015 improvements in terms of life expectancy and years of schooling have tailed off (though have not reversed) (ibid.).

The sense that Brazil's economic crisis has exerted pressure on social development outcomes is heightened when we examine the evolution of the country's HDI in regional comparative terms. Whereas between 1990 and 2000, increases in the value of the HDI modestly outpaced those of Colombia and Mexico – countries which tend to place close to Brazil in global HDI rankings – this was not the case after 2010, especially after 2015 (ibid.).

In elaborating the HDI index, UNCTAD provide alternative versions which account for differences between countries in terms of income inequality and gender development/inequality. In terms of Brazil's adjusted HDI score and related standings, these factors make a difference. In relation to income inequality adjusted HDI (IHDI), Brazil's score for 2018 stood at 0.574 compared to a regional average of 0.589. The comparable figures for unadjusted HDI were 0.761 and 0.759, respectively. In other words, adjusting for income inequality, the particularly skewed nature of Brazil's distribution pushes down Brazil's IHDI in relation to its HDI more than is the case for the region as a whole. In relation to gender, the UNDP compute HDI scores for males and females separately in attempt to discern whether there is and development gap between the two groups. For Brazil, the ratio of female to male aggregate HDI scores achieved a ratio of 0.995 in 2018, ahead of the region as a whole (0.978), and for Colombia (0.986) and Mexico (0.957), in particular (ibid.). In relation to gender inequality, Brazil performs relatively strongly in terms of life expectancy and years of schooling where female outcomes outstrip those of males. In respect to income, however, as with other Latin American countries, that accruing to males substantially exceeds that earned by females (ibid.).

Before leaving the UNDP HDI data behind it is worth finally briefly discussing the broader quality of human development indicators that are presented.[2] Countries are divided into groups, comprising, respectively, the top, middle and bottom thirds according to their ranking on each indicator. Across all 14 of the indicators just mentioned, Brazil, like Colombia, fell into the top third of countries on just one indicator while it was in the bottom third on four (in the case of Colombia, the country was placed in the bottom third for 5 indicators) (ibid.). By contrast, Mexico exhibited top third performance on four indicators. In sum, therefore, while Brazil has made undoubted social progress over the past three decades it remains the case that in key areas, it continues to lag behind its global and, indeed, regional peers.

As should be evident by now, poverty in Brazil – as elsewhere – is a multidimensional phenomenon. This is not only in terms of how it is measured; it is also the case that poverty has strong spatial, ethnic and gender-related characteristics. In terms of the spatial dimension, it has long been recognised (see Soares et al., 2016) that certain regions of the country, notably the North and North East, have lagged developmentally behind the more affluent South and South East. There are a number of complex reasons for this, to be discussed later in this chapter, but, in brief, much of the explanation centres on deficiencies in human capital, and the related failure of the North and North East to diversify sufficiently from their traditional agricultural activities.

By contrast, the South and South East have long been the focal points of urbanisation, industrialisation and the pursuit of mechanised agribusiness. In particular, the South Eastern part of Brazil, around São Paulo, became the most prosperous part of the country. That it did so arose from its role as the centrepiece of the coffee sector; the latter proved a powerful springboard for modernisation and development in the late 19th century. Moving forward to the present, Table 7.3 clearly reveals the income disparities that continue to characterise any comparison between the North/Northeast and other parts of the country. The data show that average male and female household incomes in the South East are approximately double those prevalent in the North and Northeast, a striking difference to say the least. Of course, these dramatic inter regional disparities should not conceal the fact that strong intra-regional differences exist. As is self-evident, the ostensibly prosperous and modernised conurbations of the South and South East – notably Rio de Janeiro and São Paulo – embrace significant pockets of poverty, marginalisation and, of course crime.

Two other features which become obvious following even a cursory glance at Table 7.3 centre on income disparities according to gender and ethnicity. As the data make clear, across the nation as a whole and in each constituent region, incomes tend to be lower, on average, for women and people of colour. The disparity is especially acute in the case of ethnicity: for Brazil as a whole, average monthly incomes for whites are approximately double that for non-whites. Adding to the picture, it is important to take into account that the spatial distribution of ethnic groups throughout Brazil is far from even, with a relatively greater preponderance of whites in the affluent South and East compared to the less prosperous North and North East. Taking these considerations on board it becomes apparent that poverty – or affluence – in Brazil have striking and ethnic and spatial components: elements which have accentuated political and cultural controversies around social development. What, however, the snapshot of data presented in Table 7.3 conceals is the surprising progress which has been made in recent years in addressing poverty as it has affected disadvantaged population groups and regions.

Osorio (2019) examines the evolution of poverty by ethnic group over the 2004–14 period, a space of time bookended by the introduction of the *Bolsa Família* conditional cash transfer programme and the eruption of the political

TABLE 7.3 Household income per capita, 2018 by region, gender and ethnic group

Monthly household income per capita (R$)

| | Gender | | | | | | | | Ethnic group | | | | | | | |
| | Male | | | | Female | | | | White | | | | Non-White | | | |
	Average	CV (%)	Median	CV (%)	Average	CV (%)	Median	CV (%)	Average	CV (%)	Median	CV (%)	Average	CV (%)	Median	CV (%)
Brazil	**1,350**	**1.4**	**809**	**0.7**	**1,324**	**1.4**	**798**	**0.9**	**1,846**	**2.0**	**1,039**	**1.1**	**934**	**0.8**	**630**	**0.5**
North	891	2.6	503	3.2	882	2.6	498	3.4	1,362	4.8	710	3.7	773	2.0	477	1.9
Northeast	812	1.7	483	2.0	818	1.8	484	2.2	1,120	2.8	617	2.8	714	1.4	472	1.2
South East	1,663	2.6	980	1.3	1,618	2.4	966	1.4	2,130	3.3	1,181	1.5	1,099	1.3	797	1.0
South East	1,624	1.7	1,063	1.4	1,589	1.6	1,045	1.4	1,783	1.7	1,172	1.4	1,088	1.7	847	1.4
Centre-West	1,570	2.5	963	1.7	1,487	2.4	941	1.9	1,945	2.8	1,136	2.1	1,281	2.3	853	1.2

Source: Author elaboration from IBGE: Pesquisa Nacional por Amostra de Domicílios Contínua, 2018.
CV = Coefficient of Variation.

and economic crisis which was to unseat President Dilma Rousseff. The study evaluates the fortunes of three defined ethnic groups, *pretos, pardos* and *brancos*[3] as revealed by the application of poverty lines ranging from US$ PPP 0.10 to 10.00 per day. The results are very interesting. A significant decline in poverty was experienced between 2004 and 2014 and this was "greater among *pretos* and *pardos* than among *brancos*, leading to a decrease in the racial inequality of poverty" (ibid., p. 6). In terms of the degree of this decline in inequality, for poverty lines below US$1.00 per day, inequality fell between 20 and 40%, while for poverty lines in the region of US$3.00 per day, the fall was smaller, around 10%. For poverty lines defined above US$4.00 per day the reduction of racial inequality between 2004 and 2014 was most significant as between *pardos* and *brancos*: between *pretos* and *brancos*, the reduction in inequality ranged from 10% to 20%. Between *pardos* and *brancos* the reduction in inequality exceeded 20% for poverty lines measured at US$ 6.00 per day and up (ibid., p. 27). Summarising his study Osorio (2019) holds that

> although it has declined, the racial inequality of poverty remains very high. In 2014, the level of poverty indicators for *pretos* and *pardos* was almost equal to that of *brancos* in 2004. In 2004, on the average of the poverty lines considered, the odds of *pretos* being poor were 2.5 times greater than *brancos*'; and the odds of *pardos* was 3.2 times higher. In 2014, the odds of pretos being poor was still 2.1 times greater than *brancos*', while that of *pardos* remained 2.6 times greater.
>
> *(ibid., pp. 6–7)*

The reasons which underpin these interesting dynamics are complex and will be assessed later in this chapter. For the time being, though it is important to note that the economic crisis which erupted after 2013 has slowed or arrested the movement towards reduced ethnic inequalities with respect to poverty. Supporting this conclusion, the ratio of average non-white to white household income in Brazil remained stable, at 0.51, between 2014 and 2018 according to data provided by the most recent household income survey.

Turning to the evolution of regional disparities, the past two decades have generally seen a decline in income and poverty differentials between Brazil's constituent states. In particular, according to a wide-ranging study by Goes and Karpowicz (2017), income variation between states fell considerably between 2004 and 2014 while, interestingly, the variation of within state income inequality fell. Comparing the two years in question, the standard deviation of state Gini coefficients declined from 0.035 to 0.033. Critically, the authors find that, in Brazil's poorest regions, the North and North East, incomes for the lowest deciles of the population grew more rapidly than in the traditionally more prosperous regions of the South, South East and Centre West (ibid., p. 8). These trends – pointing to improvements in Brazil's poorest regions over time – are reflected in broader poverty measures. Soares et al. (2016) demonstrate that over the 2003 to 2013 period the incidence of poverty in the Northeast fell from approximately 42% to 22% of the population. Extreme poverty (indigence) declined from approximately 16% to 10% of the population over the same period (ibid., p. 8). The Northeast actually performed better than Brazil as a whole according to these metrics and certainly better than the neighbouring North region. However, even in the latter region, significant reductions in poverty were experienced, at least up to 2013, according to a multidimensional survey carried out by Silva et al. (2017).

The reasons underpinning this process of regional convergence will be discussed later in the chapter. Again, however, it needs to be pointed out that available evidence indicates that regional convergence and, more specifically, the deepening social and economic inclusion of the North and Northeast have slowed since the early 2010s (Goes & Karpowicz, 2017). Some indication of this is provided by data taken from the IBGE National Household Survey. Whereas in 2012 average per capita household incomes were, respectively, 68% and 61% of the national average in the North and North East, by 2018 the equivalent figures were 66% and 61%. This again indicates the broader distributional and regional consequences of the deep crisis into which Brazil's economy fell after 2013.

Policy responses and their effectiveness

Thus far, this chapter has reviewed trends in poverty and inequality, highlighting the fact that for a two-decade period stretching from the early 1990s to the mid-2010s, significant progress was made. This of course was prior to a deep economic crisis in which notable reversals were experienced. In what follows, an attempt is made to understand the factors, underpinning these dynamics, especially the transition from the high poverty, high inequality regime that preceded the Real Plan to the more pro-poor growth epoch which has followed it. In particular, the analysis focuses on the role of policy, not just in terms of explicit anti-poverty and redistributional measures, but also on the contributions of macroeconomic policy, in particular, its counter-inflationary component. First, however, and in order to provide necessary background, it is worth very briefly considering developments in the three decades leading up to the launch of the Real in 1994.

Poverty, inequality and the policy environment, 1964–94

The 30 years separating Brazil's military coup in 1964 and the introduction of the Real in 1994 comprised an economically and socially tumultuous period. During this time the pursuit of reduced poverty and inequality more often than not took a back seat to the quest for structural transformation and, towards the end of the period, the containment of hyper-inflation. Following the military coup in 1964, the authorities prioritised accelerated growth through partial economic liberalisation and the promotion of non-traditional exports. This "Post ISI" strategy certainly proved effective in elevating growth rates, which, by the late 1960s and early 1970s were averaging over 5% per annum. However, as Fishlow (1972) made clear in a landmark article, whatever benefits this accelerated dynamism may have bought, they needed to be set beside the emergence of increased income inequality. The fact was, as Fishlow made apparent, that the economic policy programme of the military government was not configured to address the income inequality which had long characterised Brazilian society and, by the time of the article, was only widening. Nor was policy at the time centred on explicit poverty alleviation measures.

As Brazil moved into the mid-1970s, the eruption of the 1973 oil crisis and the global recession which followed it prompted a change in economic strategy. This centred on a return to a more traditional ISI policy framework in which the establishment of basic industries and the expansion of energy and transportation infrastructure assumed a high priority (Baer, 2013). Again, the military government, still in power, did not place any emphasis on social policy. On the distributional front Hoffmann (2018) points out that among the economically active population inequality in the distribution of income actually widened. Hoffmann argues that this was the case partly because of increased female participation in the labour market, a group which typically receives lower pay (ibid., p. 469). Turning to the issue of poverty, developments in the 1970s were more favourable than might be thought. This outcome which can in part be traced to growing female labour market participation, but also to the reasonably robust growth which still endured. According to an important pan Latin American retrospective study by Londoño and Székely (2000), between 1970 and 1980, the absolute numbers of those living in moderate poverty in Brazil declined by 13.12%, while the numbers of those living in extreme poverty fell by 10.1%. This compares with declines for Latin America as a whole of 23.3% and 15.46% (for moderate and extreme poverty, respectively) over the same period.

Whatever progress had been made in the 1970s was confined to poverty rather than distributional outcomes and reflected the trickle down (principally employment) implications of above historical average economic growth. Social policy remained constrained in scope and principally confined to those who participated in formal labour markets and were able to access benefits from contributory social insurance schemes. Little in the social policy field was to change in the 1980s and the early 1990s, yet the challenges to human development were only to intensify given the economic crisis into which Brazil would plunge.

The crisis of the 1980s sprang in large part from a combination of international recession, global monetary crisis and a wave of debt defaults, especially in Latin America. In the case of Brazil, the burden of international sovereign debt accumulated during the 1970s became impossible to service in the new scenario and in 1987 the country entered partial default. The response of the international financial institutions was to impose stringent structural adjustment policies. These obliged the authorities to trim spending sharply, drastically narrowing the scope for spending on social programmes. Thus, any possibility of mitigating the social effects of wider recession was severely limited. Matters were made more challenging by the fact that inflation became high and persistent in the 1980s. High inflation eroded the real incomes of those who were unable to protect them through wage indexation or the ownership of interest-bearing assets. The group of affected individuals and households centred on the poorest who tended not to participate in formal labour or financial markets.

Unsurprisingly, the 1980s, known throughout the region as "the lost decade", turned out to be a dismal era from a social development perspective. Londoño and Székely (2000) estimate that the numbers living in moderate poverty in Brazil rose by 34.75% 1980 to 1990 while those in extreme poverty rose by 23.75%. For Latin America as a whole the equivalent figures were 54.11% (moderate poverty) and 37.14% (extreme poverty) (ibid., p. 124). Between 1981 and 1989, the value of Brazil's Gini coefficient rose from 0.574 to 0.625 indicating that income inequality rose steeply in line with poverty. Ferreira et al. (2007) attribute the increase in income inequality to two key factors: the rise in inflation (the mechanism described in the previous paragraph) and perhaps paradoxically a gradual rise in the educational level of the labour force. The latter, so the authors argue, benefitted the restricted sub-groups of the population who had benefited from more extensive education and had managed to translate this into greater productivity and earnings (ibid.).

The 1990s dawned with the accession to office of the first popularly elected president in almost 30 years. Yet democratic mandate or no, the administration of President Collor do Melo did not in general prioritise social programmes, focusing instead on countering hyperinflation. The one social policy innovation that did emerge during this period was entitled the *Previdência Social Rural*, a measure introduced in 1991. This provided a pension for informal workers in the primary sector (agriculture, fishing and mining) whom previously had not been covered by any such arrangement. As time went on, this measure was to help address rural poverty in quite a significant way.

However, more immediately, the monetary shocks which formed the centrepiece of President Collor's macroeconomic policy between 1990 and 1993 did little to arrest the growth in poverty. According to Ferreira et al. (2007) the proportion of those living below the administrative poverty line rose from 31.5% to 32.6% between 1989 and 1993, although there was a (very) modest reduction in income inequality between the two years.

Stabilisation, the rise of social development policy and the pursuit of pro-poor growth: 1994–2014

The two decades following the adoption of the *Real* in 1994 witnessed a flourishing in policy innovation designed both to stabilise the economy, but also to address ingrained income inequality and poverty. The change in policy environment reflected three key factors. In the first place, the international economic backdrop facing Brazil improved noticeably following the end of the 1980s. Access to foreign capital – both through foreign direct investment and portfolio flows – grew significantly. This occurred as the debt adjustment crisis of the 1980s passed, global financial innovation proceeded apace, and international investors responded favourably to Brazil's market reform programme. An important feature of the improving international context comprised a gradual recovery in commodity prices, a factor assisted by the growing prominence of the Chinese economy. This would greatly assist Brazil's traditional export sectors. This, in turn, would impel accelerated growth, creating greater fiscal headroom for social spending programmes.

The second key feature, identified by Alston et al. (2016), was the emergence of a domestic political consensus around the need for socially progressive reforms. Such a consensus was conspicuously lacking during the years of military rule. However, with the maturing of Brazil's democracy and the internalisation of social democratic ideals,[4] the political mainstream mobilised behind a more socially inclusive development strategy. Third, after years of fruitless experimentation, the authorities managed to configure a macroeconomic stabilisation strategy that was able to address the realities of inflation in Brazil, and to take advantage of the country's increasing economic openness.

In terms of progress of the policy reform agenda over the 1994–2014 period, it is possible to identify two main phases. The first, stretching between 1994 and 2003, emphasised the control of inflation. During this period modest social reforms also were rolled out, as resources became available and the political will solidified behind the idea of socially inclusive development. The second phase, spanning 2003–14, retained the main counter-inflationary elements of the first phase, but radically stepped up pro-poor policy interventions. These embraced, notably, the launch of an ambitious conditional cash transfer programme, the *Bolsa Família* (Family Grant).

The discussion now turns briefly to the policy innovations undertaken in each of these two phases. As will be argued shortly, during the first phase, the most impactful on distribution and poverty was macroeconomic stabilisation brought on by the Real Plan. The mechanisms of the Plan have already been discussed so there is no need to repeat them here. Still, it is worth reiterating just how successful it was in eliminating hyperinflation. Between 1994 and 1996 consumer price inflation fell from quadruple to single digits, a development which would greatly assist Brazil's poor in defending the real value of their earnings. Beyond the achievement of price stability itself, the most striking accomplishment of the Plan was to facilitate transition to a low inflation environment without sacrificing growth (Giambiagi & Moreira, 1999). Thus, from 1994 onwards (with, admittedly, an interruption around 1998–99), poorer income groups were able to benefit from the opportunities (employment and otherwise) conveyed by an expanding economy.

Overshadowed by the Real Plan to some extent, were the explicit social policy achievements of the Cardoso administrations during the 1994–2003 period. An important measure – aimed at tackling poverty in the elderly – came in 1996 with the introduction of the *Benefício de Prestação Continuada*. This is a pension, equivalent to one minimum salary, targeted initially at people over the age of 70 or with disabilities. Those eligible need to live in households where income stands at a quarter of the minimum wage or less (Barrientos, 2018, p. 517). A higher profile measure, the *Bolsa Escola*, emerged in 1995. This was initially a trial programme, undertaken by some municipalities and championed by the Governor of the Brasília Federal District, Christovam Buarque. The *Bolsa* provided financial support to selected families to maintain their children at school. It was initially targeted at municipalities where there was a high incidence of child labour in hazardous environments. The trial programmes proved, by and large, highly successful. As such, they attracted considerable domestic and international attention. By 2001 the *Bolsa Escola* had been rolled out as a federal programme and would form the basis of the globally renowned *Bolsa Família* introduced by President Lula in 2004. Also, during 2001 (the penultimate year of the Cardoso administration), the Ministry of Health introduced the *Bolsa Alimentação* (Food Grant) programme. This was targeted at pregnant women and small children and had the aim of reducing infant malnutrition and mortality (ibid., p. 519).

The election of President Lula to office in 2002 marked a watershed moment for the evolution of social policy in Brazil. Throughout the four terms of PT administration that were to follow, explicit policies designed to tackle poverty and inequality assumed top priority, arguably for the first time in Brazil's history. On reaching office the new President moved quickly, establishing two new programmes, the *Auxílio Gás* and the *Fome Zero* initiative. The first programme provided support for low income families to buy gas – the main cooking fuel in Brazil – while the second (translated into English as the Zero Hunger initiative) provided financial and in-kind support for low income families to access food. Both of these early efforts came to be overshadowed by the launch in 2004 of the *Bolsa Família* programme. The *Bolsa* came to be viewed as the major social policy achievement of the Lula administration and, arguably represented the biggest expansion of the social safety net since the Vargas labour reforms of the 1930s.

The programme built explicitly on the experience of the earlier, more experimental *Bolsa Escolar* but was rolled out on a far more extensive, national basis. According to Campello and Neri (2013), who provide a detailed account of the programme's evolution, from a standing start in 2004, by 2013 the *Bolsa* covered no fewer than 13 million people. Like the *Bolsa Escolar* before it, the *Bolsa Família* is a conditional cash transfer programme whereby households below a certain income threshold (currently R$140 per month) receive a benefit of R$32 per month per vaccinated child attending school. For households with incomes below R$70 per month, the *Bolsa* provides a top up benefit of R$70 per month.

The conditionality attaching to the *Bolsa* arises from the necessity for children to attend school regularly and to be vaccinated when required. The idea here is to prevent the inter-generational transmission of poverty. By ensuring that children in poor households receive adequate schooling, the expectation is that they would be better equipped for more productive adulthoods. The relative contribution of the *Bolsa* to the alleviation of poverty and the fall in income inequality is a hotly debated – and studied – issue, and one which will be examined very shortly. Before engaging with it, however, it is worth acknowledging the tremendous technical and organisational achievement that the *Bolsa* represents. Campello and Neri (2013) illustrate the considerable administrative challenges which had to be overcome in rolling the programme out. Not the least of these was the creation of a robust database of claimants and an electronic payments system to enable those eligible to draw on the funds to which they were entitled. It is also worth noting that the *Bolsa*, for all its scale, consumes only around 1% of GDP on an annual basis. Considering the concrete impacts of the programme, this is a very modest sum.

Beyond the *Bolsa Família*, the PT years saw the unfolding of many other social policy initiatives. Among these were the ethnic quota schemes for higher education institutions, already discussed in Chapter 5. The latter drew on the same intellectual inspiration as the *Bolsa* in that it saw enhanced investment in education for disadvantaged groups as the key to breaking cycles of poverty. Another very important initiative – *Minha Casa, Minha Vida* (My House, My Life) centred on the increasing public provision of social housing. Biderman et al. (2018) provide a very detailed account of this programme, in particular, focusing on its effects on urban sprawl. Launched in 2009 *Minha Casa, Minha Vida*, by mid-2016 had invested R$318bn constructing 4.4m housing units. The idea of the programme was to given low-income households the opportunity to purchase residential property at subsidised mortgage rates. Financing was provided by the Federal savings bank, the Caixa Econômica Federal. Despite the achievements of the programme in rolling out more housing stock Biderman et al. (2018) sound a note of caution around the location of the new developments; these are not always conducive to sustainable urban development or the provision of convenient employment opportunities for residents (ibid.)

Having sketched out the changing social and macroeconomic policy landscape, how effective, in truth, were these policy shifts in driving improved poverty and distributional outcomes? Focusing on developments during the first half of 1994–2014 period, Ferreira et al. (2007) argue that the reduction in inequality accounted "for almost half of the decline in the more bottom-sensitive poverty measures, like the squared poverty gap" (p. 2). The fall in inequality, so the authors argue, stemmed from three key factors. The first concerns education, variations in the acquisition of which accounts for something like a third of differences in income between households. Since the returns to education were falling during the period concerned, this helped to drive down inequality. That this was the case has also been established in a range of other high-quality studies (see Firpo & Portella, 2019).

The second key driver relates to Brazil's agricultural revolution. Rising output and productivity in that sector has helped to narrow the gap between urban and rural wages, not only reducing inequality (both interpersonal and regional) but also driving down rural poverty. The third factor driving reduced inequality – and also poverty – has been the expansion in transfer payments. Over the course of the 1994–2004 period, as has been seen, there was a notable multiplication in the number and scale of social programmes. Ferreira et al. (2007) point out that over this decade "the population share receiving income from this source has almost doubled, from 16% to 30%, and inequality among recipients has also fallen" (ibid., p. 3). Forming a background to all these processes, the 1994 to 2014 period witnessed the ending of hyper-inflation thanks to the success of the Real Plan. Thus, an important driver of poverty and inequality was removed from the equation.

Consideration of the ten-year period preceding the introduction of the *Bolsa Família* thus offers obvious evidence that drivers of poverty and inequality (or their reduction) have multifarious drivers connected with the returns to human capital, labour market structures and macroeconomic stabilisation. The provision of an enhanced social safety net therefore must form only part of a broader explanation of inequality and poverty trends. This conclusion, it turns out, also holds when the post 2004, *Bolsa Família* period is considered.

Sotomayor (2019) conducted a major econometric study using data drawn from the Brazilian national household survey to determine the main factors underpinning poverty and inequality trends in the 2000s and early 2010s. The study clearly establishes the role of labour market changes during this period as the prime influence on outcomes. There are a number of elements here. In the first place, increasing labour force participation drove up the number of average incomes per household, i.e. the dependency ratio fell. Added to this effect, and very important according to the author,

> increased educational attainment, with associated earnings growth, accounted for well over half of the post-*Real* Plan reduction in poverty and up to 38% of that taking place during the upturn. Household incomes also grew as a result of changes in skill prices, which explain about a quarter of the fall in the headcount ratio that occurred during the 2000s and the early 2010s.
>
> *(ibid., p. 13)*

In relation to skill prices, the data indicate an interesting process whereby a combination of two factors were at work. In the first place, improved educational attainment meant a greater proportion of households were able to benefit from higher skilled, higher paid employment. However, for those in lower skilled occupations, wage rates were greatly boosted, not only by a tightening labour market[5] but also by sharp increases in the minimum wage,[6] a policy choice that became a hallmark of successive PT administrations. Sotomayor estimates that rises in lower skill prices "were responsible for over 80% of the equalizing skill prices effect" (ibid., p. 13).

The sense that factors around the labour market were the most important source of poverty and inequality reductions is echoed in a study by Ferreira et al. (2017). Examining the 2003–12 period, in particular, the authors find that the predominant drivers[7] of reductions in inequality were connected with reductions in the experience premium. Again, labour market dynamics evolved here in such a way that lower skilled occupations received an earnings boost relative to higher skilled ones. As can be imagined, such a development would tend to favour lower income households, especially given the fact that, during the relevant period, rates of employment were increasing.

A very significant finding from the Ferreira et al. (2017) study surrounds pay differentials relating to gender and ethnicity. Developments here help explain why, as established earlier in this chapter, poverty rates fell especially sharply for women and people of colour over the first decade and a half of this millennium. Ferreira et al. (2017) establish that over this period the urban-rural, male-female and white-non-white wage gaps noticeably narrowed. Why would this have been the case? There are three broad complementary explanations here. In the first place, the recovery of the rural economy, boosted by rising commodity prices and more effective farming practices, drove rural wages upwards at a faster rate than their urban counterparts. Such a development was of particular benefit to the traditionally poorest of Brazil's rural regions, the North East. Here, significantly, the relative concentration of people of colour is higher than the urbanised South and South East. Second, people of colour have traditionally had less access to education than their white counterparts due to discrimination and adverse patterns of educational funding (Rands Barros, 2018). With reductions in the skills premium, this disadvantage, for a while at least, bore down less on earnings. However, Ferreira et al. (2017) also stress the importance of regulatory change affecting labour markets: better enforcement of labour market equality and access provisions over the first decade and a half of this millennium opened up employment opportunities to traditionally disadvantaged population groups. This allowed them to access rapidly rising wages.

As with the general picture surrounding poverty and inequality, positive developments concerning population groups and regions were driven, not only by labour market dynamics but (to a lesser extent) by direct social policy measures. The rise of conditional cash transfer programmes, notably the *Bolsa Família*, exercised a critical influence in lifting people out of extreme poverty (Campello & Neri, 2013) though their role was more marginal in terms of people higher up the income scale, including those upwardly mobile elements who would be termed "the new middle class." However, such programmes undeniably had a strong direct impact on women (who were usually designated as the recipients of this transfer payment) and on the North and Northeast. In relation to the Northeast, by the beginning of the last decade, no fewer than 52% of all transfers connected with the *Bolsa* were directed at the region. It was also the case that, in relation to its modest economic scale, the Northeast region received a disproportionate tranche of federal funding, not only relating to conditional cash transfer programmes, but also connected with public sector employment and infrastructure projects. Such categories of spending rose considerably under the administrations of Presidents Lula and Rousseff, leading to allegations of vote-buying from their political opponents.

Social policy, poverty and inequality: developments since 2014

As evident from earlier in this chapter, the period since 2014 has witnessed a partial reversal of the social progress which has generally marked the past three decades. According to standard headcount measures, the incidence of poverty has increased while there is evidence to suggest that income inequality has been on the rise again. These unwelcome developments have coincided, on the political front, with the unravelling of the broad social democratic consensus that hitherto had characterised successive administrations' approach to social development. The fracturing of the broad coalition for progressive social change alluded to by Alston et al. (2016) was crystallised in the election of President Jair Bolsonaro in October 2018. Since coming to power, the new administration has emphasised the pursuit of economic efficiency rather than pro-poor development as its principal socio-economic objective. To what extent has this shifting policy landscape influenced poverty and distributional outcomes?

In responding to this question, the first point worth noting is that, while the political character of the administration may have changed radically between 2014 and the present there has been little change in the constellation of explicit anti-poverty measures in force. The *Bolsa Família*, the flagship policy of the Lula government, remains in place as do earlier pro-poor reforms, for example, the rural pensions scheme. However, the resources targeted at these initiatives has come under severe strain, especially as a result of the Bolsonaro administration's self-imposed spending cap. In 2019, the government began to control the numbers of new *Bolsa* claimants, leading to the accumulation of a waiting list of those who wished to sign up for the scheme's benefits.

According to one of Brazil's leading quality broadsheet newspapers, the *Folha de São Paulo*, by January 2020 around 1 million families were waiting to have their claims processed with the poorest municipalities particularly badly affected (*Folha de São Paulo*, 10 February 2020). This development comes against a background of cuts in the *Bolsa Família* budget allocation: this was due to shrink from R$32.5bn to R$29.5bn between 2019 and 2020.[8] Other important social programmes such as *Minha Casa, Minha Vida* have also seen funding cut. However, running counter, to these developments has been the passage of a pension reform package in late 2019 (see Chapter 5). This is supposed to have favourable distributional consequences. At the time of writing, however, it was too early to assess whether these have been borne out in reality. In addition, forced to respond to the outbreak of the Corona virus crisis in the first half of 2020, the authorities have boosted spending on the *Bolsa* while introducing an emergency benefit for informal workers.

Putting these developments together, however, it is highly doubtful that they will place Brazil in a stronger position to meet its social challenges. This is especially troubling given the nature of the macroeconomic environment that has been facing Brazil's poorer citizens since 2014. While inflation has fallen to record lows, any favourable impacts need to be set beside the surge in unemployment and contraction in output that accompanied the recession of 2014–17. Recovery for the following two years was weak, with the economy forecast to tip into recession once more in 2020 in the wake of the COVID-19 pandemic. These adverse trends have been strongly associated with rises in poverty and pressure on wage levels. Existing social provision, impacted by spending cuts, has not been sufficient to offset these severe macroeconomic and labour market headwinds. Against this background, it should hardly be surprising that progress on reducing poverty and inequality has come to an effective halt since the middle of the 2010s. The question now is whether progress can be resumed. It is to this issue that we now briefly turn in the conclusions.

Conclusions

This chapter has examined the challenges that Brazil has faced over the long term to ensure that social outcomes match economic progress. Following an era in which tackling poverty and inequality assumed a low priority, the early to mid-1990s saw the start of a two-decade period in which an expansion in the scope of social policy accompanied much improved macroeconomic and labour market conditions. Combined, these factors brought about progressive reductions in poverty and inequality. The evidence strongly suggests that improved employment conditions, above all, were responsible for the progress made, not least in regard to the regional, gender and ethnic dimensions of social development. After 2014, however, the emergence of an economic crisis, combined with declining emphasis on social policy to halt the march towards reduced poverty and inequality.

At the beginning of the 2020s, the question is whether the progress the characterised the 1994–2014 period can be resumed. In very large part, the evidence uncovered in this chapter suggests that this will depend on how quickly the labour market can recover from the twin shocks of the 2014–17 economic crisis and the 2020 COVID-19 pandemic. While one might hope for regained momentum in the social policy sphere, this appears unlikely in the short term given fiscal constraints and the ideological character of the Bolsonaro administration. Leaving these considerations aside, the achievement of better distributional and poverty outcomes will require that attention be paid to a range of other issues that, so far, have remained under-addressed. In particular, a range of structural obstacles to accelerated social progress needs to be overcome. These partly centre on issues discussed elsewhere in this volume, specifically growth volatility

(Chapter 1), unequal access to skills and education (Chapter 3) and the income concentrating effect of state spending (Chapter 5). However, there are some other factors at work which also require a response. They include issues around infrastructure and regional connectedness, crime and security, health and, potentially, land distribution.

Notes

1 See, for example, Abreu (1989).
2 These are as follows according to the relevant report:

> The indicators on quality of health are lost health expectancy, number of physicians, and number of hospital beds. The indicators on quality of education are pupil-teacher ratio in primary schools, primary school teachers trained to teach, percentage of primary (secondary) schools with access to the internet, and the Programme for International Student Assessment (PISA) scores in mathematics, reading and science. The indicators on quality of standard of living are the proportion of employed people engaged in vulnerable employment, the proportion of rural population with access to electricity, the proportion of population using improved drinking water sources, and proportion of population using improved sanitation facilities.
>
> (ibid., p. 7)

3 Translated into English these approximate respectively to Black, Mixed and White, being the three standard ethnic groups employed for statistical purposes by the IBGE's National Household Survey.
4 Which had achieved what amounted to hegemonic status among the Western democracies following the economically orthodox 1980s.
5 Partly connected with, as we have seen, an agricultural renaissance.
6 This rose by around 70% during the economic upturn that followed the start of the 2000s.
7 In fact, accounting for two-thirds of the reduction in the Gini.
8 But will probably not due to the Coronavirus pandemic (see below).

8

ENVIRONMENTAL CONSIDERATIONS

Of all the pressing issues facing Brazil, those surrounding the environment are, from an international perspective at least, probably the highest profile. There are some good reasons for this. Above all, Brazilian national territory embraces a large portion of the most biodiverse region on earth, the Amazon basin. Within this unique biological sphere reside countless thousand species of plants, animals, birds and insects. This represents an endowment far richer than any to be found in the temperate latitudes of North America, Europe or Asia. To add to this priceless heritage, the Amazonian region is home to a wide range of indigenous peoples, each with their own languages, culture and customs.

As is universally recognised, however, the Amazon basin is among the most threatened natural habitats on Earth. It has suffered consistent depredation. This has occurred as Brazil's agricultural frontier has extended, the mining sector has expanded, and informal settlement by outsiders have permeated even its remotest corners. The threat to biodiversity, in and of itself, is a pressing problem for the planet. However, in recent years, this threat has become enmeshed with another concern. This centres on the fact that depletion of the Amazonian rainforest is diminishing one of the globe's great carbon sinks. This, in turn, is actively accelerating the progress of climate change. At the same time, increasing settlement of the Amazon basin by outsiders threatens the way of life, and even the existence, of indigenous peoples. In contrast to newcomers, the latter have constructively co-existed with their environment for thousands of years.

While the fate of the Amazon commands most global attention, Brazil presents a range of other pressing environment concerns. In relation to the biodiversity theme, the Amazon is far from the only threatened, naturally rich biome within Brazil's national frontiers. To take one example, in the West of the country, Brazil plays host to one of the world's most extensive and biodiverse wetland areas in the world, the Pantanal. To take another, along the Atlantic coast a unique stretch of tropical forest, the *Mata Atlântica*, forms another important – and much depleted – natural habitat.

Environmental issues extend, of course, beyond biodiversity and climate change. There exist other areas of concern. A long-established environmental preoccupation surrounds air pollution, principally from transportation and industrial sources. The scope of this has long been troubling, especially in terms of its impact on public health and social development in Brazil's sprawling megalopolises. In addition, pollution of soils and river systems has long proved an unfortunate adjunct of industrial, agricultural and mining activity. The 2019 environmental disaster following the failure of a mine tailings dam in Brumadinho, Minas Gerais state, is a case in point.

All of these issues suggest (to put it at its mildest) that the development process in Brazil has not always fully taken into account its broader environmental impacts. Against this background, the purpose of this chapter will be to examine the environmental consequences of Brazil's economic emergence. Particular emphasis will be placed on the role of public policy. Here, an attempt is made to assess the success encountered by regulation and enforcement to mitigate the impacts of economic development on the broader natural environment. To achieve this objective, this chapter adopts the following structure.

Following this introduction, the chapter begins by briefly analysing the changing profile of the environment in Brazil's development process. Despite initial attempts to protect sensitive forested areas in the 1930s, by and large, environmental considerations occupied a marginal position in the policy calculus surrounding Brazil's decision to pursue structural transformation of its economy. This section of the chapter goes on to show how this began to change from the 1980s onwards, coincident with the return to civilian rule. The past 30 years have seen far more concerted attempts to mitigate the environmental impacts of economic development, though as the discussion makes clear, progress has been far from steady. This especially applies to the period following the eruption of economic crisis in Brazil in 2013–14.

Having sketched out the broad evolution of the development-environment nexus over the long term, the chapter then turns its attention to three critical environmental themes. The objective here centres on evaluating Brazil's performance in each area, with consideration being given to evaluating the effectiveness of policy measures. The key environmental topics to be reviewed in this section comprise biodiversity and deforestation, the energy mix and climate change. By way of a conclusion, the chapter considers the likely trajectory of environmental policy over the medium to long term, and whether the adverse trends currently being experienced are likely to be reversed.

The role of the environment in Brazil's development process over the long term – a brief overview

For a very long time, the environmental impacts of progress and structural transformation occupied a marginal position in the public and policy debate in

Brazil surrounding the development process. As in the case of critical social issues around poverty and access to education, environmental considerations were
subordinated to a determination to engender industrialisation, rapid urbanisation
and a reshaped role for Brazil in the international division of labour. Why was
this the case? One explanation relates to the economic paradigms which helped
frame policy decisions. The structuralist school of thought, which dominated
economic thinking in Brazil from World War II to the 1980s, took surprisingly
little account of the environmental consequences of rapid economic growth. In
one sense, this is not surprising since, unlike neoclassical economics, the structuralist paradigm does not possess a rigorous framework to account for externalities.[1] The presence of such a framework would have allowed for a more explicit
calculus of the social – including environmental – costs of development. Instead,
structuralist economists and policymakers predominantly focused on the nar-
rower economic (rather than environmental) benefits alleged to arise from rapid
industrialisation (Bielschowsky, 1988).

The subordination of environmental considerations to the pursuit of economic progress was not simply a function of the hegemony of a particular economic paradigm. It was also the product of the constellation of political forces
and interests. These were at work during the period stretching from the *Estado
Novo* in the 1930s to the return to civilian rule in the mid-1980s. There are a
number of dimensions to this. In the first place, up until the late 1960s and 1970s
an environmental consciousness movement had yet to meaningfully evolve at
the national or global level. Elements of civil society who would come together
and advocate in favour of environmental sustainability had still to coalesce. At
the same time, a strong axis of shared interests binding industrialists, the political
leadership and technocrats steered policymaking in favour of industrial and infrastructural development (Schneider, 2004).

The bias in favour of industrial developmentalism found its keenest expression in the expansion of Brazil's energy infrastructure. In particular, the period
stretching from the 1950s to the 1980s, would see a vast increase in Brazil's
hydro-electric generating capacity, much of it encroaching on environmentally sensitive areas (Souza Braga, 2020). Such was the strategic imperative of
the pursuit of hydro-electric capacity that the state itself, either through federally or state government-controlled energy utilities, directly commissioned
the construction of dams and related infrastructure. In the Amazon basin, in
particular, the pursuit of hydroelectric projects formed part of a wider scheme
to open up the region to development. Hence, in the 1950s and 1960s the Free
Trade Zone of Manuas (Zona Franca de Manaus) was founded in the Amazon's
largest settlement with the intention of kickstarting industrial development.
The Zone would go on to evolve into a national centre for electronics production and light manufacturing. More notoriously, 1972 saw the inauguration
of BR 230, the Trans Amazonian highway, a 4,000 km long road eventually
designed to link the Northeast coast, to Manuas, and onwards to Boa Vista
in the West. The highway became internationally criticised for its impact on
deforestation.

Given the fact that such projects did arouse hostility, at least in the minds of affected communities, it might be expected that active opposition might have built up to them. To a limited extent this is true. Still, for many years, opposition was held severely in check by the fact that Brazil had ceased to be a pluralist, representative democracy. As Souza Braga (2020) points out, the role of the military in quashing dissent proved a critical component in Brazil's drive towards hydroelectricity in the 1960s and 1970s. The containment and management of potential opposition, more often than not, comprised an extensive propaganda campaign rather than the meting out of heavy-handed repression (ibid.).

Although protection of the environment was never a key priority during Brazil's industrialisation process, it is worth pointing out that there were a few legislative developments which would later form the basis for a more comprehensive policy approach. Moura (2016) highlights, the two best known, respectively, the Código de Águas (Water Code) and the Código Florestal (Forest Code). Both these measures, dating from 1934, provided a rudimentary level of environmental protection. The Water Code expressly forbid development which would pollute wells or springs while the Forest Code mandated that owners of forested land would be obliged to maintain 50% of it (later 80%) untouched. Enforcement of the Forest Code was, however, far from always effective. By the 1970s, growing global and national environmental consciousness had even begun to filter through to the military government, which, as the decade wore on, gradually loosened its repressive grip on society and allowed Congress to reconvene. In 1973 an important milestone was accomplished when the Federal Government for the first time established an agency dedicated to environmental issues. The agency, termed Secretaria Especial de Meio Ambiente (Special Secretariat for the Environment) would spawn parallel bodies at the state and local level (ibid., p. 15).

Despite these developments, it was not until the 1980s and 1990s that environmental considerations were more fully factored into strategy regarding Brazil's development process. This period marked the dawn of a far more comprehensive policy framework, characterised by additional monitoring and enforcement bodies, fresh legislation and growing activism on environmental matters by the Brazilian government in international fora. As if to mark Brazil's more serious commitment to the environment, Brazil's first popularly elected administration in three decades co-organised and hosted the Rio Earth Summit in 1992 (ibid.).

What factors account for this striking change of direction? The most obvious driver here was the transition to civilian rule after 1985. As a result of this, the administration was far more directly accountable to an increasingly environmentally aware population than had been the case under the military. At the same time, the domestic political profile of environmental issues had been steadily rising for years, partly as a result of consciousness raising by activists and non-governmental organisations. Two high profile *cause celèbres* also stood as rallying points for popular opinion. One was the national and international outrage caused by the assassination of renowned Amazonian environmentalist and rubber tapper, Chico Mendes in 1988. The other surrounded the fate of residents of the town of Cubatão, an industrial centre close to the Port of Santos in São Paulo state. By the 1980s, levels of pollution from nearby petrochemical complexes had become so severe that birth defects and chronic ill health had come to plague the community. On top of this, in 1984, an oil spill resulted in a fire which caused the death of over 90 residents. Unlike events in the Amazon, those in Cubatão were located in the heart of Brazil's developed and industrialised South East and were harder for the political and business elite to ignore.

Also of relevance to the growing profile of environmental issues, at a time when a newly democratic Brazil was opening up to foreign trade and investment, decision-makers and voters alike became much more susceptible to the currents of international opinion. Against this background, the influence of international NGOs and foreign governments became more salient in the domestic policy discourse surrounding the environment. Finally, it is worth pointing out that, by the early 1990s, the structuralist paradigm which had hitherto framed the economic policymaking process was in abeyance. The rise of more orthodox approaches created space for more formal consideration of the negative externalities generated by Brazil's development strategy.

Given the change in political and global context in from the 1980s onwards, what were the main changes in policy terms? The most significant institutional development at the federal level was the unification of previously separate bodies. Agencies charged with environmental supervision of forests, rubber cultivation, fisheries and general environment oversight were combined into one mega-agency, IBAMA (Instituto Brasileiro do Meio Ambiente e dos Recursos Naturais – Brazilian Institute for the Environment and Natural Resources) in 1989. At the same time, and in keeping with the decentralising ethos of Brazil's 1988 Constitution, a series of environmental licensing, monitoring and enforcement bodies were created at state and municipal level (ibid., p. 17). In 1991, with support from the World Bank, a new programme, the Programa Nacional do Meio Ambiente (National Environment Programme), was introduced with the aim of providing the financial means to enable critical federal environmental projects. Underscoring the new political priority ascribed to environmental issue, 1992 (the last year in office for President Collor de Melo) saw the creation of the MMA, the Ministério do Meio Ambiente (Environment Ministry).

Beyond institutional innovation and restructuring, the past three decades have seen some very important developments in policy terms. Further details of these initiatives and their results will be revealed later in this chapter but for the time being it is worth providing a broad overview of the key measures introduced. Among the most significant was legislation passed in 1997 updating the Código das Águas and tightening up its provisions surrounding pollution and conservation. The legislation accompanied the creation of a new regulatory body, the Agência Nacional das Águas (National Water Agency), reflecting the fact that provision of water and sewerage services was, thanks to the privatisation programme, increasingly in the hands of privatised operators.

The new millennium saw an acceleration in the pace of environmental legislation with the focus, in particular, centring on conservation of rainforest areas and their biodiverse habitats. The landmark legislation in this respect was 2012's new Forest Code. In particular, this extended protection of forested land in private hands. In the case of the Amazon region private landowners would now be required to set aside 80% of their forested land in its natural state compared with 20% for the rest of the country (Machado, 2016). The Forest Code, reflecting advances in technology, also introduced an electronic registration and satellite monitoring system, allowing a database of land use to be created. This system, known as SICAR (Sistema Nacional de Cadastro Ambiental Rural – National Rural Environmental Registration System) forms a core means of regulating land use in environmentally sensitive areas.

Two other pieces of legislation are also worth briefly noting at this point. First, and of significance for the maritime environment,[2] and reflecting the liberalisation of the oil exploration and production sector, Law 9966 of 2000 set out a legal and regulatory framework tasked with preventing pollution generated by the expanding offshore industry. Second, and of growing relevance as Brazil entered the 2010s, Law 12187 of 2009 created the legal framework for the establishment of a national policy on climate change.

Since 2015 it is noteworthy that the pace of environmental legislation has slowed considerably. The current administration of President Bolsonaro has proven sceptical of the climate change agenda pursued by its predecessors and has cut funding for projects in this area. At one point it appeared likely that the Environment Ministry (MMA) would be extinguished or folded into another ministry; however, at the time of writing this development had not materialised. Among the very few environmental initiatives to get off the ground since the election of the new administration in 2018 has been one discouraging littering. It can be argued that this represents, from the perspective of powerful producer interest groups, a relatively uncontroversial and benign policy development.

Brazil's environmental track record and the role of public policy

The previous section sketched out in broad terms the changing priority ascribed to the environment in Brazil's development process over the long term. Having accomplished this, the discussion now turns to an evaluation of Brazil's environmental performance in recent years and the possible relationships this has with the evolution of public policy. To start with, the analysis centres on the critical theme of biodiversity and deforestation.

Biodiversity and deforestation

Despite environmental depredation Brazil remains the most biodiverse country on Earth hosting, it is estimated, 12–15% of all known species (OECD, 2015).

The most biodiverse of all zones centre on forested land which accounts for almost two thirds of the national territory. Of all the forested areas, by far the largest is represented by the Amazonian basin, though the Mata Atlântica, the Atlantic Forest, remains of significance, accounting for 13% of Brazil's land area, as opposed to 49% for the Amazon (ibid.). The global significance of Brazil's forests is hard to overstate. In addition to their rich endowment of lifeforms, they also act as a major absorber of carbon. As previously mentioned, the Amazon also forms home for thousands of indigenous people, with unique cultures, languages and customs. In many cases, these communities have had little contact with the outside world and continue to pursue their traditional lifestyles. In and of itself, this represents a priceless facet of humankind's common heritage. However, as is universally recognised, Brazil's forests, their communities and natural habitats have for long been under assault. Since 1990, a year which marked the effective start of Brazil's trade and market liberalisation policies, approximately 10% of forested land has been lost. What general forces have been behind this process?

In order to answer this question, it is important to bear in mind that Brazil's forests, the Amazonian biome, in particular, present rich commercial opportunities for those willing to endure the logistical, health and security challenges implicit in operating there. There is nothing especially new about this. In the late 19th century the Amazon basin became, for a while, the world's leading centre for rubber production, a development which encouraged urban expansion (in Manuas and Belém) and the expansion of river and even rail transportation in the region (De Paula, 1982). Later on, in the 20th century, the Ford Motor Corporation would try to shift rubber production in the region away from traditional tapping towards plantation and systematised cultivation. However, this venture was not a success. In any event, by that stage the global centre of production had shifted to the Malay Peninsula. Despite the decline of the rubber sector, as the 20th century progressed, commercial exploitation of the Amazon increased apace. This development had three main sectoral dimensions, centring on agricultural, energy and mining activities.

Mueller and Mueller (2016) in analysing the remarkable success of Brazilian agriculture – at least in terms of productivity and boosting global market share-point out that one of the key features of the process resided in an expansion of the agricultural frontier. For certain crops, for example, soya, this involved cultivation in the hitherto largely unexploited tropical savannah region known in Brazil as the *Cerrado*. The *Cerrado* itself represents an important biodiverse habitat. However, the growth of soya cultivation enhanced the availability of an important animal feedstock and opened up the possibility of stepping up ranching and beef production in more marginal areas. Once again, expansion of the agricultural frontier resulted. Partly thanks to improving transportation infrastructure cattle rearing could be potentially accomplished – following forest clearance – in the Amazon. Hence, as Walker and Moran (2000) point out the Amazonian region witnessed in the final half of the 20th century a significant rise in ranching and, associated forest clearance. This was not only accomplished by large concerns; small scale family enterprises also became involved.

Besides agriculture, the other key encroachment of economic development into the Amazonian rainforest centred on Brazil's expanding hydroelectric programme. Further details of this are set out later in this chapter. However, for the time being suffice to say that in a number of locations, from the Tucuraí to the giant Balbina projects, dam infrastructure has changed patterns of water flow as well as opening up previously remote regions to external development. The expansion of attempts to tap the water resource of the Amazonian region for energy generation accelerated notably after the military government's adoption of the Second National Development Plan (PNDII) in 1974 (Souza Braga, 2020).

Whereas hydroelectric projects represent the outcomes of state policy, the Amazonian region has also been threatened by smaller-scale, often informal, private ventures. This particularly applies to the case of gold mining and logging. Here, activities are frequently carried out illegally, in defiance of increasingly rigorous legislation. By the 1990s there were more than 1 million *garimpeiros* (informal miners) located in mining camps throughout the Brazilian Amazon (Barreto et al., 2006). The impacts of the mining sector are considerable. Sonter et al. (2017) estimate that between 2005 and 2015 9% of all Amazonian deforestation can be attributed to mining activities. The area of cleared land here represents more than ten times the actual extent of the mining leases themselves, reflecting the broader impacts mining has in terms of leading to the development of ancillary infrastructure and human settlement (ibid.). Besides deforestation, a particular problem stemming from the mining operations was mercury pollution, a by-product of the refining process (Barreto et al., 2006).

From the discussion so far, the impression may have been created that, in the face of relentless commercial exploitation, the process of accelerating deforestation is inevitable and unstoppable. However, such an impression would be misleading. Examining Figure 8.1 it becomes apparent that between around 2004 and 2015, the rate of deforestation slowed dramatically.

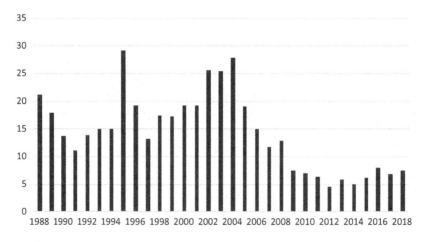

FIGURE 8.1 Rate of deforestation (1,000s sq. km per year).
Source: Author elaboration from INPE data.

What factors lay behind this process? The first major driver of declining rates of deforestation centred on better regulatory and legal frameworks and more rigorous enforcement of the related legislation. With the advent of the administration of President Lula in 2003, environmental protection assumed a much higher political priority, a factor which was to endure under his successor, Dilma Rousseff. One product of this, as already discussed was a radically revised and strengthened Forest Code, introduced in 2012. However, over the 2000s more policy initiatives came into play, for example, 2004's Action Plan for Combating Deforestation in the Amazon. Integrating federal, state and municipal agencies the plan, using satellite imagery data, provided for real time monitoring of deforestation. It also enabled law enforcement officials to be rapidly sent to areas where breaches of legislation were taking place (ibid.). Compared with previous attempts to check deforestation, the new framework had real "teeth" and proved far more pro-active. An important quantitative study conducted by Assunção et al. (2015) attempted to gauge the impact of government policies on the observed decline in deforestation after 2004 and concluded that they were significant. On the basis of simulations, the authors suggest that some 73,000 km^2 of forest, which otherwise would have disappeared, were protected between 2005 and 2009 as a result of policy shifts. However, the authors also point to the role of softening commodity prices, which would have diminished the economic viability of clearing forest to engage in primary production.

Whereas in the middle of the 2010s it appeared that deforestation was under an unprecedented measure of control, more recent developments suggest a more troubling turn of events. As the data in Figure 8.1 indicate, the pace of deforestation has begun to accelerate once more: between 2014 and 2018 the annual total of forested land cleared rose from 5,000 to 7,500 km^2. Between August 2018 and July 2019 alone, deforestation rose by 30% compared with the same period a year earlier: the highest net loss since 2008 (*New York Times*, 18 November 2019). As part of this process, over the course of 2019 a series of ferocious forest fires affected the region. These events drew wide international attention and, indeed, condemnatory comments from the French President, Emanuel Macron.

What factors might be at work in explaining this surge in deforestation? In the first place, apart from anything else, recent trends suggest that the weight of legislation alone is not sufficient to keep deforestation from accelerating. Compared with the late 1990s and early 2000s, when deforestation was also gaining pace, the legislative frameworks and monitoring systems are now considerably better developed. Therefore, explanations other than inadequate regulation need to be sought. These focus on the political environment, the level of enforcement, general economic conditions and climatic variation.

In terms of the political environment, there is no doubt that the administration of Jair Bolsonaro, elected in 2018, is closer to the interests of the agricultural and mining sectors than were its three predecessors. Against this background, and with fresh spending curbs in place, it is perhaps not coincidental that the power and capacity of environmental agencies has recently been weakened. According to a Human Rights Watch Report issued in September 2019[3] the weakening of the state[4] has coincided with a new phase of deforestation where criminal gangs and networks have become important instigators of the deforestation process. Such groups have been connected with 28 deaths as they have enforced their will. Elements of civil society – including indigenous people – resisting the clearances have been targeted by these criminal bands. Given the remoteness of locations, corruption and the resource challenges facing overstretched law enforcement agencies, investigations leading to the arrest and conviction of perpetrators are rendered especially challenging.

Depending on one's political standpoint, it may be tempting to lay the blame for accelerated deforestation entirely at the door of the Bolsonaro administration. Of course, the reality is inevitably more complex. In particular, it is important to note that the start of the rise in deforestation coincided with the entry of the Brazilian economy into crisis around 2014–15. This development occurred under a political leadership considerably more attuned to environmental concerns than its successors. While rigorous studies relating to the drivers of recent deforestation have yet to emerge, it seems likely that the onset of economic crisis, in triggering increased marginality and deprivation, may have increased the incentive for many to engage in illegal forest clearance. Certainly, it is the case that informal mining and agriculture represent options for those who have lost livelihoods in the formal sector. Another important factor to take into account centres on climatic variation, whether man-made or otherwise. In this connection it is important to note that the surge in forest fires in 2019 came in the wake of unusually dry conditions.

Beyond the issue of deforestation lie other threats to biodiversity in Brazil. In particular, the country plays host to one of the world's richest habitats for aquatic life, being the location for the world's largest contiguous mangrove swamps (OECD, 2015, p. 193). However, something like a quarter of these have been lost and only 1.5% of marine areas are subject to protective measures (ibid.). Brazil's biodiverse littoral has come under intense pressure over the past two decades in response to increased coastal development. Some of this, especially in the North East, has resulted from state-driven projects to improve port infrastructure and ramp up oil refining capacity. In many ways, Brazil's threatened coastlines represent a new frontier for conservation. Partly to safeguard marine biodiversity, but also to protect valuable offshore natural resources, the Brazilian Navy in 2004 designated an area stretching 200 km offshore as an exclusive economic zone. This has been branded the Amazônia Azul (Blue Amazon) (Weisebron, 2013). In practice, it would appear that the focus of state policy, in terms of resources committed, has focused on the development of offshore oil reserves, especially around deposits to be found in the pre-salt layer off the South East coast. Practical marine conservation measures have struggled to catch up with the pace of exploitation of marine resources, whether in terms of hydrocarbons, or in terms of fishing (where the catch rose by no less than 15% between 2000 and 2013) (OECD, 2015, p. 193).

Turning to the broader picture of biodiversity, an important and troubling indicator is presented by the incidence of threatened species. Of over 12,000 fauna species that were examined, 1,173 were assessed as threatened in 2014 according to data reported by the OECD's 2015 Environmental Performance Review of Brazil. These included "110 mammal, 234 bird and 409 marine and freshwater fish species" (ibid., p. 195). Regarding threatened plant species, in terms of biome, the most challenged area was not the Amazon but rather the Atlantic Forest where just over 40% of species were deemed to be at risk. This compares with an equivalent figure of just under 20%, still a huge and worrying proportion, for the Amazon itself. With regard to these forest habitats, the concern must be that following the increase in the pace of deforestation since 2014, the proportion of threatened species must have increased. This would have occurred despite targeted initiatives to safeguard threatened species launched around the turn of the last decade.

The energy mix and the role of renewable energy sources

Given Brazil's poor environmental image globally, it is perhaps surprising that it has succeeded more than most large economies in developing renewable and low-carbon energy sources. In 2016 around 44% of all energy was generated from renewable sources compared with a world average of just 14% (Balança Energetica Nacional – National Energy Balance (BEN), 2018). However, examining data trends over time, it becomes apparent that, while overall production of renewables has been rapidly increasing since 1990, it is also the case that production of non-renewables – specifically oil and gas – has also sharply increased. Indeed, this has happened at such a pace that the overall share of renewables in the national energy matrix has slightly declined, from 47.9% to 44.2% (Table 8.1).

Examining the issue of electricity production more specifically, a particular – and longstanding feature – of Brazil's energy mix becomes apparent: the central role of hydroelectricity. According to data presented in the 2018 edition of the National Energy Balance, in 2017, 65.2% of all electricity was generated by hydro sources with nuclear, oil, wind and solar, biomass, natural gas and coal accounting for, respectively, 2.6%, 2.5%, 6.9%, 8.2%, 10.5% and 4.1%. Thus, in

TABLE 8.1 Energy production by source Brazil, selected years (Ktoe)

Year	Coal	Natural gas	Nuclear	Hydro	Biofuels and waste	Oil	Wind, solar, etc.	Total	Percent renewables [a]
1990	9,671	3,334	583	17,774	47,765	58,894	0	138,021	47.9
2000	13,015	8,131	1,575	26,174	46,626	88,228	138	183,749	40.6
2010	14,468	23,666	3,784	34,677	81,607	104,729	3,653	266,584	46.4
2017	16,783	32,526	4,101	31,892	86,450	110,721	4,549	287,022	44.2

Source: Author elaboration based on data from IEA World Energy Balances 2019.
a Hydroelectric, biofuels and waste, wind and solar.

respect of electricity generation, Brazil leans more heavily towards the utilisation of renewable sources than is the case for other usage categories, for example, transport. What factors help explain patterns of renewable energy development in Brazil, and is the role of renewables likely to increase over the future as the global quest to tackle climate change unfolds?

The centrepiece of Brazil's movement towards greater use of renewable energy sources has been its hydroelectricity programme. Interestingly, development of this on a large scale began in the 1950s. This was some time before environmental considerations were to become a primary motivation driving the use of cleaner forms of energy worldwide. In the case of Brazil, significant investments in hydroelectric power schemes emerged as part of the country's industrialisation strategy. They reflected the fact that, besides possessing many suitable locations for the construction of dams and associated infrastructure, Brazil had not at the time developed large scale on or offshore oil and gas reserves. In developing the capacity to supply energy to an increasingly urbanised, industrialised nation, hydroelectric power held the potential to generate significant recurrent savings in terms of energy imports. As time went on, the state became an increasingly important actor in the hydro-electric programme, especially following the formation of the federally owned Eletrobrás generation and transmission utility in 1961 (Leite, 2014).

Under the military government and its Second National Development Plan of 1974 the pace of hydroelectricity project development increased. Why was this? Aside from opening up remote areas of the country to development (a strategic objective), increasing the supply of electricity from local renewable sources promised to constrain further oil and gas imports, at the time cripplingly expensive. As a result of these developments and the continued high priority ascribed to hydro-electric schemes following the end of military rule, installed capacity rose from approximately 10,000 to 62,000 gigawatts between 1970 and 2000. By 2015 capacity had risen further to around 80,000 gigawatts.[5]

However, as is clear from the data in Table 8.1, the share of hydropower in Brazil's national energy matrix has not risen over the past 30 years. Part of the reason for this centres on the fact that the development of hydroelectric schemes is now facing more environmental opposition than was the case in the military period (Souza Braga, 2020). This is best exemplified in the case of the Belo Monte dam project where NGOs and local people mounted effective opposition to the scheme, ultimately reducing the size of the reservoir area it encompassed. However, another factor relates to the role of climatic variation. During the 2012 to 2014 period Brazil experienced particularly dry conditions with rainfall well below recent averages. This encouraged the construction and activation of thermal power plants which proved increasingly necessary to help meet surging demand for electricity. The development of thermal sources for electricity generation had been encouraged by the liberalisation of the electricity generation, transmission and distribution sectors in the 1990s. Opened up to private (often foreign multinational) participants with experience in the thermal field, these new players were able to take advantage of more readily available gas thanks to accelerating national production and imports from Bolivia.

Another important factor in constraining the relative expansion of hydroelectric power in the overall national energy balance has been the rise in biofuels, especially sugar cane-derived ethanol. As Table 8.1 indicates, energy output generated through biofuels and waste approximately doubled in absolute terms between 1990 and 2017. As in the case of hydroelectricity, the roots of Brazil's biofuel boom can be traced back to an earlier era, the 1970s, when policymakers, rather than pursuing any environmental goal were seeking to reduce the coefficient of oil imports. The PROALCOOL programme, launched during this era, provided subsidies for ethanol-based fuels for road vehicles. Working in conjunction with the programme, Brazil's (foreign enterprise-controlled) automotive industry developed engines that could run on pure ethanol or a blended combination of ethanol and gasoline. During the 1970s and 1980s production of ethanol rapidly expanded, though by the 1990s and early 2000s the technical limitations of pure ethanol engines had resulted in a drop off in sales of vehicles using these powerplants (Stolf et al., 2020). The industry responded by developing a new generation of flex fuel vehicles, which using better fuel injection and combustion technology, could avoid some of the performance penalties associated with earlier technologies. As a result, sales and production of ethanol have managed to hold their own. Indeed, according to Goldemberg (2018), by 2003 "ethanol became fully competitive with gasoline without any subsidies" (p. 365).

However, the most dramatic change over the last 30 years has related not to production of renewables but rather to a sharp rise in Brazil's capacity to extract and refine hydrocarbon fuels domestically. The pursuit of greater domestic production of oil and gas has been a strategic priority of consecutive administrations, stretching from the military governments of the 1970s and 1980s to the present day. Contreras (1993) and later Paduan (2016) both provide very engaging accounts surrounding the central role of Brazil's state-controlled oil company, Petrobrás, in this process.

Starting in the 1970s but accelerating in the following three decades, Petrobrás and, later, foreign oil multinationals would open up onshore and offshore oil and gas fields. With respect to offshore oil exploration and production, the technical challenges involved were particularly daunting given the deep water in which the bulk of Brazil's reserves are encountered in the Campos, Espirito Santo and Santos Basins, off the South Eastern coast. Progress in developing these fields was sufficiently impressive that by 2006, Brazil had for the first time became self-sufficient in oil. While a booming economy caused oil demand to outstrip growing domestic supply from 2007 to 2012, by 2013 Brazil had once again achieved the long-sought goal of self-sufficiency. By 2019 annual oil production had surpassed 1 billion barrels for the first time, assisted by the coming on stream of the recently developed pre-salt reserves (*Folha de São Paulo*, 23 January 2020). Alongside the boom in oil production, Brazil was able to develop domestic supplies of natural gas: by 2019 annual production had reached 44.7bn cubic meters (ibid.). These impressive figures were achieved despite the internal disruption to Petrobrás investment projects in the wake of the *Lava Jato* corruption scandal.

Considering Brazil's recent energy trends in the round, it become obvious that, given the strategic priority ascribed to developing the hydrocarbons sector, there are clear limits to the extent to which the role of renewables in the national energy mix can increase. The pre-salt fields, in particular, are relatively immature and offer considerable scope for further development. Also, with hydrocarbons prices falling to near record lows in the wake of the 2020 Covid-19 global pandemic, the economic attractiveness of renewables will be diminished at least in the short term.

Climate change

Brazil was an early and enthusiastic participant in global agreements to combat climate change. The Rio Earth Summit in 1992 gave rise to the United Nations Framework Convention on Climate Change (UNFCC) which Brazil was the first country to sign (Ludeña & Netto, 2011, p. 6). Later, in 2009, the administration of President Lula succeeded in passing legislation (Law 12187) which mandated voluntary limits on greenhouse gas emissions. These were scheduled to fall by 36.1–38.9% by 2020 (ibid.). In 2016, despite the end of PT government and the accession to office of a centre-right figure, President Michel Temer, Brazil once again illustrated its commitment to climate multilateralism and international cooperation by signing the Paris Agreement within the United Nations Framework Convention on Climate Change.

This agreement required on Brazil's part that it emitted no more than 1.3 giga tonnes of carbon dioxide by 2025, this to include the impacts of Land Use, Land Use Change and Forestry (LULUCF). Excluding LULUCF related emissions, the agreement requires Brazil by 2025 to emit carbon dioxide at no more than 5% and 75% above 2010 and 1990 levels, respectively. For 2030 the target ceilings are more demanding still: carbon dioxide emissions should not exceed 58% above 1990 levels and 6% below 2010 levels. Despite scepticism towards the Paris Agreement, the Bolsonaro administration has not withdrawn from it and the official position is that Brazil remains committed to meet the obligations undertaken.

At first sight, given the rapid growth of Brazil's economy (up until 2013–14) and ongoing deforestation, meeting these carbon emissions targets might seem an unlikely prospect. In fact, and perhaps surprisingly, Brazil's track record has not been unfavourable. Some summary statistics serve to illustrate this point. Taking into account LULUCF, CO_2 emissions in Brazil rose from 823 million tonnes (MT) in 1990 to 2679 MT in 2004. However, subsequently, emissions fell sharply, reaching 290 MT in 2012 before picking up somewhat to 353 MT in 2018.[6] The key factor underpinning this comparatively favourable performance (at least between 2004 and 2012) was the successful mitigation of forest clearance-related emissions (Viola & Franchini, 2019).

As seen earlier in this chapter, better legislation and more effective enforcement exercised a significant impact on deforestation, helping by extension to constrain emissions. Subsequent to 2012, however, a pick up in the pace of deforestation has accompanied a modest rise in CO_2 emissions. Also of concern, if one excludes the impact of forestry, then CO_2 emission levels have generally (modestly) risen over time. Between 1990 and 2014, such emissions rose from 563 to 1,080 MT before falling back to 1,013 MT in 2018. Where do these trends leave Brazil in terms of meeting its obligations under the Paris Agreement? Attending the Madrid Climate Summit in late 2019, Brazil's climate minister Ricardo Salles, was quoted by Reuters as saying that Brazil had already met most of its commitment to cut CO_2 emissions by 37% in relation to 2005 levels (Reuters, December 2, 2019). However, the recent reversal of favourable trends concerning emissions (taking into account LULUCF) must call this into question, especially given the probable impact of severe forest fires in 2019.

Looking ahead more broadly, it is clear that Brazil's success in combatting global climate change will hinge in large part on its success in slowing the pace of deforestation and in mitigating the effects of deforestation where this does take place. While it is true that, compared to most major economies, Brazil enjoys a high incidence of low carbon dioxide-emitting energy sources in its energy mix,[7] the hydrocarbons sector has experienced rapid expansion in recent years. At the same time, it is clear that future expansion of hydro-electric power generation will encounter more political and environmental obstacles than it did in the past. Thus, adherence to international agreements on climate change is likely to offer yet another major challenge to policymakers.

Conclusions

This chapter has illustrated the challenges which Brazil has repeatedly encountered in reconciling economic development with environmental sustainability. The squaring of this circle is always difficult in any setting. This is doubly so in Brazil given its pivotal global role as a hub of biodiversity and location for much of the Amazon, the world's greatest rainforest. For much of its history, Brazil lacked a systematic, properly enforced policy framework to help balance the competing interests of economic progress and environmental protection. Once embarked on a path of rapid industrialisation in the mid-20th century, the result was environmental depredation on a huge scale. Large swathes of the Amazon, the Atlantic Forest and other valuable habitats were lost to development, whether in the form of human settlement, extractive activities or the ever-advancing agricultural frontier. As this process unfolded, so greenhouse gas emissions rose while air, soil and water pollution became critical issues in urban, as well as many rural locations.

Fortunately, from the 1970s onwards growing environmental awareness helped prompt the development of a more robust legislative, institutional and enforcement framework. Progress here reached its apogee in the 2000s and 2010s.

This period saw broadly successful initiatives aimed at countering deforestation, loss in biodiversity and rising carbon dioxide emissions. At the same time, thanks to earlier investment in hydroelectricity and biofuels, Brazil came to enjoy – by global standards – very significant sources of renewable energy.

Since the mid-2010s though, the picture has darkened. While earlier legislation remains in place its enforcement has been undermined by budget cuts and reduced political commitment. Consequently, rates of deforestation have climbed while available evidence suggests that carbon dioxide emissions have risen in tandem. At the same time, partly thanks to the boom in hydrocarbons exploration and production, a limit may have been reached with respect to the participation of renewables in the overall energy mix.

Does the future hold out any prospect of a return to a greater emphasis on environmental sustainability? The answer rests largely on political developments, both in terms of the domestic sphere, but also in terms of the weight of international pressure that might be brought to bear on the current and future administrations. At the start of the 2020s economic pressures (partly induced by the COVID-19 pandemic), have pushed environmental issues down the list of political priorities. This, of course, is in the context of an administration already lukewarm (at best) towards this area of policy. In this connection, pressure exerted by international opinion and domestic environmental advocates will be especially important in enhancing the profile of issues such as deforestation and climate change in the minds of Brazil's political leadership. In the longer term, after elections in 2022, it is possible that a fresh, more centrist administration may come to power. If so, a renewed policy commitment to environmental sustainability could emerge. Brazil could then once more fully engage with the complex task of reconciling economic progress with environmental responsibility and protection of its priceless natural heritage.

Notes

1 For an extensive discussion of the structuralist paradigm, see Kay (1989).
2 Sometimes referred to in Brazil as the Amazônia Azul or Blue Amazon.
3 *Rainforest Mafias: How Violence and Impunity Fuel Deforestation in Brazil's Amazon*, New York: Human Rights Watch, September 2019.
4 The number of IBAMA field investigators, for example, halved from 1,600 to less than 800 between 2009 and 2019.
5 Data provided by Empresa de Pesquisa Energética (EPE).
6 Data Source: Climate Analytics and the New Climate Institute – Climate Tracker.
7 Principally thanks to the high preponderance of hydro-electricity.

9

CONCLUSIONS – TOWARDS A MORE PROMISING FUTURE

The emergence of the Brazilian economy as a major global force has been a long and tortuous process. Rapid progress has, at regular intervals, been eclipsed by profound crises, which have threatened not only hard-won achievements, but, to pessimists, have also lent credence to the view that Brazil may be incapable of embarking on a path of steady, sustainable economic and social development. So it is that at the very beginning of the 2020s Brazil finds itself entering another deep recession, brought on in part by the global and domestic repercussions of the COVID-19 pandemic. To add to the current economic malaise, Brazil also faces a deep political crisis that threatens to engulf the presidency. It is sobering to reflect on the fact that the country confronted similarly unfavourable political and economic circumstances as recently as the mid-2010s.

Faced with all of this, it is hard not to conclude, as this volume has repeatedly argued, that Brazil's economy remains beset by structural difficulties which require urgent resolution. The scale and scope of these issues can seem daunting. Yet it is easy to be too pessimistic. Recent history demonstrates that change and effective reforms can occur and that seemingly impregnable barriers to accelerated economic and social progress can be overcome. Between 1994 and 2014 the emergence of a broad political consensus behind economic reform did produce some favourable results. Hyperinflation was brought to an end, the incidence of poverty declined, the distribution of income became less skewed and progress was even made in reconciling economic development with environmental sustainability. These developments coinciding with one another appeared to demonstrate to the wider world that the Brazilian economy had come of age and was at last realising its vaunted potential.

Of course, as this volume has made clear, this "development model" could not last indefinitely. In particular, its effectiveness rested heavily on favourable commodity prices. Too little was done to create new comparative advantages that would have ridden to the rescue once demand for Brazil's key natural resource-based exports softened. Still, whatever their shortcomings or omissions, reforms instituted during the 1994–2014 period have exercised lasting positive effects, especially in the social sphere. More generally though, and to repeat the point, the period demonstrates that Brazil is capable of embracing extended periods of reform with associated economic and social progress.

Looking to the future, on the not unrealistic assumption that change is possible, what path should reform take? The answer to this question involves getting to grips with the structural factors that have been holding the Brazilian economy back. It is these very features, of course, which formed the core preoccupations of this book. Structural impediments to accelerated, sustainable and inclusive growth represent decisive factors in accounting for Brazil's volatile boom-bust trajectory over the past few decades. They also, by extension, frame the conditions whereby Brazil, like many other newly industrialised, emerging economies, appears to be caught in a middle-income trap.

Brazil, in common with its regional counterparts, notably Mexico and Argentina, and even some of its Asian emerging market peers such as India, has struggled to close the growth and standard of living gap with the advanced countries. While liberal market reforms and increased social investment have boosted productivity and effectively addressed extreme poverty, they have not proven sufficient to generate sustained improvements in economic performance of the type experienced in, for example, South Korea. The latter economy has now achieved standards of living roughly equivalent to the Western industrialised economies. In doing so, it offers a rare example of a country which, thanks to effective development policies (notably heavy investment in human capital), has managed to break out of the middle-income trap. The contrast between the extreme competence demonstrated in South Korea's management of the COVID-19 crisis and the disarray surrounding Brazil's encapsulates the gulf in development that now separates two countries. In this connection it is sobering to note that in the 1960s and 1970s development literature both countries were considered near equivalents as newly industrialising economies.

The argument throughout this book has been that durable solutions to Brazil's problems – and a way out of the potential middle-income trap – will require building on past achievements and tackling chronic structural weaknesses. The latter features are often embedded in paradoxes and/or the existence of dualism. To take one example of these, consider Brazil's world-leading firms in areas such as agribusiness and aerospace and contrast them with the bulk of enterprises in the industrial sector. These remain characterised by insufficient competitiveness and only survive because of comparatively high levels of protection. To take another example, contrast the generally skilful stewardship of monetary policy with the fiscal profligacy that has all too often characterised the management of Brazil's public finances. Yet another example is provided in the field of education and training. Despite the advent of higher education quotas for disadvantaged students, there exists an enormous divide in terms of quality between the educational opportunities on offer to the élite and those available to the mass of the population. This especially applies to primary and secondary education.

The general point here is that while Brazil has developed pockets of excellence, often demonstrating world-class virtuosity, these do not represent the totality of the country's economic reality. Put bluntly, there is a need to learn from where success has been achieved and apply the lessons more broadly in other sectors, firms and policy spheres. In highlighting the policy-relevance of structural constraints enmeshed in paradoxes and dualism, this conclusion is in clear analytical alignment with the work of the Latin American structuralist economists. However, in contrast to more traditional structuralist perspectives, more extensive state intervention may not always be the answer. In part this reflects the fiscal exhaustion of the state. At the same time though, there is a need to recognise the scope for inefficiency, rent-seeking and corruption which have all too often characterised state-directed attempts to induce structural change. Thus, wherever possible, the emphasis should lie in building up private sector capacities and resilience. Before turning to the question of where priority areas for reform should lie, it is worth engaging with a broader contextual question. This relates to the degree of economic openness likely to be embraced in the future. It also concerns the likely future regional and global economic context within which the Brazilian economy will need to compete.

Between the end of military rule in 1985 and the beginning of the current millennium, the direction of travel regarding Brazil's external economic environment was quite unambiguous. Propelled by the rise of market-friendly economic ideologies in the Western economies, structural adjustment in many developing and emerging countries, and the demise of central planning in the transition economies, global markets moved steadily towards greater openness. As part of this process, countries around the world, and certainly within Latin America, reduced tariff and non-tariff trade barriers. They also scaled down obstacles to inward foreign direct investment and instituted domestic market liberalisation which aimed at increasing competition.

Thus, when Brazil instituted its first tentative trade and market liberalisation efforts under the Sarney administration in 1987, and intensified them further at the beginning of the 1990s under Collor, it formed part of a much broader global and regional trend. Still, while adherent to these Washington Consensus-style reforms, it could not be said that Brazil was in any sense a pioneer or a particularly enthusiastic exponent of them. In contrast to Chile, for example, Brazil was late in implementing trade and market reforms. Also, the depth of the changes realised paled by comparison with that of Chile. In the case of the region's other two large economies, Argentina and Mexico, liberal reforms also went faster and further. By the beginning of the 2000s, progress on the trade and market reform agenda had effectively ground to a halt in Brazil. Indeed, the next decade and a half saw efforts to bring the state back in. Selected sectors even witnessed the partial reintroduction of *de facto* import substitution. Only with the election of the Bolsonaro administration in October 2018 has the course been set firmly once more in the direction of trade and market opening. However, looking ahead, questions must arise as to whether this prospectus of economic liberalism will play out in actuality.

The first note of caution which needs to be sounded regards what may amount to "a reversion to the mean" surrounding Brazil's policy stance towards integration with the global economy. As discussed in Chapters 2 and 4, the roots of statism and economic autarchy run deep in Brazil's economic DNA. They certainly impart significant inertial moment when sweeping economic reforms are on the table. The practical implication of this is that reformers pursuing greater economic openness always need to overcome political and institutional resistance both within the state – which still controls surprisingly large parts of the productive sector – and the private sector. It is also the case that, unlike in the United Kingdom or the United States, for example, the Brazilian economics profession is not dominated by those for whom free trade and free markets are articles of faith. As seen in Chapter 1, home-grown structuralism, has been, and remains a significant intellectual force. This inevitably feeds through into the policy sphere.

The second note of caution concerns likely trends in the broader regional and global economies. Unlike the 1980s and 1990s, the pursuit of free trade and open markets has become openly contested in certain quarters. This is the case not least in the United States under the Trump administration. Disquiet over the impacts of free trade and foreign investment flows is likely to persist, and not just in the United States. In particular, in the wake of the COVID-19 crisis, high level concern in the UK and the EU is being openly voiced concerning the role of China in the global economy. Against this background, those advocating greater economic openness in Brazil may not benefit from the global tide moving unambiguously in their direction.

Despite these caveats, the broad conclusion must be that the global economy will remain reasonably open, with promising opportunities on offer to those who can effectively compete and innovate within it. In the particular case of Brazil, concrete facts on the ground that point in this direction. In the first place, even in regard to the United States, there are indications that the two countries are beginning to move towards a bilateral free trade agreement. This follows a summit meeting between Presidents Bolsonaro and Trump in 2019. If nothing else this development indicates that, when the United States deems a country a strategic partner,[1] liberalised trade agreements are possible. Far more advanced in development is the EU-Mercosul free trade agreement. If ratified by national governments the agreement which has been reached would open up Brazil's comparatively heavily protected industrial sector to European competition. By the same token, Brazil would have greatly enhanced access to EU markets for its highly competitive agricultural produce.

Closer to home, Mercosul itself remains largely intact, anchoring free trade between Brazil and its neighbours to the South. Also within the region, Brazilian advocates of trade and market openness can generally call on support from their counterparts in Chile, the continent's most liberal economy. In addition, it is worth noting that despite nationalist rhetoric from elements of the administration, Brazil remains committed to multilateralism in international economic relations. Over the past three decades, Brazil has carved out a reputation for its active participation in major global economic governance institutions, notably the World Trade Organization. It seems highly unlikely that given the institutional and foreign policy capital tied up in this that Brazil will pursue radical, unilateral economic nationalism.

Accepting that Brazil will continue to face a broadly open global economy and that the drift of domestic policy is in favour of global integration rather than economic autarchy, where should reform efforts be concentrated? The broadest and perhaps most ambitious area for reform lies in the need more to create more efficient, non-natural resource-based sectors and firms to emulate the achievements of Brazil's renowned agricultural, oil and mining sectors. In other words, in the future, and given the volatility of (currently soft) commodity prices, there is a need to build up new sources of comparative advantage. This will necessarily involve improving process efficiencies in relevant sectors, but will also require the accumulation of fresh indigenous technological capabilities. In sectoral terms, where might the emphasis lie? In many ways it would make sense to build on pre-existing capabilities, identifying areas where Brazil may be able to build up comparative advantages reasonably quickly. Sectors such as pharmaceuticals, enterprise management software, eco-tourism and fuel-efficient vehicles present interesting opportunities in this regard but there are many other possibilities.

The challenge, of course is how to convert aspiration to build up these new comparative advantages into reality. An old-style dirigiste, state-driven import substitution approach risks replicating the inefficiencies and strategic mistakes of the past. Instead, the emphasis should be placed on removing structural obstacles to investment, entrepreneurial risk-taking and investment in challenging technologies. Central to achieving this, and of vital necessity in their own right, is the pursuit of further areas for reform set out below. Among other objectives, suggested reforms here would attempt to recast business–state relations, improve access to private sector capital, enhance human capital and facilitate a more predictable macroeconomic environment.

Turning to the first area of reform, state-business relations, Brazil's recent experience (not least the *Lava Jato* crisis) demonstrates the importance of tackling the duality which appears to exist concerning the phenomenon of insider versus outsider firms. This binary divide has created a world in which firms with close relationships to the state help to frame policy, fund political parties and are first in the line to receive lucrative government contracts and access to official finance. Outsider firms, have no such opportunities; this represents one of the reasons for chronic under-investment and precarity among large swathes of the private sector. Effective reform of state-business relations, increasing transparency and creating a more level playing field, could potentially enhance access to capital and official procurement for previously excluded firms. Reductions in clientelism and corruption would allow for more genuine, merit-based competition between firms as they sought to gain favours from the state. The result would be a fillip for efficiency where success would depend on commercial competence, and would no longer be determined by membership of opaque networks.

As part of the objective of facilitating a more hands-off approach between the state and business and to boost investment, it also vital that steps be taken to improve the functioning of domestic capital markets. As revealed earlier in this volume, despite record low base interest rates, accentuated interest rate spreads make access to private sector loans expensive for the corporate sector. As a result, either investment projects are not realised, but where they are this is facilitated through channelling of retained earnings or recourse to official credit, most often via the BNDES.

Encouragingly, reforms to the stock market have made it easier for insurgent enterprises to raise capital via share issues. However, this model of finance may not be suitable across the productive sector where, in many cases, entrepreneurs do not want to see their ventures become publicly traded. Unlocking more affordable commercial interest rates will involve further measures around bankruptcy reform and creditors' rights. However, they will also require a deconcentration of Brazil's highly oligopolistic banking system. There are signs that change may be in the air with the rise of Fintechs and new models of financial institution such as XP Investimentos. However, banking regulators and competition authorities will need to take more active steps to open up the market while, of course, exercising appropriate prudential oversight to ensure capital adequacy and financial stability.

Recurrent failure to invest sufficiently in human capital is a common thread running through the fabric of structural impediments to sustainable, inclusive growth in Brazil. Deficient and unequal access to high quality training and education means lower productivity across Brazil's supply side. It also places barriers in the way of firms' attempts to adopt new technologies, production processes and enter new markets. More obviously, there is an indisputable connection between lack of access to training and education and the inter-generational replication of poverty.

Fortunately, over the past three decades Brazil's performance in developing human capital, has improved, thanks to greater investment in public education and, of course, the *Bolsa Família*. However, a lot remains to be done, not least in the field of vocational education, and in tackling still significant regional and ethnic disparities. Progress across these dimensions has, unfortunately, slowed since the mid-2010s. This is thanks in part to fiscal stringency. However, it also stems from the collateral effects of a culture war. This has seen conservative figures in the current administration take aim at what they regard as corrosive progressivism in the educational establishment. While it will be important to resume progress on the human capital front, related to the need to tackle poverty and to develop new comparative advantages, it is also vital to ensure reductions take place in barriers to labour market participation, whether these are geographic or based on population group. Evidence from 2000s and early 2010s suggests that opening up labour markets to previously excluded groups was among the most powerful drivers of reductions in poverty and income inequality. Connectedly, and to arrest troubling recent rises in poverty, it will be desirable to boost productivist social programmes. The objective here will be to tackle long standing disparities and reduce intergeneration poverty transmission, while avoiding welfare dependence

Among the paradoxes impeding economic and social progress has been the contrast between Brazil's effective monetary management and the failure to get a proper grip on fiscal performance. At the time of writing, monetary policy had departed from its usual – cautious – trajectory. In mid-2020 the authorities had just initiated a programme of quantitative easing to counter the recessionary effects of the COVID-19 crisis. Once the crisis abates, however, it can be expected that monetary policy will return to its previous pattern, with inflation targeting comprising again its central feature. With these conditions in place, the authorities must try to build further on fiscal reform agenda to align it to more responsible monetary policy stewardship. Fiscal reform, especially around taxes and social security, should aim at freeing up resources for initiatives aimed at boosting competitiveness and realising much-needed social investment. With an effective set of fiscal reforms in place, Brazil would be much better placed to address a range of structural issues around infrastructure, human capital development, poverty and innovation.

If there is one obvious lesson that can be drawn from Brazil's development experience it surrounds the damage wrought from failure to fully incorporate environmental considerations into the economic policy calculus. As a result, over the past few decades, rapid economic development has been achieved at the expense of environmental depredation. Between the start of the millennium and the mid-2010s, real progress was made in trying to remedy this longstanding issue. In particular, rates of deforestation rapidly slowed. Subsequently, however, deforestation has accelerated while policymakers have adopted a more sceptical posture towards environmental issues in general, and international climate change accords, in particular. The challenge for the future will be to resume progress and protect Brazil's astonishing biodiversity for posterity. By embracing new sectors and technologies, the pursuit of accelerated growth need not involve further depredation of pristine rainforest, nor need it compromise Brazil's commitments to current or future climate accords.

From the discussion so far, it should be clear that placing Brazil's economy on a trajectory for accelerated, sustainable and inclusive growth will require a broad array of reforms. Accomplishing these will obviously entail resource costs. What is more, aspects of them will certainly prove politically contentious. Given this, what are the likely prospects for reform over the longer term? The current administration of President Jair Bolsonaro set out on its course with a market liberalisation agenda. This was heavily influenced by Finance Minister, Paulo Guedes, a figure aligned with free-market, Chicago School approaches. Thus, further privatisation, trade liberalisation and fiscal and monetary orthodoxy formed the core economic policy agenda for the incoming administration. This can be characterised as an attempt to shrink the state and deal with the inefficiencies accumulated during the PT years (2003–16). Initially some success was encountered, with privatisations announced, and a complex social security reform passed in November 2019.

The picture has become somewhat murkier as the administration approaches the mid-point of its term in office. Not only has the COVID-19 crisis exposed serious divides in the President's cabinet and widened bitter political divisions on a national basis; it has also wrought profound social and economic damage. Aside from Brazil's worryingly high death toll from the virus, the crisis has exposed deficiencies in the country's health system, pushed the nation into recession, and increased rates of poverty. In an attempt to respond to these events, the authorities have enacted emergency economic measures, the most important being an unprecedented programme of quantitative easing from Brazil's Central Bank. This has clearly changed the basis – temporarily at least – of Brazil's macroeconomic framework.

More broadly though, the need to respond to fast moving events, alongside the introduction of emergency measures will likely see elements of the reform programme – on both fiscal and market liberalisation – encounter delay. In terms of a very important element of the reform agenda – recasting the state-business relationship – the prospects of change have in all likelihood been damaged by the departure in mid-2020 of Sergio Moro, the Justice Minister. Mr. Moro was, of course, at the centre of attempts to clean up state-business relationships, having directed the Lava Jato investigations of the mid-to-late 2010s. Weakened by Mr. Moro's departure, and even at growing risk at the launch of impeachment proceedings against him, President Bolsonaro may find it much harder to forge the consensus necessary to proceed with further reforms.

In the longer term, the COVID-19 crisis will inevitably recede but in all likelihood, it will leave behind a Brazilian economy scarred and, in more need than ever of confronting its structural deficiencies. It is possible that the passing of the crisis and a broader reflection on its causes and consequences could then catalyse renewed structural reform efforts. At the same time, presidential and congressional elections scheduled for 2022 have the potential to produce a new administration, committed to a pragmatic programme of meaningful reform. Were this to be the outcome, Brazil would have a good chance of resuming the path of progress interrupted with the outbreak of political and economic crisis in the mid-2010s. For the sake of such an important global economy, and a nation of such great talent and potential, it must be hoped that this is the case.

Note

1 The US administration has even floated the idea of Brazil becoming a NATO member.

BIBLIOGRAPHY

Abreu, M. 1990. *A Ordem do progresso: Cem anos de política econômica republicana, 1889–1989*, Rio de Janeiro: Elsevier.

Abreu, M. 2004. 'Trade liberalization and the political economy of protection in Brazil since 1987', *INTAL-IADB Working Papers*, SITI 08b.

Acemoglu, D. & J. Robinson. 2012. *Why Nations Fail: The Origins of Power, Prosperity, and Poverty*, New York: Crown Publishing Group.

Addis, C. 1999. *Taking the Wheel: Auto Parts Firms and the Political Economy of Industrialization in Brazil*, University Park, PA: Penn State University Press.

Afonso, J., E. Araújo & B. Farjado. 2016. 'The role of fiscal and monetary policies in the Brazilian economy: understanding recent institutional reforms and economic changes', *The Quarterly Review of Economics and Finance*, 62: 41–55.

Agenor, R. & P. Montiel. 2015. *Development Macroeconomics*, Princeton, NJ: Princeton University Press.

Aghion, P., P. Howit & D. Mayer-Foulkes. 2005. 'The effect of financial development on convergence: theory and evidence', *The Quarterly Journal of Economics*, 120(1): 173–222.

Alston, L., M. Melo, B. Mueller & C. Perreira. 2016. *Brazil in Transition: Beliefs, Leadership and Institutional Change*, Princeton, NJ: Princeton University Press.

Amann, E. 2000. *Economic Liberalisation and Industrial Performance in Brazil*, Oxford: Oxford University Press.

Amann, E. 2017. *Brazil and Its Development Challenges: A Personal View*, Inaugural Address, Leiden: Leiden University.

Amann, E. & W. Baer. 2000. 'The illusion of stability: the Brazilian economy under Cardoso', *World Development*, 28(10): 1805–19.

Amann, E. & W. Baer. 2005. 'From the developmental to the regulatory state: the transformation of the government's impact on the Brazilian economy', *The Quarterly Review of Economics and Finance*, 45(2–3): 421–31.

Amann, E. & W. Baer. 2006. 'Economic orthodoxy versus social development? The dilemmas facing Brazil's labour government', *Oxford Development Studies*, 34(2): 219–41.

Amann, E. & J. Cantwell (eds.). 2012. *Innovative Firms in Emerging Market Countries*, Oxford: Oxford University Press.

Amann, E. & P.N. Figueiredo. 2012. 'Brazil', in E. Amann & J. Cantwell (eds.) *Innovative Firms in Emerging Market Countries*, 210–47, Oxford: Oxford University Press.

Amsden, A. 1992. *Asia's Next Giant: South Korea and Late Industrialization*, New York: Oxford University Press.

Anuário Brasileiro de Educação Básica. 2019, São Paulo: Moderna.

Arantes, F. & F. Cazeiro Lopreat. 2017. O novo consenso em macroeconomia no Brasil: a política fiscal do plano real ao segundo governo Lula, *Revista de Economia Contemporânea*, 21(3): 1–34.

Arbix, G. 2019. 'Innovation in Brazil since 2003: advances, incoherencies and discontinuities', in E.B. Reynolds, B.R. Schneider & E. Zylberberg (eds.) *Innovation in Brazil: Advancing Development in the 21st Century*, 73–90, London: Routledge.

Assunção, J., C. Gandour & R. Rocha. 2015. 'Deforestation slowdown in the Brazilian Amazon: prices or policies?' *Environment and Development Economics*, 20: 697–722.

Ayres, J., M. Garcia, D. Guillen & P. Kehoe. 2019. 'The monetary and fiscal history of Brazil, 1960–2016', *IDB Working Paper Series*, N° IDB-WP-990.

Baer, W. 2013. *The Brazilian Economy: Growth and Development*, Boulder, CO: Lynne Rienner.

Baer, W. & C. McDonald. 1998. 'A return to the past? Brazil's privatization of public utilities: the case of the electric power sector', *Quarterly Review of Economics and Finance*, 32(3): 503–23.

Banco Central do Brasil (BCB). 2018. *Relatório de Economica Bancária*, Brasília: Banco Central do Brasil

Barbosa Filho, F. & R. de Moura. 2012. 'Evolução Recente da Informalidade no Brasil: Uma Análise Segundo Características da Oferta e Demanda de Trabalho', *FGV-IBRE Texto Para Discussão* No. 17.

Barreto, P., C. Souza, R. Noguerón, A. Anderson & R. Salamão. 2006. *WRI Report: Human Pressure on the Amazon Forests*, Washington, DC: World Resources Institute.

Barrientos, A. 2018. 'Anti-poverty transfers and poverty reductions', in E. Amann, C. Azzoni & W. Baer (eds.) *Oxford Handbook of the Brazilian Economy*, 511–34, New York: Oxford University Press.

Barros, A. 2015. 'Expansão da educação superior no Brasil: limites e possibilidades', *Educ. Soc., Campinas*, 36(131): 361–90, Abr.–Jun.

BBC Brasil. (2019). 'Os seis números que resumem os seis meses da educação na gestão Bolsonaro', 30th June 2019.

Belassa, B. 1965. 'Trade liberalization and "revealed" comparative advantage', *The Manchester School*, 33(2): 99–123.

BEN. 2018. *Balanço Energético Nacional 2018*, Rio de Janreiro: Empresa de Pesquisa Energética.

Bernard, A., V. Smeets & F. Warzynski. 2017. 'Rethinking deindustrialization', *Economic Policy*, 32(89): 5–38.

Biderman, C., M. Hiromoto & F.R. Ramos. 2018. 'The Brazilian Housing Program Minha Casa Minha Vida: effect on urban sprawl', *Lincoln Institute of Land Policy Working Paper*, WP18CB2.

Bielschowsky, R. 1988. *Pensamento Econômico Brasileiro*, Rio de Janeiro: IPEA.

Bolognesi, A. 2018. 'Desafios do setor eletrico', in G. Oliveira (ed.) *Desafios da Infraestrutura no Brasil*, 183–206, São Paulo: Trevisan.

Bresser Pereira, L.C. 2018. 'Brazil's macroeconomic policy institutions', in E. Amann, C. Azzoni & W. Baer (eds.) *Oxford Handbook of the Brazilian Economy*, 221–42, New York: Oxford University Press.

Campello, T. & M. Neri. 2013. *Programa Bolsa Família: Uma Decada de Inclusão e de Cidadania*, Brasília: IPEA.

Campos, P. 2019. 'Os efeitos da crise econômica e da operação Lava Jato sobre a indústria da construção pesada no Brasil: falências, desnacionalização e desestruturação produtiva', *Mediações Londrina*, 24(1): 127–53, Jan.–Abr.

Caro, R. 2015. *The Power Broker: Robert Moses and the Fall of New York*, London: Bodley Head (originally published in 1974).

Cassiolato, J.E., Lastres. H. & Soares, M.C. 2014. 'The Brazilian national system of innovation: challenges to sustainability and inclusive development,' in Gabriela Dutrénit & Judith Sutz (eds.) *National Innovation Systems, Social Inclusion and Development*, Chapter 3, 68–101, Cheltenham: Edward Elgar Publishing.

de Carvalho. 2019. Seminário FGV de Direito e Economia Regulação e Concorrência no SFN –Uma Nova Agenda, Powerpoint presentation available at: https://www.bcb.gov.br/conteudo/home-ptbr/TextosApresentacoes/Apresenta%C3%A7%C3%A3o_CV_Semin%C3%A1rio%20FGV_15.02.19.pdf

Castelan, D. 2010. 'A implementação do consenso: Itamaraty, Ministério da Fazenda e a liberalização brasileira', *Contexto Internacional*, 32(2): 563–605.

Cavalcante, L. & F. De Negri. 2015. 'Consensos e dissensos sobre a evolução da produtivide na indústria brasileira', in L. Cavalcante & F. De Negri (eds.) *Produtividade no Brasil: Desempenho e Determinantes*, 2: 541–63, Brasília: IPEA-ABDI.

Chang, H.J. 2002. *Kicking Away the Ladder: Development Strategy in Historical Perspective*, London: Anthem Press.

Chiarani, T. & da A. Silva. 2019. 'International trade in goods by technological intensity: the Brazilian case 1996–2010', in E. Grivoyannis (ed.) *International Integration of the Brazilian Economy*, 143–86, New York: Palgrave.

Cimoli, M., G. Dosi & J. Stiglitz. 2009. *Industrial Policy and Development: The Political Economy of Capabilities Accumulation*, Oxford: Oxford University Press.

Cline, W. 1985. 'International debt: from crisis to recovery?', *American Economic Review*, 75(2): 185–90, Papers and Proceedings of the Ninety-Seventh Annual Meeting of the American Economic Association (May).

CNI. 2019. *Competitivade Brasil 2018–19*, Brasília: CNI.

Colman, D. & F. Nixson. 1994. *Economics of Change in Less Developed Countries*, New York: Harvester Wheatsheaf.

Columbia Center on Sustainable Investment & Fundação Getúlio Vargas (CCSI-FGV). 2018. *The Top 20 Brazilian Multinationals: A Long Way Out of the Crises*, New York: CCSI-FGV.

Contreras, E. 1993. *Os Desbravadores: A Petrobrás e a Construção do Brasil Industrial*, Rio de Janeiro: ANPOCS.

Cowan, B. 2016. 'Holy ghosts of Brazil's past', *NACLA Report on the Americas*, 48(4): 346–52.

Cysne, R. 2002. 'Micro and macroeconomic aspects of the reforms', in *Brazil in the 1990s: An Economy in Transition*, 39–88, London: Palgrave/St. Antony's College.

Dahlman, C. & C. Frischtak. 1993. 'National systems supporting technical advance in industry: the Brazilian experience', in R. Nelson (ed.) *National Innovation Systems: A Comparative Analysis*, 414–50, New York: Oxford University Press.

Doctor, M. 2016. *Business State Relations in Brazil: Challenges of the Port Reform Lobby*, London: Routledge.

Dulci, O. 2002. 'Guerra fiscal, desenvolvimento desigual e relações federativas no Brasil', *Revista de Sociologia e Política*, 18: 95–107, Jun.

Dunning, J. & S. Lundan. 2008. *Multinational Enterprises and the Global Economy*, Cheltenham: Edward Elgar.

Ebenstein, L. 2015. *Chicagonomics: The Evolution of Chicago Free Market Economics*, New York: St Martin's Press.

Economist Intelligence Unit. 2019. *Brazil Country Report*, November, London: Economist Intelligence Unit.

Economist Intelligence Unit. 2020. *Brazil Country Report*, January, London: Economist Intelligence Unit.

Eichengreen, B., D. Park & K. Shin. 2012. 'When fast-growing economies slow down: international evidence and implications for China', *Asian Economic Papers*, 11(1): 42–87, February.

Eichengreen, B., D. Park & K. Shin. 2014. 'Growth slowdowns redux', *Japan and the World Economy*, 32: 65–84.

El País. 22nd August 2019. 'Bolsonaro's ambitious privatization package goes from the Post Office to the Jericoacora concession'.

Etchemendy, S. & I. Puente. 2017. 'Power and crisis: explaining varieties of commercial banking systems in Argentina, Brazil and Mexico', *Journal of Politics in Latin America*, 9(1): 331.

Evans, P. 1995. *Embedded Autonomy: States and Industrial Transformation*, Princeton, NJ: Princeton University Press.

Felipe, J. 2012. 'Tracking the middle-income trap: what is it, who is in it, and why? Part I', *ADB Economics Working Paper Series* No. 306, Economics and Research Department, Asian Development Bank, Manila.

Ferraz, J.C., H. Rush & I. Miles. 1992. *Development, Technology and Flexibility: Brazil Faces the Industrial Divide*, London: Routledge.

Ferreira, A. 2010. *História da Educação Brasileira: da Colônia ao século XX*, São Carlos, SP: EdUFSCar.

Ferreira, F., S. Firpo & J. Messina. 2017. 'Ageing poorly? Accounting for the decline in earnings inequality in Brazil, 1995–2012', *IZA Institute of Labour Economics Working Papers*, IZA DP No. 10656.

Ferreira, F., P.G. Leite & J.A. Litchfield. 2007. 'The rise and fall of Brazilian inequality', *Re Vista*, Spring.

Ferreira, P. & C. Araujo. 2006. 'On the Economic and Fiscal Effects of Infrastructure Investment in Brazil', *FGV Ensaios Econômicos*, No. 613, 1–28.

Figueiredo, P., M. Pinheiro, B. Cabral, F. Queiroz, F. Perin & R. Wegner. 2018. *Imperativo do Fortelicimento da Competividade Industrial no Brasil*, Rio de Janeiro: FGV Editora.

Financial Times. May 8th 2020. 'Brazil approves quantitative easing to fight coronavirus woes'.

Financial Times. December 6th 2019. 'Brazil's booming credit markets fan hopes of "revolution"'.

Financial Times. January 22nd 2019. 'Brazil's Jair Bolsonaro pledges to open up economy'.

Financial Times. June 30th 2019. 'EU-Mercosur trade deal: what it all means'.

Financial Times. August 14th 2018. 'Is the structure of the UK economy leading to poor productivity?'.

Firpo, S. & A. Portella. 2019. 'Decline in wage inequality in Brazil: a survey', *World Bank Policy Research Working Papers*, 9096.

Fishlow, A. 1972. 'Brazilian size distribution of income', *The American Economic Review*, 62(1/2): 391–402.

Flamini, V. & M. Soto. 2019. 'Doing more with less: how can Brazil foster development while pursuing fiscal consolidation?', *IMF Working Paper*, WP/19/236.

Fleury, A, M. Fleury & F. Borini. 2013. 'The Brazilian multinational's approach to innovation', *Journal of International Management*, 19: 260–75.

Folha de São Paulo. 10th February 2020. 'Bolsonaro trava Bolsa Familía em cidades pobres e fila chega a 1 milhão'.

Folha de São Paulo. 23rd January 2020. 'Brazilian oil and gas production breaks record in 2019'.

Fonseca, P., A. Cunha & J. Bichara. 2013. 'O Brasil na era Lula: retorno ao desenvolvimentismo?', *Nova Economia*, 23(2): 403–28, maio-agosto.

Frenkel, R. & M. Rapetti. 2010. *A Concise History of Exchange Rate Regimes in Latin America*, Washington, DC: Center for Economic and Policy Research.

Frischtak, C. 2019. 'Science and innovation in Brazil: where to now?', in E.B. Reynolds, B.R. Schneider & E. Zylberberg (eds.) *Innovation in Brazil: Advancing Development in the 21st Century*, 93–119, London: Routledge.

Garcia-Escribano, M., C. Goes, & I. Karpowicz. 2015. 'Filling the gap: infrastructure investment in Brazil', *IMF Working Papers*, 15–180.

Giambiagi, F. 2007. *Reforma da Previdencia: O Encontro Marcado*, Rio de Janeiro: Campus.

Giambiagi, F. & A. Além. 2001. *Finanças Públicas*, Rio de Janeiro: Editora Campus.

Giambiagi, F. & M.M. Moreira (eds.). 1999. *A Economia Brasileira nos Anos 90*, Rio de Janeiro: BNDES.

Giambiagi, F. & G. Tinoco. 2019. 'O teto do gasto público: mudar para preservar', *BNDES Textos para Discussão* No. 144.

Góes, C. & I. Karpowicz. 2017. 'Inequality in Brazil: a regional perspective', *IMF Working Papers*, WP/17/225.

Goldemberg, J. 2018. 'Energy in Brazil: past and future', in E. Amann, C. Azzoni & W. Baer (eds.) *Oxford Handbook of the Brazilian Economy*, 358–76. New York: Oxford University Press.

Gomes, J. & F. Vieira. 2009. 'O campo da energia elétrica no Brasil de 1880 a 2002', *Revista da Administração Pública*, 43(2): 295–321, Mar./Abr.

Gonzaga, G. & J. Assunção. 2010. *Educação Profissional no Brasil: Inserção e Retorno*, Brasília: SENAI.

Gordon, R. 2016. *The Rise and Fall of American Growth*, Princeton, NJ: Princeton University Press.

de Graaf, G. 2007. 'Causes of corruption: towards a contextual theory of corruption,' *Public Administration Quarterly*, 31(1): 39–86.

Greenwood, J., J. Sanchez & C. Wang. 2010. 'Financing development: the role of information costs', *American Economic Review*, 100(4): 1875–91.

Hall, P. & D. Soskice. 2001. *Varieties of Capitalism: The Institutional Foundations of Comparative Advantage*, Oxford: Oxford University Press.

Hoffmann, R. 2018. 'Changes in income distribution in Brazil', in E. Amann, C. Azzoni & W. Baer (eds.) *Oxford Handbook of the Brazilian Economy*, 467–88. New York: Oxford University Press.

Holland, M. 2019. 'Fiscal crisis in Brazil: causes and remedy', *Revista de Economia Política*, 39(1): 88–107.

Hymer, S. 1976. *International Operations of National Firms: A Study of Foreign Direct Investment*. Cambridge, MA: MIT Press.

IDB-WEF. 2019. *Improving Infrastructure Financing in Brazil*, Geneva: IDB-WEF.

IPEA/World Bank. 2011. *Ponte sobre o Atlântico: Parceria Sul-Sul para o Crescimento Brasil e África Subsaariana*, Brasília: IPEA/World Bank.

Irajá, V. 2019. 'A reforma silenciosa de Paulo Guedes para revolucionar a máquina federal' *Veja*, 13th December 2019.

Joaquim G. & B. Van Doornik. 2019. 'Bank competition, cost of credit and economic activity: evidence from Brazil', *Central Bank of Brazil Working Papers*, No. 508.

Kay, C. 1989. *Latin American Theories of Development and Underdevelopment*, London & New York: Routledge.

Kerche, F. 2018. Ministério público, lava jato e mãos limpas: uma abordagem institucional', *Lua Nova*, 105: 255–86.

Kohli, A. 2004. *State-Directed Development: Power and Industrialization in the Global Periphery*, Cambridge: Cambridge University Press.

Krueger, A. 1974. 'The political economy of the rent-seeking society', *American Economic Review*, 64(3): 291–303.

Krugman, P. 1991. 'Myths and Realities of US Competitiveness', *Science* 254(5033): 811–15.

Krugman, P. & J. Rotemberg. 1991. 'Speculative attacks on target zones', in P. Krugman & M. Miller (eds.) *Exchange Rate Targets and Currency Bands*, 117–32, Cambridge: Cambridge University Press.

Kume, H. 1996. 'Política de importação no Plano Real e a estrutura de proteção efetiva', *IPEA Texto para Discussão* 0423.

Lall, S. 1992. 'Technological capabilities and industrialization', *World Development*, 20 (2): 165–186.

Lall, S. 2000. 'The technological structure and performance of developing country manufactured exports, 1985–1998', *Oxford Development Studies*, 28(3): 337–69.

Leite, A. 2014. *A Energia do Brasil*, São Paulo: Lexikon.

Lisboa, E, R. Godinho & L. da Silva. 2018. 'Fintechs in Brazil: opportunities or threats?', *International Association for Management of Technology IAMOT 2018 Conference Proceedings*, 22–26th April, Aston University, Birmingham, England.

Little, I., T. Scitovsky & M. Scott. 1970. *Industry and Trade in Some Developing Countries: A Comparative Study*, London: Oxford University Press for the OECD.

Londoño, J.L. & M. Székely. 2000. 'Persistent poverty and excess inequality: Latin America, 1970–1995', *Journal of Applied Economics*, 3(1): 93–134.

Love, J. 1971. *Rio Grande Do Sul and Brazilian Regionalism, 1882–1930*, Stanford, CA: Stanford University Press.

Ludeña, C. & M. Netto. 2011. 'Brazil: mitigation and adaptation to climate change', *IDB Technical Note 622*.

Machado, F. 2016. *Brazil's New Forest Code: A Guide for Decision-Makers in Supply Chains and Governments*, Brasília: WWF Brazil.

Madeiros, M., R. Barbosa & F. Carvalhaes. 2018. *Educational Expansion, Inequality and Poverty Reduction in Brazil: A Simulation Study*, Working Paper, Available at: https://papers.ssrn.com/sol3/papers.cfm?abstract_id=3189211

Magalhães, G. & R. Castioni. 2019. 'Educação profissional no Brasil – expansão para quem?' *Ensaio: avaliação e políticas públicas em educação*, 27(105): 732–54, Out./Dez.

Marques, F. 2019. 'Ciclo interrompido', *Pesquisa FAPESP*, 275: 36–41.

Mazzucato, M. & C. Penna. 2016. *The Brazilian Innovation System: A Mission-Orientated Policy Proposal*, Brasília: CGEE.

MEC. 2018. *Projeto914BRZ1050.3–CNE Estudo Comparado Sobre Ensino Superior no Brasil, Europa e Estados Unidos*, Brasília: MEC.

Micco, A. & N. Pérez, *Determinants of Maritime Transport Costs (April 2002)*, IDB Working Paper No. 371, 1–49.

Morais, J. 2013. *Petróleo em Águas Profundas: Uma História Tecnológica da PETROBRAS na Exploração e Produção Offshore*, Brasília: IPEA.

Morceiro, P. 2018. 'Evolution and sectoral competitiveness of the Brazilian manufacturing industry', in E. Amann, C. Azzoni & W. Baer (eds.) *Oxford Handbook of the Brazilian Economy*, 243–65. New York: Oxford University Press.

Morceiro, P. & J. Guilhoto. 2019. 'Desindustrialização setorial e estagnação de longo prazo da manufatura brasileira', *FEA-USP Working Paper Series*, 2019-01, 1–28.

Moura, A. 2016. 'Trajetória da política ambiental federal no Brasil', in M. Moura (ed.) *Governança Ambiental no Brasil: Instituições, Atores e Políticas Públicas*, 13–43, Brasília: IPEA.

De Moura Castro, C. 2018. 'The development of Brazilian education: a tale of lost opportunities', in E. Amann, C. Azzoni & W. Baer (eds.) *Oxford Handbook of the Brazilian Economy*, 489–510. New York: Oxford University Press.

Mourougane, A. & M. Pisu. 2011. 'Promoting infrastructure development in Brazil', *OECD Working Papers*, No. 898.

Mueller, B. & C. Mueller. 2016. 'The political economy of the Brazilian model of agricultural development: institutions versus sectoral policy', *Quarterly Review of Economics and Finance*, 62(C): 12–20.

Mussachio, A. & S. Lazzarini. 2014. *Reinventing State Capitalism: Leviathan in Business, Brazil and Beyond*, Cambridge, MA: Harvard University Press.

Nelson, R. ed. 1993. *National Innovation Systems: A Comparative Analysis*, New York: Oxford University Press.

Netto, V. 2016. *Lava Jato*, Rio de Janeiro: Primeira Pessoa.

Neves, C. 2017. 'Higher education institutions and systems, Brazil', in J. Shin & P. Teixeira (eds.) *Encyclopaedia of International Higher Education Systems and Institutions*, Dordrecht: Springer.

New York Times. November 18th 2019. 'Amazon deforestation rose sharply on Bolsonaro's watch'.

Nunes, S. 2013. *The Brazilian Fiscal Responsibility Law: Rules, Results and Challenges*, PowerPoint presentation available at: https://www.joserobertoafonso.com.br/attachment/15925

Ocampo, J.A. & J. Ros. 2012. 'Shifting paradigms in Latin America's economic development', in J.A. Ocampo & J. Ros (eds.) *Oxford Handbook of Latin American Economics*, 3–25, New York: Oxford University Press.

OECD. 2015. *Environmental Performance Review: Brazil*, Paris: OECD.

OECD. 2019a. *Education at a Glance, 2018*, Paris: OECD.

OECD. 2019b. *Education at a Glance: Brazil Country Note, 2018*, Paris: OECD.

Oliva, B., F. Ribeiro & A.P. Souza. 2015. 'O Retorno da educação profissional no mercado de trabalho: evidências a partir de dados longitudinais', FGV São Paulo Business School CIMICRO No. 31 Working Paper 393, 1–38.

Oliveira, F. & Diasoto G. 2015. '*A reforma tributária: removendo entraves para o crescimento, a inclusão social e o fortalecimento da federação*', *Revista Política Social e Desenvolvimento*, São Paulo: Plataforma Política Social, ano 03, novembro.

Oliveira, G. (ed.). 2018. *Desafios da Infraestrutura no Brasil*, São Paulo: Trevisan.

Olson, M. 1965. *The Logic of Collective Action*, Cambridge MA: Harvard University Press.

Orair, R. & S. Gobetti. 2019. 'Tax reform in Brazil: Guiding principles and proposals under debate', *International Policy Centre for Inclusive Growth Working Papers*, No. 182, 1–28.

Orair, R. & S. Gobetti. 2017. 'Do expansionismo a austeridade: política fiscal em period recente', *Boletim de Análise Político-Institucional*, No. 12, Jul.–Dez., 51–60.

Da Costa Oreiro, J. & L.F. de Paula. 2019. 'A economia brasileira no governo Temer e Bolsonaro: Uma avaliação preliminar', *Mimeo*, Available at: https://www.researchgate.net/publication/336147850_A_economia_brasileira_no_governo_Temer_e_Bolsonaro_uma_avaliacao_preliminar

Osorio, R. 2019. 'A disigualdade racial da pobreza no Brasil', *IPEA Textos para Discussão*, No. 2487.

Özden, C. & F. Parodi. 2004. 'Customs unions and foreign investment: theory and evidence from Mercosur's auto industry', *Central Bank of Chile Working Papers*, No. 282.

Paduan, R. 2016. *Petrobras. Uma História de Orgulho e Vergonha*, São Paulo: Objetiva.

Paiva, M. 2012. *BNDES: um banco de história e do futuro*, São Paulo: Museu da Pessoa.

De Paula, J. 1982. 'Notas sobre a economia da borracha no Brasil', *Estudos Economicos*, 12(1): 63–93, Abr.

Philippon, T. 2019. *The Great Reversal: How America Gave up on Free Markets*, Cambridge, MA: Belknap Press.

Picanço, L., A. Allen & M. Prado. 2018. *Economy and Trade – Brazil 2018 Understanding the Issues*, Washington, DC: Woodrow Wilson Center.

Pieri, R. 2018. *Retratos de Educação no Brasil*, São Paulo: Insper.

Pinheiro, A.C. 1999. 'Privatização no Brasil: Por quê? Até onde? Até quando?', in F. Giambiagi & M. Moreira (eds.) *A Economia Brasileira nos Anos 90*, 147–82, Rio de Janeiro: BNDES.

Pinheiro, A.C. 2011. 'Two decades of privatization in Brazil', in W. Baer & D. Fleischer (eds.) *The Economies of Argentina and Brazil*, 252–79. Cheltenham: Edward Elgar Publishing.

Pinheiro, A.C. 2018. 'The rise and fall of state enterprises', in E. Amann, C. Azzoni & W. Baer (eds.) *Oxford Handbook of the Brazilian Economy*, 701–17. New York: Oxford University Press.

Pompermayer, F. 2018. 'Desafios do setor de ferrovias', in G. Oliveira (ed.) *Desafios da Infraestrutura no Brasil*, 280–92, São Paulo: Trevisan.

Ponticelli, J. & L. Alencar. 2016. 'Court enforcement, bank loans and firm investment: evidence from a bankruptcy reform in Brazil', *Central Bank of Brazil Working Papers*, No. 425.

Porter, M. 1990. *The Comparative Advantage of Nations*, London: Macmillan.

Prado, M. & L. Carson. 2018. 'Corruption scandals, the evolution of anti-corruption institutions and their impacts on Brazil's economy', in E. Amann, C. Azzoni & W. Baer (eds.) *Oxford Handbook of the Brazilian Economy*, 741–68. New York: Oxford University Press.

Prebisch, R. 1949. *The Economic Development of Latin America and its Principal Problems*, E/CN.12/89, United Nations publication, Sales No. 50.II.G.2, New York: United Nations.

Quaglino, M. & J. Dias. 1993. *A Questão do Petróleo no Brasil: Uma História da Petrobras*, Rio de Janeiro: CPDOC: PETROBRAS.

Quian, R, J. Araújo & A. Nucifora. 2018. *Brazil's Productivity Dynamics*, Washington, DC: World Bank.

Ramamurti, R. & J. Singh. 2009. *Emerging Multinationals in Emerging Markets*, Cambridge: Cambridge University Press.

Rands Barros, A. 2018. 'Brazil's Northeast', in E. Amann, C. Azzoni & W. Baer (eds.) *Oxford Handbook of the Brazilian Economy*, 446–467. New York: Oxford University Press.

Reuters. 26th June 2018. Update 1 – 'Brazil lowers inflation target to 3.75 pct in 2021'.

Reynolds, E.B., B.R. Schneider & E. Zylberberg (eds.). 2019. *Innovation in Brazil: Advancing Development in the 21st Century*, London: Routledge.

Roett, R. 2011. *The New Brazil*, Washington, DC: Brookings Institution.

Rufín, C. & L. Manzetti. 2019. 'Institutions and policy choices: the new left in Brazil', *Iberoamericana – Nordic Journal of Latin American and Caribbean Studies*, 48(1): 40–52.

Russell, V. 2018. 'Liverpool 1985: the council that tried to set an illegal budget', *Public Finance*, October 8th issue.

Sá, C. 2016. 'The rise and fall of Science Without Borders', *International Higher Education*, No. 85, Spring 17–18.

Santana, M., M. Ararat, P. Alexandru, B. Yurtoglu & M. Rodrigues da Cunha. 2008. *Novo Mercado and Its Followers: Case Studies in Corporate Governance Reform*, Washington, DC: International Finance Corporation.

Schmitter, P. 1974. 'Still the century of corporatism', *Review of Politics*, 36(1): 85–121.

Schneider, B.R. 2004. *Business, Politics and the State in Twentieth Century Latin America*, Cambridge: Cambridge University Press.

Schneider, B.R. 2009. "Hierarchical market economies and varieties of capitalism in Latin America', *Journal of Latin American Studies*, 41(3): 553–75.

Schneider, B.R. 2015. 'The developmental state: comparative and historical perspectives', *Revista de Economia Politica*, 35(1): 114–32.

Schwartzman, S., E. Krieger, C.O. Bertero & F. Galembeck (eds.). 1995. *Science and Technology in Brazil: A New Policy for a Global World*, Rio de Janeiro: Editora da Fundação Getúlio Vargas.

Silva, N. & S. Saccaro. 2019. 'Efeitos de crédito do BNDES na sobrevivência das firmas Brasileiras', *IPEA Textos Para Discussão*, No. 2531, 1–44.

Da Silva, A., J. Soares de Souza & J. Araújo. 2017. 'Evidences on multidimensional poverty in the Northern Region of Brazil', *Brazilian Journal of Public Administration*, 51(2): 219–39, Mar.–Apr.

Silva, M. 2002. 'Plano Real e âncora cambial', *Revista de Economia Política*, 22(3), julho–setembro.

Soares, S., D. Suarez, L. de Souza, L. Rodrigues, W. da Silva, F. Silveira & A. Campos. 2016. 'Poverty profile: the rural North and Northeast of Brazil', *International Policy Centre for Inclusive Growth (IPC-IG) Working Papers*, No. 136.

Soares da Silva, M. 2015. 'Financial and economic development nexus: evidence from Brazilian municipalities', *Central Bank of Brazil Working Papers*, No. 399.

Sonter, L.J., D. Herrera & D. Barrett. 2017. 'Mining drives extensive deforestation in the Brazilian Amazon', *Nature Communications*, 8: 1013.

Sotomayor, O. 2019. 'Growth with reduction in poverty and inequality: did Brazil show the way?' *The Journal of Economic Inequality*, 17: 521–41.

Souza Jr., J. 2014 (ed.). *Evolução Recente das Políticas Monetárias e Cambial e do Mercado de Crédito no Brasil*, Rio de Janeiro: IPEA.

De Souza, P., F. Vaz & L. Paiva. 2018. 'Efeitos redistributivos da reforma da previdência', *IPEA Texto Para Discussão*, No. 2424.

Souza Braga, F. 2020. *A Ditadura Militar e a Governança da Água no Brasil: Ideologia, Poderes Político-Econômico e Sociedade Civil na Construção das Hidreletricas de Grande Porte*, PhD. Thesis, Leiden University.

Stolf, R. & A. Rodrigues de Oliveira. 2020. 'Success of the Brazilian alcohol program (proálcool) – a decade-by-decade brief history of ethanol in Brazil', *Engenharia Agrícola*, 40(2): 243–8, Mar./Apr.

Sunkel, O. 1993. *Development from within: Toward a Neostructural Approach for Latin America*, Boulder, CO: Lynne Rienner.

Svensson, L. 1992. 'An interpretation of recent research on exchange rate target zones', *Journal of Economic Perspectives*, 6(4): 119–44.

Thorp, R. 1998. *Progress, Poverty and Exclusion: An Economic History of Latin America*, Washington, DC: IADB.

Torres, E., L. Macahyba & R. Zeidan. 2014. 'Restructuring Brazil's national financial system', *University of Manchester IRIBA Working Papers*, No. 06.

Torres, E. & R. Zeidan. 2016. 'The life-cycle of national development banks: the experience of Brazil's BNDES', *Quarterly Review of Economics and Finance*, 62: 97–104.

Triches, D. & L. Bertrussi. 2017. 'Multicointegração e Sustentabilidade da Política Fiscal no Brasil com Regime de Quebras Estruturais (1997–2015),' *Revista Brasileira de Economia*, 71(3): 379–94.

UNCTAD. 2019. *Human Development Report 2019*. New York: UNCTAD.

UNCTAD. 2019. *World Investment Report 2019*: Special Economic Zones: Geneva: United Nations Conference on Trade and Development.

Vallaverde, J. 2017. *Perigosas Pedaladas: Os bastidores da Crise que Abalou o Brasil e Levou ao Fim o Governo Dilma Rousseff*, São Paulo: Editora Geração.

Velloso, F., A. Villela & F. Giambiagi. 2008. 'Determinantes do "Milagre" Econômico Brasileiro (1968–1973): Uma análise empírica', *Revista Brasileira Econômica*, 62(2): 221–46 Abr.–Jun.

Versiani, F. 2018. 'The colonial economy', in E. Amann, C. Azzoni & W. Baer (eds.) *Oxford Handbook of the Brazilian Economy*, 17–39, New York: Oxford University Press.

Villalobos, C. & S. Klasen. 2016. 'The impact of SENAI's vocational training program on employment, wages, and mobility in Brazil: lessons for Sub Saharan Africa?' *The Quarterly Review of Economics and Finance*, 62(C): 74–96.

Viola, E. & M. Franchini. 2019. *Brazil and Climate Change: Beyond the Amazon*, London: Routledge.

Walker, R. & E. Moran. 2000. 'Deforestation and cattle-ranching in the Brazilian Amazon: external capital and household processes', *World Development*, 28(4): 683–99.

Weisebron, M. 2013. 'Blue Amazon: thinking the defence of Brazilian maritime territory', *Austral: Brazilian Journal of Strategy & International Relations*, 2(3): 101–24.

Weyland, K. 1993. 'The rise and fall of President Collor and its impact on Brazilian democracy', *Journal of Interamerican Studies and World Affairs*, 35(1): 1–38.

Williamson, J. (ed.). 1990. *Latin American Adjustment: How Much Has Happened?*, Washington, DC: Institute for International Economics.

World Bank. 2012. *How to Decrease Freight Logistics Costs in Brazil*, Washington, DC: World Bank.

World Bank. 2017. *Um Ajuste Justo, Analise da Eficiência e Equidade do Gasto Público no Brasil*, Washington, DC: World Bank.

World Bank. 2018. *Doing Business 2019: Training for Reform – Brazil*, Washington, DC: World Bank.

World Economic Forum. 2018a. *The Global Competitiveness Report 2018*. Geneva: World Economic Forum.

World Economic Forum. 2018b. *Brazil Competitiveness and Inclusive Growth Lab Report*, Geneva: World Economic Forum.

Younsi, M. & A. Nafla. 2019. 'Financial stability, monetary policy, and economic growth: panel data evidence from developed and developing countries. *Journal of the Knowledge Economy* 10, 238–60.

INDEX

Note: **Bold** page numbers refer to tables, *italic* page numbers refer to figures and page numbers followed by "n" denote endnotes.

Printed in the United States
By Bookmasters